A Therapist's Guide t
Writing in Psychotherapy

This guide practically aids mental health professionals in understanding and improving their therapeutic and academic writing, demonstrating how the written word is an invaluable tool to document, assess, and promote change with those in and outside the therapy room.

Exploring the various ways writing occurs in psychotherapy professions, Michael D. Reiter comprehensively covers the range of the written word, from progress notes and assessment documentation, to journaling and therapeutic letters, as well as contacting larger systems such as report writing and grant applications. Chapters are formatted to include the purpose and function of a particular type of writing before providing multiple examples so therapists can apply this in their own practice. This book aims to help all therapists, regardless of academic training or therapeutic modality, to incorporate these ideas into their work.

This book is designed for mental health professionals in a variety of settings, including counselors, therapists, social workers, family therapists, and clinical psychologists. This book is useful for graduate students as well as those already in practice.

Michael D. Reiter, PhD, is a licensed marriage and family therapist in the state of Florida and an AAMFT-approved supervisor. He has taught family therapy courses for more than 20 years and written 11 psychotherapy books and co-edited two books on therapy with couples.

A Therapist's Guide to Writing in Psychotherapy

Assessment, Documentation, and Intervention

Michael D. Reiter

Routledge
Taylor & Francis Group

NEW YORK AND LONDON

Designed cover image: © Getty Images

First published 2023
by Routledge
605 Third Avenue, New York, NY 10158

and by Routledge
4 Park Square, Milton Park, Abingdon, Oxon, OX14 4RN

Routledge is an imprint of the Taylor & Francis Group, an informa business

© 2023 Michael D. Reiter

The right of Michael D. Reiter to be identified as author of this work has been asserted in accordance with sections 77 and 78 of the Copyright, Designs and Patents Act 1988.

Library of Congress Cataloging-in-Publication Data
Names: Reiter, Michael D., author.
Title: A therapist's guide to writing in psychotherapy : assessment, documentation, and intervention / Michael D. Reiter.
Description: New York, NY: Routledge, 2023. | Includes bibliographical references. | Identifiers: LCCN 2022060763 (print) | LCCN 2022060764 (ebook) | ISBN 9781032279336 (hardback) | ISBN 9781032279343 (paperback) | ISBN 9781003294702 (ebook)
Subjects: LCSH: Psychotherapy—Authorship. | Communication in psychiatry. | Medical writing.
Classification: LCC RC437.2 .R45 2023 (print) | LCC RC437.2 (ebook) | DDC 616.89/14—dc23/eng/20230406
LC record available at https://lccn.loc.gov/2022060763
LC ebook record available at https://lccn.loc.gov/2022060764

ISBN: 978-1-032-27933-6 (hbk)
ISBN: 978-1-032-27934-3 (pbk)
ISBN: 978-1-003-29470-2 (ebk)

DOI: 10.4324/9781003294702

Typeset in Times New Roman
by codeMantra

This book is dedicated to Thursday, Mika, Mr. Friendly, Sushi, Emi, Piper, and Buddy. Thank you for being a companion on the journey.

Contents

Figures

Table

Preface

I have been a psychotherapist for more than 30 years now. For more than 20 of them I have been a full-time faculty member, training students on the philosophy and practice of psychotherapy. I have also engaged in a lot of writing about therapy. In 2020, I began writing an article about a specific type of therapeutic letter that I had found myself constructing and giving to my clients. I was also training/supervising students in a university-based therapy clinic and would train the therapists to write a therapy letter in the format I had developed. I brought on board my graduate assistant, April Brown, to help write the article, *Temporal Therapeutic Letters: Utilizing Time as a Structural Guide*, which was published in the *Journal of Systemic Therapies* (Reiter & Brown, 2020). Afterward, I realized there hadn't been, to my knowledge, a book on writing therapeutic letters. I began to consider doing so. However, a bigger understanding came to me; psychotherapists use writing in many more ways than just therapeutic letters. They do so when they write progress notes, construct their contractual forms, contact other service providers, and get clients to write for their own benefit. Further, I realized that there hadn't been a book that had explored the variety of writing psychotherapists engage in. Thus, the impetus for this book was born. In thinking about this, I also realized that much of the writing that occurs in therapy doesn't happen alone. Thus, I asked some of my friends and colleagues to join me for certain chapters, which is why you'll see different co-authors (Chapter 3 was written completely by Sara Ferguson, who has much more expertise than me in psychological assessment writing). I'm very glad I was able to collaborate with each of them. It is very nice when you get to work with people you enjoy. My hope is that there will be much in this book that you will find useful for your work with your clients. Some information may be old hat, while other information is new. We tried to provide many examples of writing so that you can have a more in-depth understanding of their possibilities. Please feel free to use, adapt, or ignore whatever you find that will be most useful for you—and most importantly useful for your clients—in your psychotherapy practice.

Acknowledgments

I want to thank all of my co-authors: Myron Burns, April Brown, Pei-Fen Li, Sara Ferguson, Lori Pantaleao, Jessica Popham, Kelsey Railsback, Natalie Rothman, Kayleigh Sabo, and Shaelise Tor. Thanks also to my editor at Routledge, Heather Evans, who has been supportive of this and my other projects with Routledge. To all of the Routledge support staff, especially Upasruti Biswas, my utmost appreciation. And to my students whom I learned with about writing in psychotherapy along the way....

About the Editor

Dr. Michael D. Reiter, PhD, LMFT, has been a practicing family therapist for more than 30 years. Michael is a licensed marriage and family therapist in the state of Florida and an approved supervisor through the American Association of Marriage and Family Therapy. From 1999–2022, he was a faculty member at Nova Southeastern University, teaching in the Division of Social and Behavioral Sciences, Clinical Psychology, Mental Health Counseling, and most recently in the Department of Family Therapy. Michael has been heavily engaged in scholarship, having written 11 books, including *Therapeutic Interviewing* (2nd ed. Routledge, 2022), *Systems Theories for Psychotherapists* (Routledge, 2019), *Family Therapy: An Introduction to Process, Practice and Theory* (Routledge, 2018), *Case Conceptualization in Family Therapy* (Pearson, 2014), and *The Craft of Family Therapy* (Routledge, 2nd ed., 2021), which was co-written with Dr. Salvador Minuchin, founder of Structural Family Therapy. Michael's books have been translated into Spanish, Polish, Chinese, Italian, and Korean. He has also co-edited two books with Dr. Ron Chenail: *Behavioral, Humanistic-Experiential and Psychodynamic Approaches to Couples Counseling* and *Constructivist, Critical, and Integrative Approaches to Couples Counseling*. Both books were published in 2017 by Routledge. Michael has also published more than 20 journal articles and presented at state, national, and international conferences regarding a variety of therapeutic interventions and models.

Contributors

April Brown, MS, is a licensed marriage and family therapist residing in Miami, FL. She is a doctoral candidate in Family Therapy at Nova Southeastern University. April is the owner of a group private practice for couples and mothers postpartum; her clinical work centers on a systemic and narrative approach. Writing, specifically letter writing, is an integral part of the therapy process with her clients.

Myron J. Burns, PhD, is currently an associate professor in the Department of Psychology and Neuroscience at Nova Southeastern University College of Psychology. He has instructed a variety of courses in psychology, counseling, and substance abuse. Dr. Burns has worked with individuals, families, first responders, and military personnel on stress management, depression, and drug use.

Sara Ferguson, PsyD, is a licensed clinical psychologist with specialty training in forensic psychology. She provides psychotherapy and psychological assessment services to individuals across the lifespan in a south Florida private practice. Dr. Ferguson's research and publication interests emphasize at-risk youth needs, including adolescent suicide and violence prevention, juvenile offending, school shootings, and forensic psychological assessment.

Pei-Fen Li, PhD, is an associate professor in the Department of Couple and Family Therapy at the Dr. Kiran C. Patel College of Osteopathic Medicine, Nova Southeastern University. She is a licensed marriage and family therapist and AAMFT-approved supervisor. Her research interests include dyadic analyses of couples' relational characteristics on their well-being, application of MFT models in Eastern cultures, acculturation of immigrant families, reentry experiences of international students, and solution-focused brief therapy intervention with parents of children with Autism.

Lori Pantaleao, PhD, is an assistant professor of Family Therapy in the Department of Couple and Family Therapy of the Dr. Kiran C. Patel College of Osteopathic Medicine at Nova Southeastern University and serves as the assistant program director for the MS students. Lori is a dually licensed clinician in mental health counseling and marriage and family therapy; she is a certified addiction professional and a certified telehealth practitioner. Lori has presented solutions-focused brief therapy training concepts at national and international conferences. In addition, Dr. Pantaleao is an editor for *The Qualitative Report* and holds a Certificate in Qualitative Research.

Jessica Popham, PhD, is an assistant professor of psychology and practicum coordinator at Albizu University. She is a licensed marriage and family therapist and approved supervisor of the American Association of Marriage and Family Therapy. She has presented nationally and internationally at conferences on family therapy, qualitative research, adoption, and clinical application.

Kelsey Railsback, PhD, is a licensed marriage and family therapist. In addition to instructing family therapy courses and practicums at Touro University Worldwide, she has an international life coaching practice and works as a guest editor for *The Qualitative Report*. She is passionate about growing an ethical qualitative research community. Her clinical interests include a focus on social justice and working with marginalized populations, and she has presented nationally on her research and clinical work with sexual survivors and sexual offenders.

Natalie Rothman, PhD, is an assistant professor of Family Therapy in the Department of Couple and Family Therapy of the Dr. Kiran C. Patel College of Osteopathic Medicine at Nova Southeastern University. Natalie also serves as the interim clinical director of the Brief Therapy Institute for NSUHealth. She is a dually licensed clinician in mental health counseling and marriage and family therapy, a certified addiction professional, and a certified telehealth practitioner. Natalie has assisted in managing a thriving practice in Royal Palm Beach, Florida, and has presented at national and international conferences.

Kayleigh Sabo, MS, has a master's degree in Marriage and Family Therapy from Nova Southeastern University (NSU) and is currently pursuing her PhD in Couple and Family Therapy at NSU as well. She is a registered marriage and family intern in Florida, working toward full licensure. Kayleigh is a certified yoga instructor (RYT-200) and incorporates yoga practices into her therapeutic work. She has worked as a therapist in university and community mental health centers as well as in private practice.

Shaelise Tor, PhD, is an assistant professor at Nova Southeastern University. She holds an MS in MFT from the University of Rochester and a PhD in MFT from Syracuse University. Her research focuses on understanding cultural differences in expressions of attachment to create more culturally responsive clinical interventions. She is also clinically active and trained in Medical Family Therapy, Narrative Exposure Therapy (NET), and Assessments for Medical Gender Affirmation Procedures.

Chapter 1

Writing in Psychotherapy

Michael D. Reiter

As a psychotherapist, you likely entered this field because you wanted to continue the legacy that Sigmund Freud began about 130 years ago working in the illustrious field that had originally been called "talk therapy." You chose to become a psychotherapist because you want to help people. It is a calling—a calling that allows you to enter people's lives, usually at their lowest points, and make a difference for them. You have spent a lot of time, money, and effort in learning about people, yourself, and the tools and techniques that will help you to help your clients. Psychotherapy has likely become one of the most significant aspects of your life. Congratulations on choosing this field, as it is a noble profession.

When most people think about what occurs when someone goes to therapy, it usually involves two people sitting down across from one another and having a conversation about one of those people's problems. Somehow in this back-and-forth exchange (depending on the therapist's theoretical orientation) change happens. The medium for that change is the therapeutic talk. You have said things that impact the way the client thinks, feels, and behaves. The session usually lasts about 50–60 minutes, the client leaves, and you can think back and smile to the good work that you did with that client.

What is missing from this fantasy is the practicalities of our field. While one of our primary therapeutic tools is the words that we speak, there are additional components to what we do as psychotherapists. It is this aspect of our profession that this book focuses on—the written component. When you look at your graduate degree curriculum, you will see courses on Ethics, Techniques, Research, and Theory. You will write many papers explaining these ideas. However, what you are likely not going to study is the importance of writing in psychotherapy.

Therapists do a lot of writing. Sometimes it happens in session; however, much of the writing in psychotherapy occurs after the client has gone home and the therapist considers what happened during their time together. Each session you have with a client needs to be documented. We do so with what we call progress notes (see Chapter 2).

DOI: 10.4324/9781003294702-1

Other writing you might engage in is to various professionals involved in the treatment of the client (see Chapter 11). Therapists may also write about a case for publication, such as case studies (see Chapter 12). This has been perhaps the most educational type of writing as it is how many therapists learned how to think about and do therapy, by reading the cases of other therapists. Freud wrote extensively about his cases. This was especially important for a fledgling field. In the latter part of the 20th century, with the advent of easily obtainable recording machines, therapists were better able to provide actual transcripts of what was discussed in session. Therapists write about their case conceptualizations—how they view the theory of problem formation and problem resolution—and then apply this conceptualization to an actual case. You have likely read quite a lot of what has happened in other therapists' sessions by reading a variety of case studies in articles and books. While theory is well-and-good, therapists need to read about how theory is placed into practice.

While case studies are one way therapists use writing about therapy, they also actually use writing during the course of therapy to help the client move toward change. One of the first written accounts of the use of therapeutic writing was done by John Watkins in 1949 in the article "Poison-pen therapy." Watkins was working with a depressed and suicidal middle-aged woman who awoke during the middle of the night and wrote a 12-page letter to her mother expressing her hostility toward her. The client then had a reduction of symptoms. Watkins believed that this letter became a significant cathartic experience for her. He then experimented with what he called "poison-pen therapy" where he would have his clients, when they began to encounter feelings of hostility, write a "hate-letter" to the person. This letter was not to be sent but rather brought into therapy to be the focus of discussion. Watkins thought that shifting people from speaking to writing slowed down their thoughts and helped extend the cathartic process. He found that the best therapeutic results occurred from integrating and consolidating in session the material the client wrote in the hate-letter.

Perhaps the first book that focused on therapists writing to clients was edited by Pearson in 1965. Pearson had chaired an American Psychological Association symposium focusing on the use of written communication in therapy and put this together in *The Use of Written Communication in Psychotherapy*. Four papers are contained in this book and Pearson, in his Preface, refers to written communication as being "unorthodox." In one of these papers, Albert Ellis (1965) predicted that the use of a non-speaking process between therapist and client, including writing rather than speaking in session, writing letters to clients, having clients write notes or letters between sessions, and having clients read articles and books, would become an accepted mode of treatment. Over half a century later, written communication has become commonplace and integral in psychotherapy practice.

We are at a place in the over 100 years of therapy where working through a variety of modalities is not only acceptable but imperative. Those who conduct psychotherapy come from a variety of disciplines, including clinical psychologists, counseling psychologists, marriage and family therapists, mental health counselors, clinical social workers, psychiatrists, as well as a variety of other job titles. We mainly all do the same thing. We work with people who are experiencing some type of distress in their life and try to make their lives more functional and enjoyable. We may have different theories of the etiology of the client's problem. We may have different techniques for problem resolution. We may have different styles of working. Regardless, we are all psychotherapists who engage people in their ultimate pursuit—change. Throughout this change process, we all engage in a variety of ways that writing finds its way into our practice.

With the advent of technology, there has been an increase in the use of writing between therapists and clients. What was once thought to only be applicable when there were unique situations where the therapist and client could not physically encounter one another (for instance, if one of them moved making face-to-face visits extremely difficult) or a client had difficulty hearing or speaking (Raimy, 1965) is now considered acceptable for any client. Writing has become infused in all aspects of ethical and responsible client care. What was once viewed as unorthodox is now commonplace. What has not been considered a legitimate aspect of psychotherapy is now acceptable and beneficial.

As an example, therapists writing letters to clients (see Chapters 5 and 6) were seen as anomalies and unique. During the late 1980s and 1990s, the use of therapeutic letters came to the forefront of the therapeutic community, where therapists began researching their usage. There is now debate as to how much the technique and concepts of therapeutic writing are from the scientific paradigm or from the humanities paradigm (Wright & Chung, 2001). That is, how much can we research and formalize the impact of writing—in essence, mastery of this technique—rather than promote the healing powers of writing—the mystery of it. As is the case with most debates, there is no right side. Both aspects, the scientific and the humanistic, are always in play.

This book covers both practical writing (e.g., case notes, assessments, communications) and therapeutic writing (e.g., therapy letters, journaling). The hope is that the information provided in this book will help you become a better psychotherapist. Since therapy is more than what happens in the room, my intention with this book is to widen your lens as to how you can, should, and might utilize various types of writing in your therapy practice. Part of this writing is to ensure you are following the laws and rules of our profession. Part of this writing is to enhance your actual therapy techniques when you are with your clients. Part of this writing is perhaps for yourself, so that you can engage in self-reflection and engage in person-of-the-therapist work. However you use writing in your practice, you should understand the whys and the hows of it. This book is one component of how to do that.

Importance of Writing

Human beings have engaged in some form of writing for approximately 5,000 years. Over this time, writing has been used to document human experience, communicate with one another, inform and be informed, and express oneself. Writing has become extremely important for human existence. Think of some of the important written documents: the Magna Carta in 1215; the Gutenberg Bible in 1455; the Declaration of Independence in 1776; the Constitution of the United States in 1787; the Emancipation Proclamation in 1863; the Treaty of Versailles in 1919; and the 19th Amendment in 1920, which gave women in the United States the right to vote.

During the last 20 years, on a much more local level, writing has equaled or replaced verbally talking in how friends, colleagues, and family members communicate with one another. With the advent of technology, email, smartphones, and social media websites and apps, people have been writing to one another to stay connected, work together, and educate one another. You may be reading this book while going to a completely online university where course content is conveyed through writing on a website rather than talking with the professor and classmates live in a classroom. This very day you have probably interacted with many people by texting and/or emailing them. Most people would find it difficult to not have their cell phone with them for a week, let alone a day. This is because many of our connections to people happen through what is written either to us via texts and emails or to people via social media.

Why is writing important for people in general? Primarily, it is about communication—to family, friends, co-workers, etc. Writing also slows down our thought processes and allows us to think more clearly about what is going on for us. When we do so we are usually better able to express ourselves. In many ways, writing is a social process where it is always embodying interpersonal relationships (Litowitz & Gundlach, 1987). These authors explained that "every piece of writing presents a self and invokes an other or others, who may or may not be the consciously intended audience of the piece" (p. 85).

Writing is also a way for ideas to get circulated in society. Before the recent advent of the internet, newspapers, magazines, and books were some of the primary ways that information was provided to the masses. Think about all the written material you have read in your life. You have likely attended school for over 15 years reading hundreds of textbooks, including this textbook. You have read newspapers, material on websites, legal contracts (okay, so most of us don't fully read them—but we are supposed to!), and road signs. Now, think about all the written material you have written. This probably includes a lot of essays, exams, text messages, emails, poetry, journals, and letters. What were the various purposes of these writings? How would your life be different if you couldn't write?

Why is it important for psychotherapists to know about the various aspects of the written word in the therapy process? First, it is endemic. Writing, to various degrees, is everywhere in therapy. You cannot practice therapy without writing something. As you will see in Chapter 2, all therapists must write progress notes for each session that they have with clients. You may also write up assessments and reports (see Chapter 3) or write case summaries to be sent to the referring person or for the medical and/or legal context (see Chapter 11). These writings may never be seen by the client. Then there is the writing that you do share with the client including all the legal forms of the therapeutic contract (see Chapter 4) as well as therapeutic letters and documents (see Chapters 5, 6, and 9). For therapeutic purposes, you might even have the client engage in writing (see Chapters 7 and 8). When you finish this book, you will have a much greater appreciation that from the beginning of the therapeutic process until the end—and at all points in between—writing is an integral component of ensuring that you are doing sound and beneficial work with your clients.

Second, what is written helps to move therapy either forward or backward. Steinberg (2000) stated, "The right words capture or convey a feeling or an attitude in a way that contributes to the therapeutic process, just as the wrong words can undermine it" (p. 1). Each communication that you have with your client is potentially therapeutic. Even a text message to the client to remind them about an appointment (see Chapter 10) is part of the therapy and may be influential in the client's movement toward their goals. How you write to your client should be different from how you write to your friend or family member. How you word your forms sets the tone for the therapeutic interaction. What you put in a therapeutic letter and how you word it have a significant impact on how it is received by the client.

Third, the writing that you do in therapy represents your accountability to the field and society. Psychotherapists operate under certain guidelines, which we call ethics. We follow standard ways of being with clients, such as the notions of beneficence (doing good) and nonmaleficence (not doing harm). We also promote client autonomy, where they make their own choices for their lives. Some of the writing that we do as therapists highlights how we are living up to our ethical ideals. For instance, our informed consent form establishes the therapeutic contract including the responsibilities of both therapist and client. Our progress notes demonstrate the standard of care we provided, showing how we followed the normal practices that psychotherapists adhere to. This acts as one form of protection for our clients, ourselves, and our field. Since writing is ingrained in how people communicate and more particularly in how psychotherapists function, to be a good psychotherapist you should have an in-depth understanding of the ways we use writing in our field.

Therapy and Writing

Primarily, therapists write about clients (Bacigalupe, 1996). During a session, therapists might take notes while the client is talking. We write an assessment or biopsychosocial evaluation that tries to encapsulate who a client is, their diagnostic difficulties, and their current life problems. We may then write case or progress notes, describing our interaction with the client, what they said, how they responded to our interventions, and the goals that we have for them in psychotherapy. We might also write about the client to other people, such as a referring physician, a case summary for a judge, or even a case study for a journal article. The client's voice is usually missing in many of the therapist's writings.

Further, aspects of diversity play a role in what the therapist privileges not only during the session but what information finds its way onto the page. As Bacigalupe (1996) explained, "What we discuss and write about with clients is influenced by age, gender, race, social class and our position of often being outsiders to the world of clients" (p. 362). While we cannot remove ourselves from our social positions, we can come to recognize how they might play a role in our interactions with clients and our written output. To offset the possibility of privileging the therapist's voice over the client's, we might consider the differences between writing *to* clients and writing *with* clients.

Most therapist writing has been writing *to* clients. This comes in the form of therapy contracts and forms (see Chapter 4), therapeutic letters (see Chapters 5 and 6), documents (see Chapter 9), or technology-based correspondence (see Chapter 10). These sorts of writing help convey the therapist's ideas to the client. They may set the parameters of the therapeutic relationship, push forward the therapeutic agenda, or help in the flow of the therapeutic communication.

Writing *with* clients privileges more the client's voice. It is a way to encourage client participation in the therapeutic process. There is usually a shift when clients write from the expert knowledge of the therapist to the local knowledge of the client (Bacigalupe, 1996). Writing with clients comes in the form of client-written letters (see Chapter 7), client journaling and expressive writing (see Chapter 8), and collaborative documentation (see Chapter 2). We will talk more about the importance of this type of writing later on in this book.

Therapist's Writing Skills

How good of a writer do you think you are? When taking time to think about the answer to this question you might first go to prose—likely poetry or expressive writing such as fiction that uses metaphors, alliteration, or other advanced writing skills. There aren't many Stephen Kings, Edgar Allen Poes, or Ernest Hemingways. Next, you might think about how you did in your high school and college English classes. You learned the basic components of sentences, paragraphs, and essays. Your grades in those classes may have been internalized as to what type of writer you are. Hopefully, though, you realize that writing is a skill that is constantly being developed and that you are constantly improving.

All therapists know how to write. The question comes—do they know how to write well? Do they know how to write in a way that will correctly convey the information and messages they want to get across? Do they know how to change their writing to different recipients? Do they know how to write so that their words become interventions? Do they know the importance of writing to help clients move closer to their goals? This book is intended as one step to help therapists answer these questions, understand, and utilize writing more proficiently and effectively in their practice.

In your graduate program, you are likely to have only written term papers and essays on exams. You probably did not cover proper writing in any class. A few master's programs might spend one day talking about what will go into a progress note. However, this skill is usually learned "on the job" when you begin your first practicum placement. Some doctoral programs, especially those in clinical psychology, will have several classes where you will learn about assessment writing. Others might have an academic writing class or a grant writing class. However, most of your time in school was spent learning concepts, ethics, theory, and techniques. This is because the component of writing is a hidden aspect of our field. This aspect needs to be honed and developed.

Writing is a skill and like all skills it can be learned and improved. Skill development comes from thoughtful engagement with the material, learning fundamental ideas, and frequent practice and utilization of the skill. The good news is that whatever skill level you have, the more you engage in writing the better you will be at it. But this is assuming that not only will you write, but you will also review and examine your writing. This is like audio- or video-recording your therapy sessions and reviewing the tape. This provides you more of an outsider perspective. [And yes, I know that pretty much no one likes to watch or listen to themselves on tape, especially when watching themselves as the therapist. However, it is so useful it should be mandatory in every therapy program.] The same holds for your writing. You need to learn how to properly write in the therapeutic context as well as how to self-edit yourself. In the beginning, it could be very useful to have your supervisor or colleagues review whatever you write—progress notes, assessments, clinical forms, or therapeutic letters. Over time, by taking in other people's feedback, you will learn how to be your own editor while you are writing.

Good Writing

This book explores how therapists use writing in their practice. It is beyond the scope to go in-depth to describe the components of good writing. There are many books that do and can do that so much better than I can. However, I do want to take a few moments to review a few of the basic elements of good writing that can help you in whatever type of writing you do as a therapist.

One of the first things for you to think about when writing, as a therapist or in other aspects of your life, is purpose. Why are you writing what you are writing? Is it to document something? To convince someone? To clarify? Your purpose will inform the format and tone of what you write. If your purpose is to provide clear expectations, you will be more straightforward. If your purpose is to woo a potential romantic partner, your writing may be flowier, using metaphors and similes. Knowing your purpose is the first step to knowing what and how you want to write.

Second, you will need to think about your audience. To whom are you writing? As therapists, we tend to write to ourselves (e.g., progress notes), our clients, a referring person, or another professional. Each audience will likely lead us to include or exclude certain content and to change our narrative tone. For instance, writing to a client will lead you to write in more second person—where you are referring to the person you are speaking to (like how I am doing in this paragraph as I am writing to you). When writing up an assessment, you are likely not to write in the first or second person but rather in the third person where you are talking about the client (using his, her, or they when referring to them).

Your writing should also demonstrate clarity. As therapists, we want whoever is reading what we are writing to understand it; usually so that it is so clear they do not have to ask us any questions to understand it (an exception here is if you were writing a paradoxical letter to your client and you thought ambiguity and confusion would be therapeutic for them). Clarity is enhanced when you use clear and specific language. The reader should know exactly (as close as we can approximate to that) what you were trying to say.

Lastly, your writing should be accurate, both in content and style. As a university professor, one of the most frustrating things about grading some students' papers is when there are misspellings. Just about every word processing program has a spell-check function. Please make sure that you use it! When there are misspellings on your website or in your documents, the reader is likely to question your professionalism and abilities. Your word processing program also likely has some type of grammar check. If not, you can use one of a variety to help ensure that your writing is accurate and clear. Imagine you read the following sentence from a doctor that was going to perform a serious surgery on you:

I don't thing that there is anything wrong with its.

How comfortable would you be having that doctor operate on you? I suspect you would be like me and think, *If they are that careless in how they write, how careless might they be when performing surgery?*

Sometimes it is the little things that make a huge difference. We may not pay attention to a well-written document (usually not saying to ourselves, "Wow, there were no grammatical or spelling mistakes in my doctor's informed consent form") but we are quite likely to notice when it is poorly written ("Didn't someone proofread this? If this is the lack of attention they give to their documents, what about for my treatment?"). Even if you are a good writer, it is a good practice to have someone else look over what you've written as they may be able to see things that we did not since we know what we were trying to say.

Supervisor's Writing

The brunt of this book is about how psychotherapists utilize writing in therapy; either they are writing to or about their clients or they are having their clients write to aid in the treatment process. For those therapists who become supervisors, writing is also an integral part of their role. From contracts to feedback, supervisors provide their supervisees with written material that is used in the supervisory process.

When I teach beginning students who are practicing active listening skills, one technique I use is having them audio-record a role-play session and then transcribe it. The transcription is usually done one line at a time so that they (a) write word-for-word what the client said, (b) write down what they think the client was really trying to tell them, (c) write down what they actually said, and then (d) given (b) write what they would like to have said differently. This assignment is usually an eye-opener for the students where they can slow down their thought processes and get closer to the client's meanings and experiences. By not having the anxiety of feeling like they must immediately say something, the students are able to look at the words and digest them, providing space for a deeper understanding of the client's expression, their own expression, as well as the flow of the therapeutic conversation.

In supervision, a similar process can happen if you ask your supervisee to transcribe their actual sessions (where the session was audio/video-recorded with the client's signed permission). Transcribing sessions would likely be most useful for beginning therapists or anxious therapists, who prefer structure in supervision (Riordan et al., 2001). These authors explained the advantages of using transcriptions in supervision in that the supervisee may:

1 experience a sense of being heard in totality rather than in spot excerpts.
2 likely detect from early transcripts to later ones a change in skill attainment.
3 feel a reduced sense of supervision fear; it may be easier to look at the words than hear the words and be less time-consuming than searching through a tape.
4 not feel the separation that sometimes exists between supervisor and supervisee.
5 find a decrease in psychological distress through the actual writing process; writing closes the gap.
6 find it helpful in determining the effects of anxieties and feelings.
7 find the transcript a helpful tool in teaching corrective listening skills.
8 find it helpful in sharpening assessment skills, formulating problem statements and goals.
9 find the transcript provides complete and exact recall...
10 find that it is a rich source in which to provide support. The written word, coupled with supervisory verbal reinforcement, further enhances skill development.
11 find the transcript a good source to point out to the supervisee his or her personal growth and receptivity to supervision.
12 aid the supervisee to better provide feedback to peers.

(pp. 197–198)

Transcriptions are especially useful in "dead" supervision, where the supervisor never actually sees the supervisee working with clients. In the university clinic that I supervise in, we utilize "live" supervision, where I am watching, in the moment, the student therapists working with clients. I can talk to them immediately before and after the session, as well as call them on the phone during their session or have them take a consultation break so that I can provide feedback. However, many ideas come into play for the rest of the team behind the one-way mirror, so I have someone behind the mirror take notes about everything that is discussed while the therapist is in the room with the client. This way, when they finish, they will be given the notes and are privy to all the conversations and feedback that were given while they were engaged with the client.

Live supervision provides the supervisor with direct access to the case and the therapist's process and skills. For dead supervision, this direct access is not as available. When I meet with supervisees who are working off-campus, I am only privy to what they tell me happened. This explanation is tempered by memory, bias, and ego. Specific word choices, as well as nonverbal communication, are usually lost. This is where the use of transcripts may come into play and be useful for the supervisor, supervisee, and the supervisory process. Depending on how detailed you want the supervisee to transcribe the session, the finer details of what occurred in the therapy room can become illuminated in the supervisory room. For instance, you might include filler words such as "um" or "uh" or word repetitions like "I...I just thought that....that you wanted to...." This will give you a sense of the flow of the therapist's communication.

While using transcriptions in supervision is usually advantageous, this may not always be the case. Having their body of work—which is usually a reflection of self—on display, the supervisee might have difficulty being open and trusting the supervisor (Riordan et al., 2001). Further, the transcript may elicit fear in the supervisee where they realize that their limitations are exposed. To attempt to offset these disadvantages, you might consider how you introduce the use of transcriptions and ensure that, especially initially, you focus on the supervisee's views of their transcript—how well they think they did and areas that they want to highlight as being productive portions of the session.

Not every supervisee will be able to create transcripts of their cases, usually due to a lack of permission for recording the session by their site and/or the client. So, this form of writing in supervision may not always occur. However, what is likely to be a mainstay in most supervisory relationships is the written evaluation. Besides exploring self-of-the-therapist, counseling skills, and therapist models, supervisors tend to provide an overview evaluation. For those supervisors working with supervisees in an academic setting, this will usually come at the midterm point and/or end of the semester. For non-academic supervision, you might decide to provide periodic written evaluations— perhaps once every six months.

Written summative evaluations serve several purposes such as providing a record of the therapist's growth as well as areas of potential growth (Riordan et al., 2001). There is no set format for written summative evaluations (unless the school/agency you are working at has its own). However, these usually include discussion of the supervisee's professionalism, openness to feedback, counseling skills, case conceptualization skills, major areas of strength, and major areas of potential growth. Like most forms and written communication, it is usually a good idea to follow up the delivery of the written evaluation with a face-to-face meeting to talk about the letter, answer any questions, and collaboratively talk about where the supervisee might go from here.

Bibliotherapy

For the most part in this book, we will be talking about writing that you and/or the client engage in that happens either inside or outside the therapy room that can only occur based on the conversations that are happening between the two of you. However, you can also use the written word of other people as a tool in the therapeutic process.

Many therapists may suggest or assign a book or some other previously printed material to be read by the client outside of the therapy session. We call this type of intervention **bibliotherapy**. The root biblio- refers to books and the Greek root of therapy means healing. Thus, bibliotherapy is healing through the use of books. Riordan and Wilson (1989) defined this therapeutic tool, "Bibliotherapy refers to the guided reading of written materials in gaining understanding or solving problems relevant to a person's therapeutic needs" (p. 506).

Usually, the books that are recommended are information-giving texts; that is, they are books written by therapists for the general population that provide specific information, exercises, and suggestions for the person to overcome a certain problem. These books usually fall within the category of **self-help books** and are designed as either stand-alone or adjunctive to therapy. However, you might also suggest clients read a plethora of other genres of literature such as nonfiction, fiction, poetry, or other types of writings. Whichever writing is used, bibliotherapists tend to have four main goals:

- to improve the capacity to respond by stimulating and enriching mental images and concepts and by helping the feelings about these images to surface
- to increase self-understanding by helping individuals value their own personhood and become more knowledgeable and more accurate about self-perceptions
- to increase awareness of interpersonal relationships
- to improve reality orientation

(Hynes & Hynes-Berry, 1994, p. 24)

You might engage in bibliotherapy for one, two, three, or all four of these goals.

There are two main types of bibliotherapy: reading and interactive (McCulliss, 2011). **Reading bibliotherapy** happens when the therapist assigns articles and/or books for the client to read outside of session without discussion between the two of them. **Interactive bibliotherapy** entails the assigning of reading that is then discussed in session. This type has three key elements: participant, literature, and facilitator. For therapists like us, our client is the participant, we are the facilitator, and the reading material is the literature. Hynes and Hynes-Berry (1994) explained,

> In interactive bibliotherapy, a trained facilitator uses guided discussions to help the clinical or developmental participant(s) integrate both feelings and cognitive responses to a selected work of literature, which may be a printed text, some form of audiovisual material, or creative writing by the participant.
>
> (p. 17)

Within these two types of bibliotherapy are three categories: clinical, developmental, and client-developed. **Clinical bibliotherapy** is used with clients who have significant emotional and behavioral difficulties. This tends to happen in psychiatric units, substance abuse facilities, and other mental health centers. While these readings may be psychology/clinically related, they do not have to be. Plays, poetry, short stories, and/or novels can be used to help bring up thoughts, feelings, and situations the client may be experiencing. **Developmental bibliotherapy** is utilized more by librarians, educators, and healthcare helpers who are working with individuals not dealing with severe difficulties. These written works are suggested so the person can think about their current functioning and how it is developmentally appropriate. These resources may be considered psychoeducation, where they explore family structure, death, substance abuse, divorce, stepfamilies, or a variety of other normal life challenges and difficulties. **Client-developed bibliotherapy** occurs when clients create their own writings, such as poetry, music lyrics, and autobiographies (see Chapter 8).

When using bibliotherapy, you will do more than just suggest something for the client to read. Usually, you will discuss the process with the client so that sessions bolster the learning the client is having at home from reading and that reading bolsters the learning from sessions. You might also ask the client to do their own writing based on what they read. For instance, if reading a story about how the protagonist handles a crisis or life event, you could have the client write a different ending or they could write about what they thought of how certain characters thought and behaved. Bibliotherapy has been shown to be effective for clients dealing with a variety of presenting problems (McCulliss, 2011), particularly as an adjunctive tool in psychotherapy (Riordan & Wilson, 1989). It is important to take into consideration the client's presenting problem, the quality of the writing you are suggesting, the client's reading level, and the connection the reading has to the therapeutic goals.

One specific type of bibliotherapy is **self-help books**. If you go into one of the few remaining physical bookstores you will most likely come to a section titled, Self-Help. Here, you and your clients can find books written specifically to help people overcome a particular difficulty. There are thousands of self-help books focusing on a variety of topics such as self-esteem, depression, anxiety, and self-defeating behaviors. A subset of self-help books is **workbooks**, which require the active engagement of the reader where they are asked to do many exercises and assignments that are designed to help them to change (see Chapter 9 for more about workbooks).

Bibliotherapy is a beneficial adjunct or alternative to face-to-face psychotherapy. One of the biggest benefits is that it is quite cost-effective. The books and readings are usually available through a local library or available for purchase at low cost. Clients can also access these resources at times that may work better for them than the limited availability of most therapists. If the client wakes up at 2 in the morning and wants to be productive, they can read a chapter of a self-help book and engage in change activities.

To summarize, Hynes and Hynes-Berry (1994) provided several assumptions about bibliotherapy:

1   Bibliotherapy is an interactive process.
2   Literature is defined in the broadest sense.
3   The process described takes place in both clinical and developmental bibliotherapy.
4   The practice of bibliotherapy may take place either on a one-on-one basis or in a group setting.
5   The results of effective bibliotherapy are improved self-esteem and assimilation of appropriate psychological or social values into the participant's character and behavior.
6   Bibliotherapy is a therapy, but part of its unique effectiveness lies in its use of literature as the primary tool; in this way, bibliotherapy makes a special appeal to the health aspects of the mind, for both developmental and clinical participants...the emphasis in interactive bibliotherapy is directed more to the encouragement and reinforcement of strengths than to the diagnosis of problem areas.
7   The effectiveness of bibliotherapy depends on the facilitator's ability to choose material that speaks to the individual participant's needs and interests; to make accurate, empathic interpretations of the participant's responses; and, through literature and dialogue, to draw out deeper self-understanding. In short, a good bibliotherapist is a skilled listener.

(pp. 17–18)

At some point in your career, you are likely to ask a client to read something, perhaps inside or outside of session, that you think will be therapeutic for them. It will be important for you to have knowledge of the written material you suggest since it will likely become the mill for the grist of the next therapy session. Further, if the reading is potentially beneficial for your client, it is also potentially beneficial for you.

So, how might you introduce bibliotherapy into your therapy? You have lots of ways of doing so, regardless of whether you do so with an individual, couple, family, or group. Here is one possibility:

> There is a book that I think is extremely relevant to you and what you are going through. It is something that can potentially enhance what we are doing here. You can get the book online, buy it, or even check it out from the library. What we can do is each week talk here about how the ideas from the book impact you. What are your thoughts about that?

Once the client begins reading what you suggested, then you can engage in the various bibliotherapy steps (Hynes & Hynes-Berry, 1994). Step one is about recognition. The client recognizes something in the reading that engages them. This should pertain to the experience of personhood. At times, the recognition is direct; something happened to a character in the reading that the client has also experienced. Other times, what piqued their interest refers to beliefs, morals, and or values. When clients start recognizing connections, they usually then begin to associate these with unacknowledged feelings.

Step two of bibliotherapy is about examination. In normal reading, we might do so just for pleasure. We likely don't slow down and really scrutinize what we are reading. By recommending and assigning a reading, the client knows that you believe that what they are reading is not only relevant but, more importantly, useful for their self-growth. This process leads them to be more intentional and thoughtful in their engagement with what they are reading.

Step three focuses on juxtaposition. The client has recognized that something from the reading is meaningful to them and thus they begin to examine it more closely. In this step, the client takes these newly developed thoughts and engages in a process of comparison and contrast. By putting ideas side by side with one another, the client can hold both the old and the new. This may lead to reaffirming the old position, invalidating the old position, or adopting a new way of understanding, thinking, feeling, and behaving.

The fourth and final step is the application to self. Here, the client evaluates and integrates what they have learned and understood through the bibliotherapy process. When examining their new viewpoints, the client evaluates what these viewpoints mean for them. However, as with all therapy, it is when the client integrates the new ideas into their actions that change is truly implemented.

Bibliotherapy is one tool in your therapeutic tool pouch. One suggestion for you is to read books that you think will be personally beneficial for you before you suggest either that book or bibliotherapy in general for your clients. This will provide you with the ability to understand the process and impact of bibliotherapy.

Structure of this Book

This book is intentionally designed to be a wide-catchment endeavor. There are likely to be chapters that will be more pertinent to your specific context, clientele, and therapeutic modality. The hope is that you will find support in areas where you currently engage in writing as well as learn additional aspects of writing in psychotherapy that you can incorporate into your practice for efficiency and effectiveness.

Chapter 2 focuses on progress notes, a form of session documentation that all therapists are required to engage in. Hopefully, after reading this chapter, you will have a better understanding of why therapists write progress notes as well as learn about a variety of standard progress note formats.

Chapter 3 deals with diagnostic and assessment writing. This is usually done by therapists who must engage in biopsychosocial evaluations. The chapter also covers treatment plans as well as writing done when clients are suicidal, such as developing a safety plan.

The next few chapters focus on how therapists use writing as a means of intervention. Chapter 4 describes the various types of forms and pragmatic letters that most therapists use, such as informed consent, release of information, and welcome letters. Chapter 5 highlights many of the aspects of therapeutic letter writing—times when the therapist writes the client a therapeutic letter. These letters focus on attempts to create change for the client. Chapter 6 provides guidance on one specific type of letter, the temporal therapeutic letter.

Chapters 7 and 8 shift the script of authorship, highlighting therapeutic interventions where the client is doing the writing. Chapter 7 discusses client-written letters, where the client might write to a particular person, therapist, self, or even the problem. Chapter 8 describes how therapists might ask clients to write journals, poetry, and lyrics as a means of intervention in the therapy process.

Chapter 9 describes the use of counter-documents—documents that provide an alternative story to the problem-saturated stories clients are likely to come into therapy with. These counter-documents may include awards, certificates, or cards. The chapter also explores the construction of client genograms.

The last decade or so has seen an exponential influx of the use of technology used in the communication between therapist and client. Chapter 10 focuses on the use of writing psychotherapy via technology. This may come in the form of text messages, chats, or emails.

The last two chapters focus on the use of writing to convey information to those outside of the therapy room. Chapter 11 explains how therapists might need to engage in writing that will go to professionals in either the legal or medical context. Chapter 12 introduces how therapists write for article publication and grant writing in psychotherapy, and how clinicians might write to gain funds to help them in service or research capacities.

This chapter has introduced you to the importance of writing in psychotherapy. It is a skill, requirement, and tool that will be an integral component of your work as a therapist. I hope that much of this book can be used as a guide, allowing you to enhance and refine the various types of writing you and/or your clients engage in. Some of what you read will be immediately useful and applicable. Other ideas may serve as seeds, sprouting at some later time.

References

Bacigalupe, G. (1996). Writing in therapy: A participatory approach. *Journal of Family Therapy, 18*, 361–373.

Ellis, A. (1965). Some uses of the printed, written, and recorded word in psychotherapy. In L. Pearson (Ed.), *The use of written communications in psychotherapy* (pp. 23–36). Charles C. Thomas.

Hynes, A. M., & Hynes-Berry, M. (1994). *Biblio/poetry therapy*. North Star Press.

Litowitz, B. E., & Gundlach, R. A. (1987). When adolescents write: Semiotic and social dimensions of adolescents' personal writing. *Adolescent Psychiatry, 14*, 82–111.

McCulliss, D. (2011). Bibliotherapy. In L. L'Abate & L. Sweeney (Eds.), *Research on writing approaches in mental health* (pp. 67–83). Emerald Group Publishing.

Pearson, L. (1965). *The use of written communications in psychotherapy*. Charles C. Thomas.

Raimy, V. (1965). The use of written communications in psychotherapy: A critique. In L. Pearson (Ed.), *The use of written communications in psychotherapy* (pp. 47–65). Charles C. Thomas.

Riordan, R. J., Arthur, G. L., & Ashby, J. (2001). Some uses of writing in clinical supervision. In L. L'Abate (Ed.), *Distance writing and computer-assisted interventions in psychiatry and mental health* (pp. 191–211). Ablex Publishing.

Riordan, R. J., & Wilson, L. S. (1989). Bibliotherapy: Does it work? *Journal of Counseling and Development, 67*(9), 506–508.

Steinberg, D. (2000). *Letters from the clinic*. Routledge.

Watkins, J. G. (1949). Poison-pen therapy. *Journal of Psychotherapy, 3*, 410–418.

Wright, J., & Chung, M. C. (2001). Mastery or mystery? Therapeutic writing: A review of the literature. *British Journal of Guidance & Counseling, 29*(3), 277–291.

Chapter 2

Writing Progress Notes

Michael D. Reiter and Kayleigh Sabo

The first time a psychotherapy trainee goes into the therapy room may be one of the most anxiety-producing events in their lifetime. They have likely spent hundreds of hours reading books, sitting in classrooms listening to lectures, watching videos of other therapists, and perhaps engaging in role-play exercises so that they will be able to survive this moment—60 minutes sitting across from a person who is seeking psychological help. Once the session is over, they tend to feel relieved.

So much time had been invested in learning what to do in the therapy room that most trainees don't think about what happens when the client leaves the office. When they realize that they must document what occurred, the anxiety comes back (but perhaps not to the same degree). Every contact that you have with clients needs to be documented to ensure that there is a record of the treatment. While these contacts include phone calls (either appointment reminders or calling the client back if they tried to contact you), primarily the main contact you have with clients is the actual session. In psychotherapy, we document our sessions via progress notes. There may be several other ways to name session documentation such as case notes, session notes, or progress reports. For the purposes of this book, we will stick with **progress notes**, as this wording seems to be the most common usage.

Keeping appropriate and thorough client records is an ethical mandate. Regardless of your professional orientation, your ethical codes expect you to keep accurate and adequate records of your contact with your clients. Not only is record-keeping an ethical obligation, but it falls within the legal realm as well. Your progress notes are the documentation of what occurred in your contact with the client. Proper documentation is one way of demonstrating that you followed appropriate protocol when working with the client. This can be quite useful if you are ever subpoenaed for a court case regarding the client. The American Psychological Association (2007), perhaps the largest umbrella organization for therapists, provided guidelines for record-keeping (see Figure 2.1). While these specifically apply to psychologists, they are useful guidelines for any psychotherapist.

DOI: 10.4324/9781003294702-2

American Psychological Association Guidelines for Record Keeping

Guideline 1: Responsibility for Records: Psychologists generally have responsibility for the maintenance and retention of their records.

Guideline 2: Content of Records: A psychologist strives to maintain accurate, current, and pertinent records of professional services as appropriate to the circumstances and as may be required by the psychologist's jurisdiction. Records include information such as the nature, delivery, progress, and results of psychological services, and related fees.

Guideline 3: Confidentiality of Records: The psychologist takes reasonable steps to establish and maintain the confidentiality of information arising from service delivery.

Guideline 4: Disclosure of Record Keeping Procedures: When appropriate, psychologists inform clients of the nature and extent of record keeping procedures.

Guideline 5: Maintenance of Records: The psychologist strives to organize and maintain records to ensure their accuracy and to facilitate their use by the psychologist and others with legitimate access to them.

Guideline 6: Security: The psychologist takes appropriate steps to protect records from unauthorized access, damage, and destruction.

Guideline 7: Retention of Records: The psychologist strives to be aware of applicable laws and regulations and to retain records for the period required by legal, regulatory, institutional, and ethical requirements.

Guideline 8: Preserving the Context of Records: The psychologist strives to be attentive to the situational context in which records are created and how that context may influence the content of those records.

Guideline 9: Electronic Records: Electronic records, like paper records, should be created and maintained in a way that is designed to protect their security, integrity, confidentiality, and appropriate access, as well as their compliance with applicable legal and ethical requirements.

Guideline 10: Record Keeping in Organizational Settings: Psychologists working in organizational settings (e.g., hospitals, schools, community agencies, prisons) strive to follow the record keeping policies and procedures of the organization as well as the APA Ethics Code.

Guideline 11: Multiple Client Records: The psychologist carefully considers documentation procedures when conducting couple, family, or group therapy in order to respect the privacy and confidentiality of all parties.

Guideline 12: Financial Records: The psychologist strives to ensure accuracy of financial records.

Guideline 13: Disposition of Records: The psychologist plans for transfer of records to ensure continuity of treatment and appropriate access to records when the psychologist is no longer in direct control, and in planning for record disposal, the psychologist endeavors to employ methods that preserve confidentiality and prevent recovery.

Figure 2.1 The APA Guidelines for Record-Keeping.

Purposes of Progress Notes

Therapy is a contractual relationship where you must demonstrate your professionalism throughout the course of treatment. One of the primary ways of doing this is through accurate and thorough progress notes. These notes are written after every session that you have describing the day, time, and length of the session and what occurred. In essence, your progress note is a measure of your accountability to the community. If you were ever questioned about what happened in a session, you would be able to provide an overview via what was written in the progress note.

Given that third-party payers for therapeutic services have increased, these organizations usually require that the treatment they are paying for is relevant and useful—that it is designed to help people move quickly toward their goals. Your progress note, along with your treatment plan, is your way of documenting that you are focusing on the client's presenting concerns and are implementing a plan to address and remediate those problems. In these situations, your progress note will highlight what the problem is, what you did during the session to address the problem, the therapeutic gains the client is making, and your continued plan for the future.

Besides using progress notes to document the proper course of treatment, they are also useful to you as a way of helping to track and remember what has occurred in prior sessions. Depending on how good your memory is, and how many sessions you have each week, you may not recall where you are in the course of treatment with a particular client. By reviewing your progress notes—at least the previous session's note—you can quickly jog your memory and resituate yourself as to what you may do therapeutically with that client in the upcoming session. This might include reviewing any homework you might have assigned the previous session, picking up on a therapeutic theme that had been discussed, or identifying what interventions you previously used that either worked or did not work.

Additionally, progress notes are useful when a client transfers from one therapist to another. As long as the client has signed a release of information for the therapists to share information (see Chapter 4), reviewing another therapist's progress notes allows you to follow the course of treatment. This will enable you to determine the best possible pathways for you when you work with that client (not that you must follow the same treatment interventions of the previous therapist, but you will be privy to what has occurred, the assessment, and the past interventions; you would then be able to choose your own course of therapy). Further, you will be able to assess potential issues to treatment, such as past intent of self-harm, which interventions seemed useful, and various therapeutic themes.

Proper documentation of treatment through progress notes allows you to communicate with yourself and the community as to what occurred in your sessions. This increases your ability to protect yourself from later ethical issues and potential lawsuits. While we can never guarantee that we will not be sued, the more that we can show—through proper documentation—that we followed standard protocol, the more we can expect to have positive results within the therapy room and with the larger systems we may encounter. Somers et al. (2010) explained that progress notes are quite beneficial for therapists-in-training by ensuring legal expectations of documentation, reducing reliance on one's memory, holding the therapist accountable, highlighting appropriate services, communicating with other professionals, and supporting clinical decisions.

In summary, progress notes are written to convey information to a variety of individuals, including yourself, the client, other people who are on the treatment team (dependent on the clinical context), third-party reviewers, and the legal system. If you do not have progress notes (which should never be the case), you open yourself up for possible litigation. Thus, proper progress notes should be a consistent component of your therapeutic practice.

It is extremely important to write a progress note as soon after the session as possible. This is because the longer that you wait to write the note, the more additional information—likely from other cases—will come into your consciousness. Further, pertinent information may leave your short-term memory. At the immediate end of the session, you are likely to forget significant aspects of the session. The longer you wait, the less you are likely to recall important aspects of the session that would be important to document.

One of the worst things a therapist can do (besides serious unethical behavior) is to wait to write progress notes. Even waiting until the end of the workday is problematic. If you did this, you would likely do a very poor job since at the end of the day you are probably physically and emotionally drained and want to leave the worksite as fast as possible. Additionally, you will have forgotten many of the important facts and ideas that were discussed in the session.

Because writing accurate progress is so important in our field, many insurance companies have moved from viewing a session as 60 minutes to one that is 50 or 45 minutes long. This reduction in session length is to allow you time during that hour to write the progress note in hopes that you do so immediately at the end of the session instead of waiting until the end of the day or potentially until the next day.

There are several standard formats for writing progress notes, which we will explore for the remainder of this chapter. However, regardless of format, there is much overlap in what information gets put on paper (or on the computer). Wiger (2012) provided ten questions to be answered in the progress notes over the course of treatment. Not every session will address every question, but having these in mind when writing your notes can help demonstrate that you are providing adequate treatment:

1 What content or topics were discussed in the session?
2 How did the session address treatment plan objectives?
3 What therapeutic interventions and techniques were employed, and how effective were they?
4 What clinical observations (behavioral, affective, etc.) were made?
5 What progress or setbacks occurred?

6 What signs and symptoms of the diagnosis are present, increasing, decreasing, or no longer present?

7 How are treatment plan goals and objectives being met at this time?

8 What is the current medical necessity for services?

9 What is being done outside the session to increase effectiveness of therapy?

10 What are the client's current limitations and strengths?

(p. 148)

When writing your note, in any format, you should think about how you are addressing each of these questions. Again, you will not address every question in every note but will focus on most of them each session.

General Guidelines for Writing Progress Notes

Regardless of the progress note format, there are some general guidelines you should consider when writing. First and foremost, they should be written professionally. As best as possible, there should not be any spelling or grammatical errors. If you are manually writing the note, rather than typing them into an electronic chart, your handwriting should be legible. There may be times when you make a mistake, such as writing an incorrect word. This does not mean that you must start a brand-new note. Rather, cross out the word using just one line (so whoever is looking at the note can read what word was crossed off) and then put your initials next to the strikeout. Here is an example of how you might do this:

Client reported that he ~~partisipated~~ ^{MR} participated in a new training.

Depending on how the progress note page is structured, there may be a lot of open space in each section. For handwritten notes, it is okay if you do not fill up the available space. However, you should put a line through the open space so that no one else can come after you and fill in material. It should always be clear who put the information into the progress note. For instance, if you are conducting co-therapy, as many therapists-in-training do, you should do the progress note together, but only one of you should do the actual writing on the paper. Having two different sets of handwriting brings a little cause for concern to the reader in that someone may have come after the fact and tried to add information to the note after it was already signed.

Another guideline, regardless of the progress note format, is to try not to use many abbreviations. An abbreviation is likely useful for yourself (although there are times when you may forget what the abbreviation is referring to), but a reader other than yourself may not know it. For instance, think about what the therapist is attempting to say in this sentence written in a client's progress note:

Clt and dtr were seen using FFT during a h.v.

What did the therapist convey? You are probably taking some guesses. However, when reading someone's progress note, we do not want to have to do any guessing. It should be extremely clear what is being said and what happened. The more abbreviations you use, the greater the chance that the reader does not use the same abbreviation or acronym list. This then increases the chances that they will either not understand or misread what you wrote. The exemption here is the professional acronym used after the therapist's name where they sign the note. We are both licensed marriage and family therapists and sign our notes with LMFT rather than writing out those five words. Given that there are only a few of these acronyms (e.g., LMFT, PsyD, LCSW, LMHC), they are more easily recognizable. Perhaps you are still wondering what it was our therapist who used the four abbreviations and acronyms above was trying to say. If so, it was: client and daughter were seen using functional family therapy during a home visit. Were you able to figure it out? If not, then you can see why it is important to not use abbreviations and acronyms that often.

As a rule, write the progress note thinking that the client will read it. This will likely prevent you from writing negative opinions about the client. Clients have the right to access their official files. If you wrote something in the note that you thought might offend the client, there is the potentiality that they will request to read the chart. You do not want to offend your clients. However, you also want to be accurate in your notes. Because your progress note is the legal documentation of your contact with the client, you should be writing it expecting other people to possibly read them.

Let's take one second to discuss the difference between progress notes and psychotherapy/process notes. As explained, progress notes are the official documentation of your session. They are part of the client's official record and are potentially available to others by subpoena. **Psychotherapy notes** are only intended for yourself. They are not part of the official record and have protections given to them that standard progress notes do not. Process notes tend to be more freeform. No one else is expected to read them besides yourself. Usually, they contain ideas for you to think about after the session.

The format of progress notes will change based on what type of note you are using. In addition to the format of the note, the actual layout/structure of progress notes varies depending on where you work, what online platform the practice uses, etc. For example, with DAP notes, some platforms/note structures may ask for the start time of the session and then the duration of the session. Other platforms may not ask for the duration but rather the start and end time of the session. While these are small nuances compared to the content of the note, they are important to mention so that you are prepared to see different structures for the same type of note in different therapeutic contexts. The format of the content sections of such notes should be consistent, but the extraneous information and how it is visually formatted may change. As a reminder, the guidelines of a good progress note given previously in this chapter typically still apply regardless of note format or layout.

One final topic to mention before the different types of progress notes are explained is the **HIPAA** compliance of your progress notes. The Health Insurance Portability and Accountability Act (HIPAA) set regulations for the protection of personal client/patient information. For example, you cannot go around telling your friends and family the first and last name of your client because that information is protected health information (PHI) that can be used by others to easily identify your client.

If your therapy practice is using an online platform (e.g., Theranest, Sunwave), it should be HIPAA compliant. This means that these sites have the appropriate measures in place to meet the electronic requirements for the protection of PHI. Therefore, the progress notes that would be included in your client's file on these platforms would naturally be HIPAA compliant as well.

Even though electronic progress notes should be HIPAA compliant (assuming the therapy practice is using a HIPAA compliant platform), there are still two important clarifications to discuss regarding progress notes and HIPAA. First, some therapy practices do not use an electronic platform for their progress notes and instead handwrite them. While this method is rarer (as more and more therapists are shifting from handwritten to electronically documented notes), HIPAA compliance would then need to be met in other ways in terms of the storage of these notes (e.g., keeping notes locked in filing cabinets instead of leaving them out in the open). There are separate HIPAA requirements for hard copies of progress notes and client information in general, but it is generally more common for progress notes to be written online due to convenience.

Second, some practices ask for the content of the note to be HIPAA compliant as well. Let's say you are writing an electronic progress note, and the online platform you are using is HIPAA compliant. While it technically would not violate HIPAA if you were to include any relevant names (e.g., your client's uncle Steve) from the session, it can create more work for you in the future. If your progress notes are court-ordered to be used for a court case, for example, you would need to go back through all applicable notes and redact any names or other PHI that could be used to identify the client or other people in the client's life. It is therefore generally more commonplace to write "The client's maternal uncle" rather than "The client's uncle, Steve." So, as a general rule, you should not include the names of people the client mentioned in the session but did not attend the session.

Formats of Progress Notes

SOAP Notes

SOAP notes are one of the most utilized formats for writing progress notes as they provide a uniform and holistic means of documenting the concerns, progress, and plan of clients and therapists. SOAP stands for Subjective, Objective, Assessment, and Plan. SOAP notes are probably the most frequently utilized form of medical notes, allowing medical professionals to systematically record the contact they had with their patients and clients. Further, utilizing such a common method of documentation can provide consistency between professionals, particularly when they are working in conjunction with one another and sharing information.

The **subjective** portion of a SOAP note includes the client's statements and perceptions of their situation. That is, this is information that you receive from the client that cannot be measured during the session. Usually, in a session, you will ask the client about what has occurred to them, and you want to document what they have told you. Thus, in the subjective portion, you will document what the client told you that they felt, thought, and wanted. This section will likely also include the client's descriptions of what is occurring in their significant relationships, such as with a spouse, parent, child, friend, or work associate. There are also times when you might talk with someone (with properly documented consent) who provides you with information. Whatever they tell you is also documented in this section.

When writing the subjective portion of the SOAP note, it is important to make it clear that what is being written was said by the client. To do this, you might use phrases such as "The client stated," "The client reported," and "The client explained." The use of these types of phrases demonstrates that the information that will then be provided comes from the client rather than other sources. To make this point even more evident, you might put your client's words into this area using quotations. For example, you might write:

When asked about his mood, the client stated, "I have been pretty stable this week and feel good about myself."

However, many therapists try to keep client quotations to a minimum.

The **objective** portion of a SOAP note provides documentation of all the measurable and quantifiable data that was introduced into the session. In essence, this section is about facts. This information is important as the data can then be used as baseline measures or to determine whether progress has occurred. In this section you should report any scores from assessments (e.g., Beck Depression Inventory, Rosenberg Self-Esteem Scale), observable client actions in session (e.g., the client cried, yelled, or fell asleep), or other verifiable data.

Gateley and Borcherding (2017) provided four steps for writing good observations:

1 Begin with a statement about the length, setting, and purpose of the treatment session.
2 Next, provide a brief overview of the key deficits that are affecting the client's performance.
3 Follow the opening statements with a summary of what you observed.
4 Be professional, concise, and specific.

(p. 81)

Cameron and turtle-song (2002) recommended that when writing the objective portion, you use precise and descriptive terms and avoid modifiers such as "appeared" or "seemed." Further, they suggest avoiding value-laden language that demonstrates your personal rather than professional opinion. Rather than writing, "Client seemed to be in a bad mood as they verbally attacked me and were quite rude" you could write, "Client arrived at session complaining about me being two minutes late. She commented four times that she was frustrated with me." These guidelines should help you to be clear and focused on providing the data that was important to notate during your session.

The **assessment** section of the SOAP note describes your evaluation of the course of treatment. It is your clinical impressions and decision-making process. Here, you document the client's progress, the impact of your therapeutic interventions, and your clinical understanding of the information that was described in the previous two sections (Subjective and Objective). Wiger (2012) provided nine types of information that are usually provided in this section:

1 Effects or results of the current session
2 Therapeutic progression
3 Client's level of cooperation/insight/motivation
4 Client progress and setbacks
5 Areas requiring more clinical work
6 Effectiveness of treatment strategies
7 Completion of treatment plan objectives
8 Changes needed to keep therapy on target
9 Need for diagnostic revisions

The assessment section will usually cover the three Ps: problems, progress, and potential (Gateley & Borcherding, 2017).

The last section of a SOAP note, the **Plan**, is based on the assessment section and should explain your professional decision-making regarding the possibility of future treatment. In a nutshell, this section describes your action plan moving forward. This may include the frequency of proposed sessions, types of interventions you think might be useful, interventions that could be utilized, possible referrals, and how you might revise the current treatment plan. If you asked the client to engage in homework, you will explain here what the homework was. Figure 2.2 presents an example of a case note written in SOAP format.

Utilizing the SOAP format provides you with a clear and structured format for describing what occurred in the session and where the course of therapy is going. When writing your note, you should consider utilizing the following guidelines (Cameron & turtle-song, 2002, p. 291):

Do:

- Be brief and concise.
- Keep quotes to a minimum.
- Use an active voice.
- Use precise and descriptive terms.
- Record immediately after each session.
- Start each new entry with date and time of session.
- Write legibly and neatly.
- Use proper spelling, grammar, and punctuation.
- Document all contacts or attempted contacts.
- Use only black ink if notes are handwritten.
- Sign-off using legal signature, plus your title.

Avoid:

- Avoid using names of other clients, family members, or others named by the client.
- Avoid terms like seems, appears.
- Avoid value-laden language, common labels, opinionated statements.
- Do not use terminology unless trained to do so.
- Do not erase, use correction fluid, or in any way attempt to obscure mistakes.
- Do not leave blank spaces between entries.
- Do not try to squeeze additional commentary between lines or in margins.

While these are useful guidelines, you will need to consider whether they make sense in the context that you practice. For instance, in our clinic, we have our therapists write their progress notes in blue ink rather than black. This prevents a photocopied note to go into the official record. The blue ink is one way to authenticate that the note was written by the therapist and not reproduced.

CLIENT CASE NOTE

Date: April 18, 2023
Time: 2:00-3:00pm
Length: 1 hour
Client: Nick Bieber

Subjective: Client is a 20-year-old Caucasian male who presented to the University Student Counseling Center. Client stated, "These last few days have been quite a bog. I've been having trouble eating and sleeping." Client explained that he was happy that he had refrained from drug and alcohol use this past week.

Objective: Client continues to take his medication. He was able to attend all his classes this week but failed to turn in two assignments. He has abstained from marijuana and alcohol. Nick stated that he has slept, at most, for six hours a night.

Assessment: Client presents as calm and focused. His speech was normal and coherent. Client's affect and body language suggest a depressed mood. He was cooperative during sessions with no sign of intoxication. Client is continuing to make movements to alleviate the depression that he is experiencing.

Plan: Continue with weekly outpatient sessions. Consult with his psychiatrist to ensure proper medication management. Future sessions should focus primarily on his depressive symptoms utilizing cognitive behavioral therapy. Discussed for the client to keep a journal about his eating and sleeping habits.

Date: April 18, 2023
Therapist: *Derek Gildenlow, Ph.D., LMFT*

Figure 2.2 Example of a SOAP Note.

DAP Notes

DAP notes are another type of progress note that is frequently used in the therapy world. DAP stands for Data, Assessment, and Plan. Like SOAP notes, DAP notes easily categorize the important information that you and your client discuss during a therapy session. Because DAP notes are commonplace across multiple fields, a variety of professionals can easily understand and communicate with each other. For example, psychiatrists, primary care physicians, therapists, etc. are often in contact with one another to coordinate care for the same client/patient; DAP notes make this coordination more comprehensive and fluid.

As evidenced by their acronyms, DAP notes have fewer categories than SOAP notes. The **data** section of a DAP note is the narrative of the therapy session—this is a story you are telling about your time with your client. It is essentially a combined version of the subjective and objective portions of a SOAP note, so it usually takes up the bulk of the DAP note. In this section, you would write about what the client shared with you as well as what you observed about the client during the session. Typically, with DAP notes, it is easiest to write the narrative in chronological order. You want to paint a picture of the progression of the session, focusing on both the general themes and topics while still highlighting the most important details and reflections from the client.

In addition to the narrative of the session, this section includes your general assessment of the client's mood, affect, physical appearance, and engagement. These are significant elements to document because they are a part of your overall assessment of your client at each session. If you notice that your client starts coming to sessions looking disheveled when they are usually well-groomed, for example, it could be an indication that something might be going on in the client's life that is clinically significant to explore. Overall, this section of a DAP note allows you to reflect on past sessions and be transported back into that space with the client. It gives you and your client a summary of your work together which you can use as a reference for your present and future work in therapy.

As mentioned with SOAP notes, the language of a DAP note is also incredibly important. For example, when writing about what the client shares with you during a session, you would need to specify that the client is the one who stated this information. You would want to note, "The client stated that they were feeling overwhelmed this week" instead of "The client was feeling overwhelmed this week." This reinforces the fact that you are not making such claims, but are rather just reiterating what the client shared. Other words (e.g., reported, shared, explained) can be used in addition to "stated." You could also add in actual quotes from the client—"The client stated, 'I felt overwhelmed this week.'" As noted in the discussion on SOAP notes, however, many professionals refrain from using too many quotations from the client. This is because including them implies you were able to write down or remember the *exact* words that the client used during a session, which is not often the case.

In addition to what the client divulges in the session, the data portion of a DAP note involves your observations of the client's actions. For instance, you might say, "The therapist observed the client cry while talking about his father." In DAP notes, some therapy practices may ask you to steer clear of language that implies the actions you observe in the session are factual. This is mainly for legal purposes, as clarifying that conversations and actions are stated or observed takes away the implication that you are presenting the information as if it were absolute and, thus, it takes away your responsibility for what is noted. As a result, you want to specify that you *observed* that this happened; you want to avoid saying, for example, "The client cried while talking about his father." Other ways you could phrase these observations include "The client seemed to be" and "The client appeared to be." Not all practices may require this distinction in notetaking; however, many practices (particularly those that use insurance) train their professionals to write in this way because insurance companies usually require this language for liability purposes.

The **assessment** section of a DAP note encompasses your reflections on the information in the data section. These notations represent your professional judgments as the therapist in relation to the clinical impressions that the client gave you. This section mirrors the assessment portion of SOAP notes, so this part involves the progress of therapy (especially regarding the client's treatment goals), your perception of the client's engagement in therapy, changes in diagnoses, etc. Harm to self and others may also be included in this section when clinically relevant. For instance, if a client brings up that they feel hopeless and have general thoughts of ending their life (e.g., "It would just be easier if I weren't alive"), you need to assess the client for any intent or plan to harm themselves or others. You also need to make sure you document that you did this assessment, along with whatever outcome came about from your assessment.

The **plan** portion of a DAP note also mirrors this section found in a SOAP note. As its title implies, this section is your plan for therapy moving forward. Wiger (2012) notes that this section is based on the assessment section in both DAP and SOAP notes. With your assessment in mind, your plan focuses on both a week-to-week plan for sessions and the general plan for therapy as a whole. Wiger further outlines some specific topics that are usually included in the plan section:

- Homework assignments
- Upcoming interventions
- Content of future sessions
- Treatment plan revisions
- Referrals

These should look familiar, as these topics were discussed regarding the plan section of SOAP notes earlier in this chapter. Additionally, in some practices, the general plan for therapy could also include the frequency of the client's sessions and what program they are in. For example, some practices have designations between behavioral/mental health and substance use programs, so such practices may want you to include which specific program the client is in.

These are the general guidelines for DAP notes. Some practices might ask you to fill out your DAP notes differently or include additional information in certain sections. Some practices—in addition to the traditional sections of a DAP note—may even add in other areas of the note to fill out. For example, the non-profit practice that Kayleigh works at has the data, assessment, and plan sections of a DAP note *and* added sections entitled "session goal," "client's response to treatment," and "additional comments." This depends on the online program that the practice uses in addition to what that particular practice prefers to include in progress notes. Figure 2.3 presents a sample of DAP note.

Alternative Progress Note Formats

We have presented two of the most common formats for writing progress notes. However, these are not the only ones available. If you work in private practice, you will be able to format your notes in whatever manner you choose. You can create your own format for a progress note. Using the ideas and guidelines in this chapter, you should be able to recognize the main points you should cover in your note. Regardless of format, you should maintain consistency in how you document your sessions. Here, we present two alternative formats that you might use: STIPS and BIRP notes.

CLIENT CASE NOTE

Date: 04/18/2023
Start Time: 2:00 pm
End Time: 3:00 pm

Data: Therapist asked client for an update on his medication usage, and client reported he continues to take his medication as prescribed. Therapist reflected that during their session last week, client shared he wants to quit drinking alcohol and smoking cannabis in order to do better in school. Client stated that he did not drink or smoke the entire week. Client reported he was able to go to all his classes this past week but did not submit two assignments on time. Therapist asked client how he feels about his progress this week, and client stated that he is happy and surprised he was able to refrain from substances but that he wishes he didn't get zeroes on the assignments he didn't submit. Therapist asked about client's sleep this past week, and client had reported last week that he was having trouble sleeping recently. Client shared that he has slept, at most, for six hours per night. Client explained he is still tired and bogged down, and client stated, "I've been having trouble eating and sleeping." Therapist and client discussed that it might be useful for client to journal about his sleeping and eating habits to see how they manifest and how client is feeling about these issues he is experiencing.

Assessment: Client presented as alert and oriented during session. Client appeared to be well-groomed. Client seemed to have a depressed mood due to his body language and tone of voice. Client's affect and mood appeared to be congruent. Client was actively engaged throughout the session, and client seems to be motivated in working toward his goal of lessening his depression by stopping the usage of substances and putting more effort into school.

Plan: Therapist and client will discuss the client's journals on his sleeping and eating habits. Therapist and client will continue focusing on how factors in client's life, such as his sleeping and eating habits, affect his depressive symptoms. Client will continue to attend individual sessions once per week or as needed. Client will continue to engage in the outpatient behavioral health program.

Derek Gildenlow, Ph.D., LMFT

Figure 2.3 Example of a DAP Note.

STIPS Notes

One alternative progress note format is **STIPS notes** (Prieto & Scheel, 2002). The STIPS acronym stands for Signs, Topics, Interventions, Progress, and Special. We will explain each of these sections in turn. The first section concerns **Signs and Symptoms**, particularly the relevant changes of the presenting problem. This area highlights observable client behaviors (similar to what is assessed during the Mental Status Exam—see Chapter 3). The second section is the **Topics of Discussion** and is where the primary content of the session is recorded. The **Interventions** section describes the model-specific interventions the therapist used in session, such as an empty chair technique or therapeutic journaling. This section would also contain updates on the client's completion of homework. The fourth section is **Progress and Plan**. Here, the therapist provides a summary of the client's progress toward the treatment goals. Further, the therapist records specific treatment plans that they are intending to address for the next session. The last section, **Special Issues**, focuses on critical clinical issues such as a client's suicidality, potential or actual hospitalizations, or safety and abuse concerns. See Figure 2.4 for a sample of STIPS case note.

Prieto and Scheel (2002) found that an eye toward STIPS notes helped therapist growth in several areas. The Signs and Symptoms section focuses therapists on looking for and acquiring important facts about the client and case. This then provides them the ability to better understand the client's presenting problem as well as potential diagnoses. The Progress and Plan section encourages therapists to develop accurate treatment plans that are related to the presenting problem. Further, therapists using this model pay particular attention to a constant evaluation of whether their interventions are leading to a movement toward the goals and, if not, they will adjust their treatment. Lastly, STIPS notes help place the therapy process in a fuller context, exploring the connection between the client's presentation, the diagnosis, the treatment plan, the interventions, and the client's progress.

BIRP Notes

An additional format for progress notes is **BIRP notes**. This acronym stands for Behavior, Intervention, Response, and Plan. BIRP notes, like SOAP, DAP, and STIPS notes, help to track client progress as well as develop a plan for future treatment. They are an efficient means of documentation.

The **Behavior** section of a BIRP note documents the presenting problem. It includes both objective and subjective information. This would be what the client told you, what you noticed, and other information that

STIPS Case Note

Date: June 28, 2023
Time: 2:00pm-3:00pm
Participant: Nick Biebers

Signs and Symptoms
Mr. Biebers, a 20-year-old Hispanic male, arrived at the session on time. He appeared tired. He was well-groomed and was dressed in a t-shirt, jeans, and sneakers. His affect was appropriate to subject matter. His mood appeared down, and he explained that he had been having trouble eating and sleeping. However, he was happy that he had refrained from drinking alcohol or smoking cannabis this week. Client was engaged throughout the whole of therapy.

Topics of Discussion
Client explained that despite his difficulty sleeping he was able to attend all his classes. However, he felt bad about himself that he did not turn in two assignments. Client also discussed his difficulty eating where he does not have much of an appetite and at times feels like he is forcing himself to eat. He explained that he has continued to take his medication this week.

Interventions
Engaged in active listening and reflected his desire to continue to stop drinking and smoking. Recommended that the client keep a journal that focused on his sleeping and eating habits. The journal could explore how his eating and sleeping habits manifest as well as how he is feeling about these issues.

Progress and Plan
Client's goal continues to be decreasing his substance use and increasing his effort in school. Client was able to refrain from all alcohol and cannabis use this past week. He also attended all class sessions. However, he did not turn in two assignments. Once per week outpatient therapy is still recommended. Next session will focus on exploring the client's eating and sleeping journal and their relationship to his depressive symptoms.

Special Issues
Client continues to improve. Suicidality was assessed and client stated that he has not thought of harming himself for over three months.

Therapist: *Derek Gildenlow, Ph.D., LMFT*

Figure 2.4 Example of a STIPS Note.

would be in the Subjective, Objective, and Data sections of SOAP and DAP notes.

The **Interventions** section describes your therapeutic process; what methods you used to try to achieve the therapeutic goal. You should write this section so that another therapist understands the techniques you used as well as the rationale for them. You might explain the specific techniques that you used (e.g., empty chair, miracle question, thought stopping, etc.) as well as specific questions you asked. You will use a lot of verbs to describe what you did such as role-played, reinforced, paraphrased, taught, and reinforced.

The **Response** section documents the client's reaction to your interventions. This includes both the verbal and behavioral responses from the client. You will want to record the client's immediate reactions, especially when they seem excited or bothered by your interventions.

The last section, **Plan**, focuses on the course of therapy, particularly the next session. This includes the date and time of the next session, as well as what you plan to focus on. If you assigned any homework, it should be reported in this section. You might also write your proposed interventions for the subsequent session. If you are working from a treatment plan, you would report whether you made any changes to it. Figure 2.5 presents a sample of BIRP note.

Groups Notes

The most common formats of progress notes listed above (SOAP, DAP, STIPS, and BIRP notes) are usually written for a singular client. Even if you have a family or couple in session, there is one person in the system who is usually used as the identifiable client at the therapy practice (mainly

---

BIRP Case Note
Date: June 28, 2023
Time: 2:00pm-3:00pm
Client: Nick Biebers

Behavior
The client reports not smoking cannabis or drinking marijuana. He also stated that he is having difficulty eating and sleeping. This has impacted his depressive symptoms. Client was able to attend all his classes this week but did not turn in two assignments.

Interventions
Engaged in active listening with the client. Introduced the idea of automatic thoughts and thought stopping. Suggested paying attention to his eating and sleeping habits.

Response
The client willingly discussed his smoking and drinking abstinence. He was happy that he was able to abstain. He willingly attempted to identify what some of his automatic thoughts were regarding his school engagement. He expressed happiness at attending all his classes but was disappointed that he did not turn in two assignments.

Plan
Next session: July 5, 2023; 2pm
The client will keep a sleeping and eating journal where he will report what he ate, the time he went to sleep, the time he woke up, and his feelings about his eating and sleeping habits. Next week we will follow up on his eating and sleeping and connect them to his depressive symptoms. We will introduce thought stopping intervention.

Therapist: *Derek Gildenlow*   Ph.D., LMFT

Figure 2.5 Example of a BIRP Note.

for billing purposes). Therefore, even if you are including information about the whole family because you had a family session, the progress note is usually only under one client's name (because that person is the actual client of the practice) and is included in that person's file.

Now, let's say both partners of a couple, for example, go to the same therapy practice for individual sessions, but they have couples sessions every other week. Each of their respective therapists would need to write a progress note for their client when these joint sessions occur. However, if your primary client is a teenager, and you do family sessions with their parents every so often (who do *not* also receive individual therapy sessions at the practice), you would only need to write a note for your teenage client (as they are the official client). This makes sense, as everyone else in these family sessions is connected and/or related to the primary client in some way but is not receiving individual services/is a client on their own.

With this in mind, there is a therapeutic context that has multiple people in the session, but all people are considered to be separate, unrelated clients: group therapy sessions. Group therapy is a common therapeutic setting for a plethora of therapy practices, as it allows for a set of people who are going through a similar situation to get together and process that situation as a whole. There are groups on family dynamics, young adult career development, emotional regulation, grief and loss, and much more.

Unlike progress notes for a "single" identifiable client, progress notes for clients in group therapy do not have as consistent of a format as SOAP or DAP notes. The format and layout/structure of a group note, therefore, can look completely different in varying therapy practices, depending on the needs of the practice as well as the online platform that the practice uses. At the non-profit facility where Kayleigh works, for example, the group notes from the online platform they use have one "behavioral objectives" section that has the same information across all clients in the group. Additionally, each client then has a separate tab within the main group note wherein you would write your "clinical impressions" for that particular person, including checking off pre-inputted characteristics for mood, affect, behaviors, etc.

Groups will have a varying number of clients in them. Some groups are small, consisting of only a few clients. Many groups average six to ten clients. Other groups may have a lot of clients. We have seen some groups have over 20 participants!! These groups tend to be more psychoeducation than interactional, being used for check-ins and information dissemination rather than traditional therapy. Regardless of the number of clients in the group, each client will need to have documentation in their chart as to their participation. As you can imagine, the more clients in the group the longer it will take you after the session to fill out all the progress notes! This is one reason that having a standardized format for progress note development is important since once you learn that format you will more easily and quickly fill in the necessary sections. Next, we will talk about a way of writing progress notes that can reduce the amount of time it takes you to write up the note.

Collaborative Documentation

Usually, therapists write up their progress notes when they have time between sessions. Some therapists wait until the end of the working day to do all their case notes (we highly recommend that you do not do this). Some may wait a day, or two or three, to do their notes (which is a terrible practice). Regardless of when, after the session, you write the note, it takes time. Even using one of the previously discussed formats takes time. If you have a full day of clients, you might be writing five to ten notes. If each note took ten to fifteen minutes, you could be writing notes for up to two hours!! This next section discusses a way of writing notes that both privileges the client's voice and eliminates the time outside of the session that it would take you to write the note.

Very few clients know that the therapist writes a progress note after each session, let alone what is in the note. Therapists are not sharing their notes because they want to maintain secrecy with clients but rather likely do not see the therapeutic usefulness of disclosing the notes with the client. It is a perfunctory aspect of having a session rather than being seen as a potential intervention. But what if writing the progress note helped to add to the possible therapeutic movement for the client?

When writing the note after the session, the therapist maintains the therapeutic hierarchy and privileges their own voice over the client's voice. The more the client is unaware of the progress note the less that it can be used therapeutically. To rectify this situation, some therapists engage in what is known as collaborative documentation. One of the benefits of collaborative documentation is that it is not a specific progress note format; rather, it can be used with whatever type of note you will be using, such as a SOAP or DAP note.

Collaborative documentation occurs when the therapist and client jointly fill out the progress note. This usually occurs in the last five to ten minutes of the session. By providing feedback about the session and progress in each other's presence, misunderstandings are reduced. By hearing the other person's conceptualization of the session, the therapist and client can hear what the other person privileges from the therapeutic conversation as well as perhaps bring in new information to the discourse. Traditionally, clients may have been given access to progress notes if they specifically asked to see them (as clients do have a right to gain access to their official file) or if there was a court order. These times are usually quite rare. When this happens, the therapist provides access for the client to read the note the therapist had written, on their own after the last session. Collaborative documentation shifts this dynamic, so the note becomes a joint endeavor. DiCarlo and Garcia (2016) explained the usefulness of working together on the progress note rather than the client viewing a written document after the fact,

> Collaborative documentation, alternatively, actively solicits the client's participation in generating a meaningful, shared account of what occurred in session, including the quality of the emotional bond between the therapist and client and progress toward the agreed upon goals and tasks.

(p. 75)

Collaborative documentation provides an opportunity for feedback to occur in the therapeutic relationship. The feedback can be viewed as immediacy—where the therapist and client talk about what has occurred between them in the session. This then reduces the tendency of therapy to function from a top-down position where the therapist is the expert, and the client is passive. Rather, collaborative documentation helps to encourage bidirectional feedback, where each person's views become important (Albeck & Goldman, 1991).

Writing progress notes after the session, or if you waited until the end of the day to write all of them, you will likely be spending up to two hours writing notes. Probably, you will try to rush these notes (because you are tired and want to get home) so that they then become less accurate and less useful to you (and thus to your client). Further, you will probably not be looking forward to writing them and it will leave you feeling frustrated at the end of the workday. Collaborative documentation leads to improved time management and thus increased cost-effectiveness (Maniss & Pruit, 2018).

There is no one right way to engage in collaborative documentation. Some therapists will talk with the client and jointly construct the sentences that will go in the progress note. Other therapists might write down what the client said and then write down their own thoughts. Still, others might develop a progress note where there is a clear section for the therapist's ideas and another section for the client's ideas. There is no correct way to engage in collaborative documentation; rather, it should be done to enhance the therapeutic alliance, accurately document what occurred in the session, and be an intervention that helps to keep the therapist and client focused on what has occurred—and thus what might occur—in therapy.

DiCarlo and Garcia (2016) summarized the assumptions of using collaborative documentation, which include: heightening clients' engagement in therapy, which improves the therapeutic alliance; having clients active in the administrative aspect of therapy since their active engagement is not harmful; and enhancing collaboration, leading to increased feedback, which is associated with better clinical outcomes. We know that the more active clients are in therapy, where they are bringing forth their personal agency, the more investment and motivation they will have to engage in the therapy process and actively take steps to work toward their goals.

If you choose to utilize collaborative documentation in your work, you might do so with pen and paper writing the note together, or do so on the computer. Given the increase in therapists utilizing electronic health records, more and more therapists are directly doing their progress notes online. This may then impact the therapeutic relationship as therapists and clients might have different expectations and experiences of having computers being used during the session (Matthews, 2020). Maniss and Pruit (2018) explained,

> Collaborative documentation is a model for concurrently documenting content and process while providing behavioral health services. It incorporates the goal of a strong therapeutic alliance with the concept of shared decision-making between providers and clients and the technology of electronic health record systems.
>
> (p. 7)

Matthews suggested that to enhance the use of computers in the therapy room, therapists could provide explanations and prompting before using the computer in the session, eliciting the client's input into what gets typed, and providing a summary of the content being typed.

Chen et al. (1998) discussed the development of what they called the **therapeutic document**. This tool is used in group counseling and replaces the progress note. It is a form of collaborative documentation that both keeps a record of the therapeutic interaction and serves as a therapeutic intervention as well. In their model, they focus on three key steps. First, there is a retracing of key episodes and striking events. The therapist, immediately at the conclusion of the group session, writes key phrases related to the main events of the session. Second, the therapist refines the narratives. In essence, using verbatim dialogue from the session, the therapist writes down the meanings they make from the events that happened. Lastly, the therapist distributes the therapeutic document to all group members. They then process at the beginning of the next session the group members' reactions to the document. Questions include the participants' reactions to the document, discoveries they may have made after reading it, and the relationship it has to their current goals. Based on this conversation, those new meanings and understandings are included in the therapeutic document for that group session. One of the benefits of this process of developing the therapeutic document is that clients are provided and review the document outside of the session. Here, they are allowed to take the needed time to consider what is written and how that is related to their own growth process. Further, the document can be referred to repeatedly, giving the client more access to the explanations of the therapeutic conversations—conversations that had focused on clients' strengths, resources, exceptions, and personal agency. Chen et al. believed that, like therapeutic letters, the therapeutic document will likely lead to quicker client change and thus reduce the number of sessions a client comes to therapy.

By being involved in the session as well as the decision-making and treatment process, clients have increased investment in therapy, with heightened outcomes as a result (Maniss & Pruit, 2018). Further, clients seem to like the process. For instance, in one study, 82% of clients reported that they found engaging in collaborative documentation to be helpful or very helpful (MTM Services, 2012). Eighty percent of clients also reported feeling involved or very involved in this process. This led 70% of these clients to express their desire for their therapists to continue to use collaborative documentation. We have used collaborative documentation in our practice at a university community mental health clinic and found that almost all the clients found usefulness in it (Reiter et al., 2022). Our clients stated that jointly writing the progress note with their therapist provided them an opportunity to recall the important topics that were discussed, ensuring that the client and therapist were on the same page about goals for the session, and having a summary of what was said. Some clients even asked if we could photocopy the progress note so they could have the documentation they could refer to outside of the session that highlighted their continued movement toward their goals. However, not every client will appreciate the collaborative documentation process. We had one client who found it to be off-putting because he believed it to be gimmicky and took away from therapy time. We believe this situation might have been remedied if we had framed the use of collaborative documentation differently, explaining that this process was to ensure that we were both on the same page, summarizing the most important aspects of the session. In his case, we chose to discontinue jointly filling out the note and the therapist did so on their own after the session.

While collaborative documentation has many advantages, it might not always be useful or warranted. Albeck and Goldman (1991) suggested that collaborative documentation might not be indicated in psychiatric institutions, depending on the client's diagnosis and current functioning. Ritter (2014) cautioned that having such transparency in access to notes may not be useful for younger children or in complex family situations. You will need to evaluate the client's likely reaction to engaging in collaborative documentation and whether you think it will be useful for your client. Like our client who found it to detract from the therapy process, it is not for everyone. We recommend you try it with one or two clients whom you have a very good relationship with and who are likely to appreciate this process. See what you think about collaborating on the notes. How useful do you find it? What do you notice regarding the impact it has on the therapeutic relationship? How do you think it impacts the next and subsequent sessions? Perhaps you will consult with your client and ask them about what their experience is in doing the note together with you.

Summary

Progress notes are one of the primary methods that psychotherapists use to communicate to themselves and others what occurred during a particular session. Good documentation helps provide evidence for the course of treatment, particularly focusing on what therapists do to help clients move toward their goals. The various progress notes formats presented here are the most used ones and should serve as a good foundation for you in choosing one of them or developing your own that addresses the primary areas of good progress notes: the client's presentation, your clinical judgment, your interventions, and your short-term plan for treatment. Perhaps one of the most important things for you to do when writing progress notes is to have a supervisor or more established therapist look over your note and give you feedback and suggestions for how you might modify them so that they are accurate, ethical, and useful.

References

Albeck, J. H., & Goldman, C. (1991). Patient-therapist codocumentation: Implications of jointly authored progress notes for psychotherapy practice, research, training, supervision, and risk management. *American Journal of Psychotherapy, 45*(3), 317–334.

American Psychological Association. (2007). *Record keeping guidelines.* Retrieved from https://www.apa.org/practice/guidelines/record-keeping.

Cameron, S., & turtle-song, i. (2002). Learning to write case notes using the SOAP format. *Journal of Counseling and Development, 80*(3), 286–292.

Chen, M., Noosbond, J. P., & Bruce, M. A. (1998). Therapeutic document in group counseling: An active change agent. *Journal of Counseling & Development, 76*(4), 36–43.

DiCarlo, R., & Garcia, Y. E. (2016). Electronic record keeping and psychotherapy alliance: The role of concurrent collaborative documentation. In S. Y. Tettegah & Y. E. Garcia (Eds.), *Emotions, technology, and health* (pp. 63–82). Elsevier/ Academic Press.

Gateley, C., & Borcherding, S. (2017). *Documentation manual for occupational therapy: Writing SOAP notes* (4th ed.). Slack.

Maniss, S., & Pruit, A. G. (2018). Collaborative documentation for behavioral healthcare: An emerging practice. *Journal of Human Services: Training, Research, and Practice, 3*(1), 1–23.

Matthews, E. B. (2020). Computer use in mental health treatment: Understanding collaborative documentation and its effect on the therapeutic alliance. *Psychotherapy, 57*(2), 119–128.

MTM Services. (2012). *Implementing collaborative documentation.* (PowerPoint slides by Bill Schmelter) Retrieved from, http://www.integration.samhsa.gov/pbhci-learning- community/jun_2012_-_collaborative_documentation.pdf.

Prieto, L. R., & Scheel, K. R. (2002). Using case documentation to strengthen counseling trainees' case conceptualization skills. *Journal of Counseling & Development, 80*, 11–21.

Reiter, M. D., Bibliowicz, V., Sabo, K., Yu, X. C., Delgado, Y., Barrionuevo, D., & Rich, B. (2022). Collaborative documentation: Therapist experiences in jointly writing progress notes. *Journal of Systemic Therapies, 41*(2), 89–104.

Ritter, J. T. (2014). Transparency in the delivery of mental health care [Letter to the editor]. *Journal of the American Medical Association, 312*(6), 650.

Somers, C. V., Benjamin, J. D., & Chenail, R. J. (2010). How Master's students document stability and change within and across progress notes. *Contemporary Family Therapy, 32*, 22–38.

Wiger, D. E. (2012). *The psychotherapy documentation primer* (3rd ed.). John Wiley & Sons.

Chapter 3

Assessment Writing

Sara Ferguson

Assessment writing is a critical part of the therapeutic process. These documents typically cover evaluative aspects of the treatment process. The primary assessment documents are your patient's biopsychosocial (BPS) report and the included mental status exam (MSE), treatment plan, and treatment summary. These documents are a necessary and guiding part of the treatment process. Additional critical documents are risk assessments and safety plans, which create written records of your patient's risk-related needs and the steps for keeping them safe.

Assessment documents are both structured and flexible and should always be completed in a professional manner. These documents can always be viewed by your patients with any Health Insurance Portability and Accountability Act (HIPAA; U.S. Department of Health and Human Services, 2022) request. Moreover, they often serve as helpful records that can be shared with relevant professionals in your patient's life (e.g., psychiatrist). With these factors in mind, it is important that you are careful and thoughtful in your approach to assessment writing.

This chapter will review each assessment document in detail, including best practices guidance, stylistic preferences, and helpful examples for you to use in your own practice. Given the variable nature of mental health and clinical settings, this chapter is not exhaustive in its review of assessment documents and should be used as a building block to your clinical approaches. Moreover, the information provided is generally related to clinical work with adults and there are specific child-related aspects that have not been covered.

Biopsychosocial

When first meeting with a patient, you will likely complete a formal clinical interview that may be structured or semi-structured. The goal of this interview (often called an **intake**) is to obtain pertinent historical and current information about your patient. This includes a number of topics, ranging from education, interpersonal relationships, medical

DOI: 10.4324/9781003294702-3

conditions, and reasons for coming in for treatment, to name a few. The information gathered in this interview will act as your guide to collaboratively develop a treatment plan and form a clinical conceptualization of your patient.

Biopsychosocials are typically done in a semi-structured manner (i.e., the use of a set of prepared questions in a flexible manner), and it is important that you determine your approach prior to completing the interview. Many therapists utilize a template that is divided into sections that contain relevant questions to review; others simply use a free-hand outline of important domains. Regardless of the method you take for your interview, it is important that you thoroughly review your patient's history and current needs. Below is a list of the sections that you *must* include in your BPS interview.

- Referral Data
- Presenting Problem
- History of Presenting Problem
- Background Information/Relevant Family Information
- Historical Data: this includes historical information about a number of domains in your patient's life. The following sections must be explored:
  - Developmental history
  - Social history
  - Education history
  - Occupational history
  - Medical history
  - Psychiatric history
  - Substance use history
  - Abuse/trauma
  - Legal involvement
  - Diversity considerations
- Patient Strengths
- Mental Status Exam
- Summary/Clinical Conclusions
- Diagnostic Impressions (if appropriate)
- Treatment Goals and Strategies

In order to accurately track and obtain your patient's information, it is likely that you will take notes throughout the interview. Upon completing the intake interview, your next step will be to record the information in a formal manner, called a **BPS report**. This is a confidential document that creates a comprehensive clinical picture of your patient's history and current challenges and needs. BPS reports are a significant part of your treatment process. Depending on the nature of your practice, these reports may be shared with the patient or with other relevant providers (with appropriate consent—see Chapter 2).

BPS reports can be considered a clinical art piece, as they are intended to take the reader on a narrative journey, during which the details of your patient's life come together to paint a comprehensive clinical picture. Within this writing process, part of the artful approach includes your efforts to shape the narrative in a way that feels connected and brings the reader to a sensible clinical conclusion (i.e., diagnosis, if appropriate). At the same time, this picture must be developed in a succinct and objective manner, with an emphasis on factual information. You must be mindful to refrain from inserting opinions or judgments (e.g., "Unfortunately, the mother was unable to conceive a baby" vs. "The mother reported experiencing fertility issues").

BPS reports should be typed, with professional formatting (e.g., consistent section headers and spacing). There is not one specific way in which you are required to format your report; however, there is a general outline that should be followed that will be discussed in detail further on. Refrain from using psychological jargon in your writing; it is recommended to use around an eighth-grade education level of language. Remember, we want this information to be accessible to anyone who obtains consent to review it.

Always include how you obtained the information that you are documenting, e.g., "Mrs. Doe *reported* that she grew up in south Florida" vs. "Mrs. Doe grew up in south Florida" or "Record review confirms a historical traumatic brain injury (TBI)" vs. "The patient suffered a prior TBI." This ensures that you are relaying accurate details from the patient or their records and it reduces your liability or the potential to report something incorrectly. Another general consideration is your use of patient quotes, and this is really a matter of personal preference. The present author will utilize relevant and brief patient quotes in her BPS reports, but only when it enriches the documentation. Should you decide to use your patients' quotes, ensure that you have their permission and that you record their words verbatim and within quotes.

Additionally, it is important to note that the BPS and related assessment documents are always written in the third person. The use of first-person language (e.g., me and I) is discouraged, although it is up to you what you call yourself (e.g., therapist, clinician, provider). The sentence structure should mirror the following: "The patient and this therapist met for an intake." Lastly, be consistent in how you reference the patient throughout your documentation. It is generally recommended to utilize the patient's formal name Mr. X or Ms./Mrs. X vs. their first name only. Let's explore sections of your BPS in more detail, including relevant examples that convey stylistic approaches, as well as the necessary information to include.

Referral Data

This section should be concise and include the details regarding your patient's referral to treatment. The **Referral Data** should outline what psychological services the patient is seeking and the referring party. This information can be recorded in its own section at the beginning of your BPS, or it can be integrated into the presenting problem section.

Presenting Problem

The purpose of this section is to outline your patient's reasons for seeking treatment and how their current challenges are impacting their functioning. It should begin with a simple introduction that includes the patient's full name (and nickname in quotes, when appropriate), age, and racial and ethnic identities. This is your reader's initial introduction to your patient's concerns and the starting point of your narrative. Referral data and the place in which your patient is presenting for treatment should be recorded next. Then, you will provide specifics regarding the symptoms that your patient is reportedly experiencing, including duration, frequency, and severity, and examples of any related impaired functioning. If your patient carries a historical diagnosis that is relevant to the current clinical picture, you can include that in this section. Figure 3.1 presents a sample of the Presenting Problem section of a BPS.

Presenting Problem Example

Mr. X is a 29-year-old White-Hispanic male, who was referred to the Jon and Jane Doe Clinic by his primary care physician, Dr. Y. Mr. X reported a desire to address "a life-long struggle with [him]self." He described his presenting problems as having a negative self-perception, poor self-worth and self-esteem, depressive and anxious symptoms, and interpersonal difficulties. Mr. X reported experiencing these symptoms daily and indicated that they have begun to negatively impact his functioning. He described his life as isolated and relayed that he is distrustful of relational connections. He reported having a low mood on most days, with frequent periods of weepiness, chronic worries and feelings of tension, and loss of pleasure in previously enjoyed activities (e.g., cycling). Mr. X relayed that he is seeking therapeutic services to reduce his depressive and anxious symptoms, address his negative self-perception, and ultimately gain a more positive self-esteem and approach to interpersonal relationships.

Figure 3.1 Sample of the Presenting Problem Section of a Biopsychosocial Report.

History of Presenting Problem Example

Mr. X reported a long-term inner conflict, described as constant self-degradation and an inability to acknowledge or believe that he can do something right. Further, he reported a historical negative self-perception, low self-worth, and poor self-esteem, resulting in symptoms of depression and anxiety. Mr. X cited his childhood experience of daily verbal and emotional abuse at the hands of his mother as a crucial factor in the development of his presenting problem. He stated that he began to believe the insults that his mother called him and, as a result, was unable to acknowledge anything positive about himself.

Mr. X recalled first feeling depressed at the age of 13. He described this as a general sense of sadness and worry about the future. These episodes reportedly occurred intermittently throughout his adolescence and into early adulthood. Mr. X indicated that his depressive experience is stronger than his anxiety and related that symptoms typically increase in the context of relational conflict. Mr. X shared that he has struggled to maintain close connections with others throughout his life and is often distrustful of his friends and family members.

According to Mr. X, this has resulted in an isolated life, with little relational connections.

Figure 3.2 Sample of the History of Presenting Problem Section of a Biopsychosocial Report.

History of Presenting Problem

Upon recording the information regarding your patient's presenting problem, you will then detail the history of these issues. Construct a narrative that gives insight into how the problems started, the course of their development, what makes them better or worse, precipitating factors, and where they are problems and for whom. This section should demonstrate the impact of the patient's problems and how it led them to the present intake. Figure 3.2 presents a sample of the History of Presenting Problem section of a BPS.

Background Information

The **Background Information** section serves as an introduction to your patient's pertinent life details. It provides a window into your patient's origin story (i.e., birthplace, siblings, who raised them, where they grew up) and a description of their childhood and any significant memories.

Background Information Example

Mr. X was born in Houston, Texas and is reportedly an only child. He shared that his parents

divorced when he was six years old, at which point his father moved to another state for an

employment opportunity. He recalled being raised primarily by his biological mother and

relayed that throughout childhood, they moved often. He described his childhood as "troubled,"

namely connected to the reported verbal and emotional abuse at the hands of his mother. Mr. X

relayed that his father lost contact with his family and that he has not reestablished a

relationship. At the age of 15, Mr. X reportedly settled down in Austin, Texas, and lived there

until relocating to south Florida for college. Mr. X currently lives in Miami, Florida, in an

apartment with a roommate.

Figure 3.3 Sample of the Background Information Section of a Biopsychosocial Report.

Developmental History Example

Mr. X indicated that he was born vaginally, and no pregnancy or delivery complications were

cited. Mr. X reported that his developmental history was unremarkable. He stated that to his

knowledge, he met his developmental milestones on time.

Figure 3.4 Sample of the Developmental History Section of a Biopsychosocial Report.

You will also document your patient's current status (i.e., where they live now, marital status, if they have children, and whom they live with). Lastly, you should include relevant familial background. Figure 3.3 presents a sample of the Background Information section of a BPS.

Developmental History

Developmental History goes beyond the scope of your patient's developmental progress. This is an appropriate section to record any significant information regarding your patient's in utero development, labor (including the delivery method), and post-natal care. Note whether your patient met their developmental milestones on time and if they did not, specify the concerns reported and any interventions completed to target the needs. Figure 3.4 presents a sample of the Developmental History section of a BPS.

Social History Example

Mr. X described himself as a "loner" throughout life, indicating that it was always hard for him

to make and keep friends. Mr. X reported that his negative beliefs about himself have greatly

impacted his interpersonal style and relationships. Currently, he reported that he has limited

close friends and attributed this to his guarded nature. He indicated that this tendency is based

on his fear that close relationships will result in him being hurt by others.

Mr. X cited his relationship with his mother as "close but turbulent." He denied any other current

significant relationships. Regarding his romantic life, Mr. X indicated that he identifies as

heterosexual and reported having one long-term relationship in the past. He shared that this

relationship lasted approximately one year and ended two years prior to the intake.

Figure 3.5 Sample of the Social History Section of a Biopsychosocial Report.

Social History

Social History should paint a picture of the quality of your patient's friendships over time up to the present day. You should record all significant relationships in your patient's life (familial and friends), along with any major relational conflict or experiences of bullying/harassment. Your patient's past and current romantic relationships and desires for connectedness should be reviewed, along with their current support system. Disclosure of affectional orientation can be included in this section, along with the Diversity Considerations section. Figure 3.5 presents a sample of the Social History section of a BPS.

Educational History

In this section you will record relevant education details from your patient's history. This content will vary depending on the age of the patient. For adults, you can record a broad description regarding your patient's education history and grades. Note any significant learning, behavioral, and disciplinary issues, along with participation in extra-curricular activities. If your patient requires specialized services (i.e., accommodations or curriculum modifications), indicate the needs and interventions implemented. Additionally, you can include your patient's reported strengths and challenges in schooling (e.g., strongest and hardest subject). If your patient has gone on to achieve higher education degrees, these should be

Educational History Example

Mr. X described himself as a historically good student, citing a B average. He cited Math as his

best subject and English as his most challenging subject. He reported that he was in a general

education environment throughout schooling and never required accommodations or

modifications to his curriculum. Mr. X recalled losing motivation in high school and became

disinterested in his academics and extra-curricular activities (e.g., tennis and yearbook club). Mr.

X reported some behavioral issues in high school related to truancy. Mr. X attended Noname

Community College and obtained an associates degree.

Figure 3.6 Sample of the Educational History Section of a Biopsychosocial Report.

Occupational History Example

Mr. X reported a lengthy and varied history of employment, including sales, retail, and customer

service positions. He reported that it is difficult for him to maintain a job and that he often quits

after a few months or is fired. He reported being fired typically for missed workdays due to his

depressive experience. Mr. X denied any desire to pursue a specific career path and shared that

he does not enjoy the jobs that he has tried in the past. Currently, he works at a local cell phone

store in a sales position. Mr. X reported current financial difficulties, citing it as a major stressor.

He shared that he lives "paycheck to paycheck" and that he often runs low on resources at the

end of the month.

Figure 3.7 Sample of the Occupational History Section of a Biopsychosocial Report.

noted, including the degree type and major, when relevant. Educational certifications can be listed here as well. Figure 3.6 presents a sample of the Educational History section of a BPS.

Occupational History

Occupational History includes a broad record of your patient's past places of employment. You do not need to list every job that your patient has had. It can be helpful to try to group employment experience as shown in the example below. If there are patterns of concern regarding your patient's ability to maintain a job (i.e., recurrent firing), it is helpful to document this and the general reasons for the occupational difficulties. You can also discuss your patient's occupational skills (e.g., strength in computer processing), relevant certifications, and current employment status. Lastly, this is a logical place to discuss your patient's current financial status (e.g., middle class) and any associated needs or stressors. Figure 3.7 presents a sample of the Occupational History section of a BPS.

Medical History

The **Medical History** section centers around any significant medical-related information about your patient. You will record any prior medical diagnoses/significant illnesses, hospitalizations/surgeries, or injuries. Specific notation should be made regarding any past traumatic brain injuries (TBIs). Be sure to list your patient's past and current medication list, current treating primary care physician, date of last physical, and description of their current health. Lastly, you will want to document any significant familial medical history. Figure 3.8 presents a sample of the Medical History section of a BPS.

Psychiatric History

Psychiatric History is an important section, as it will detail any relevant psychological or psychiatric information that your patient discloses. Some of these details may be repetitive from the History of the Presenting Problem section. Record any involvement in prior psychological services (e.g., therapy or assessment), including your patient's impressions of the effectiveness (e.g., "the patient reported that at the age of 20, they engaged in individual psychotherapy for approximately one year. The patient indicated that the therapy was somewhat helpful"). You will also want to document

Medical History Example

Mr. X's medical history is significant for seasonal allergies and migraine headaches. He cited

two emergency hospitalizations, one due to gastrointestinal issues in 2009 and another related

to a broken foot in 2014. Record review indicates that Mr. X's most recent physical exam

occurred in 2021 and was unremarkable. Currently, he described himself as generally healthy.

Medical family history is significant for paternal diabetes and prostate cancer and maternal

cardiac issues.

Figure 3.8 Sample of the Medical History Section of a Biopsychosocial Report.

Psychiatric History Example

Mr. X reported a significant psychiatric history, dating back to early adolescence, including the experience of intermittent depressive and anxious symptoms. He denied ever engaging in therapeutic services in the past. Mr. X relayed that he has participated in irregular psychiatric care in the past and has tried a number of different anti-depressants (he reportedly cannot recall the names). Mr. X cited this method of treatment as generally unhelpful, which has prompted him to seek psychological assistance. Mr. X denied ever being hospitalized for psychiatric reasons. Moreover, he denied any past or current homicidal ideation. Regarding suicidal ideation, Mr. X endorsed experiencing passive thoughts of death (e.g., not wanting to wake up in the morning), without a plan or intent, throughout the course of his lifetime, with the most frequent thoughts occurring a week prior to intake. These thoughts prompted the completion of a formal risk assessment and safety plan, which is documented in his chart. Familial psychiatric history is significant for maternal depression and anxiety.

Figure 3.9 Sample of the Psychiatric History Section of a Biopsychosocial Report.

any participation in psychiatric services, including the use of psychotropic medication. Should your patient endorse this type of history, include the treating psychiatrist's name, along with any past or present medications (including regimen and dosage) that the patient reports.

You will also want to document any prior mental health diagnoses, involuntary/voluntary inpatient hospitalizations, history of suicide or self-harm attempts and current suicide/self-harm risk and history or current homicidal ideation, plans, or intent. Of note, if there are any risk concerns, your next step will be to complete a risk assessment. The steps that you take should be documented after reporting endorsed risk concerns (see Risk Assessment section for more information on this). Additionally, if relevant, you can include your patient's openness/interest in treatment. The final part of this section is your patient's familial psychiatric history. Figure 3.9 presents a sample of the Psychiatric History section of a BPS.

Substance Use History

Substance Use History should be explored with every adult patient. This includes the use of alcohol, tobacco, and any other illegal substances. Record the type of substances consumed in the past, the amount, and the

Substance Use History Example

Mr. X denied ever using illegal substances and tobacco. He indicated that he drinks alcohol

regularly, describing his use as one to two beers a day, five days a week. Mr. X denied ever

having a problem with his alcohol usage. He indicated that he does not experience withdrawals

without it and has had periods in which he has been abstinent from alcohol in the past. Mr. X

shared that he likes to have a beer after work to "unwind" and has noticed that he can

sometimes have a low mood after he drinks. He denied ever requiring intervention for his

substance use in the past.

Figure 3.10 Sample of the Substance Use History Section of a Biopsychosocial Report.

frequency. Also provide details about any significant consequences that
have occurred as a result of substance use, e.g., missed work, interpersonal conflict, and increased tolerance. Indicate whether the patient has
ever struggled with substance abuse in the past; if this is the case, document if they have required intervention. Figure 3.10 presents a sample of
the Substance Use History section of a BPS.

Abuse/Trauma History

This section may not be relevant for every patient; however, the query
is important to complete in all interviews. It is recommended that you
record any report of prior or current physical, sexual, emotional, psychological, or verbal abuse. Identify the person who completed the abuse
and whether or not there was legal or state involvement (i.e., Department
of Children and Families). Regarding details of abuse, it is imperative
that you record the type, frequency, and severity of the abuse. Indicate
whether any injuries or lasting marks occurred as a result of abuse. Corporal punishment should be included in this section, along with any other
experiences that the patient identifies as abuse and the related impact.
    Lastly, any traumatic events that the patient reports should be dis-
cussed. Details can be limited with a broad description. Be sure to include
the related impact, if relevant (e.g., "the patient reported that at the age of
five, he witnessed the accidental death of a family member. He indicated
that although it was a tragic event, it did not impact him negatively in
the long-term"). It is not appropriate to delve deeply into trauma-related
details during the intake, as it risks triggering post-traumatic stress reactions for patients. Your patient should lead these discussions and offer as

Abuse/Trauma History Example

As discussed, Mr. X reported a significant history of verbal and emotional abuse at the hands of

his mother. He recalled enduring verbal insults from his mother on a daily basis throughout his

childhood. He reported that the verbal insults have declined over time and that now his mother

is "calmer" in her old age. Mr. X also endorsed experiences of corporal punishment at the hands

of his mother, indicating that she would use a belt or wooden spoon to spank him. Mr. X denied

that these spankings left lasting marks or ever resulted in an injury. Mr. X related that this type

of punishment occurred in his later childhood and was discontinued in his teenage years. He

indicated that he never told anyone about the abuse and there was never any legal or state

involvement. No other experiences of abuse or trauma were reported.

Figure 3.11 Sample of the Abuse/Trauma History Section of a Biopsychosocial Report.

much or as few details as they can during the initial interview. Figure 3.11 presents a sample of the Abuse/Trauma History section of a BPS.

Legal Involvement

Legal Involvement is a brief section that should detail whether or not your patient has encountered the legal system. Only significant legal issues should be reported. Do not include things like parking or speeding tickets.

Diversity Considerations

This section should include a number of details that have been gathered throughout the interview. Your aim will be to cover the important factors that are unique to your patient. Generally, this is where you will expand upon your patient's identified race and ethnicity and cultural practices, particularly if they are of significance to the patient. You can also discuss religious affiliation or level of spirituality. Moreover, any disabilities or special needs can be reviewed. Affectional orientation can also be discussed in this section, particularly if your patient identifies as part of the LGBT-QIA+ community. Ensure that you utilize your patient's exact descriptions in this section, so as to reflect their personal beliefs and values. Figure 3.12 presents a sample of the Diversity Considerations section of a BPS.

Diversity Considerations Example

Mr. X shared that his family is originally from Puerto Rico and that he identifies as a White

Hispanic male. He reported that the cultural values often associated with Latinos are not

important to him and that he has always identified as more "American" than the rest of his

family. Regarding religiosity and spirituality, Mr. X indicated that he identifies as Catholic,

although he is not actively practicing. Mr. X denied any disabilities or special needs.

Figure 3.12 Sample of the Diversity Considerations Section of a Biopsychosocial Report.

Patient Strengths Example

Mr. X presented as an insightful individual with a keenness for introspection and openness to

experiences. Despite his long-term struggles with depression and feelings of inadequacy, he

maintains a relatively positive outlook on life and hope for the future. Interpersonally, he

presented as humorous, respectful, and kind, all of which will likely aid in the work toward his

desired goal of increased social contact and deeper interpersonal relationships.

Figure 3.13 Sample of the Patient Strengths Section of a Biopsychosocial Report.

Patient Strengths

It is recommended to include a section that highlights your patient's strengths. These are important protective factors that will help to guide your treatment planning. Be creative in your review of strengths and consider those that are particularly relevant to the therapeutic process (e.g., insight, openness). Figure 3.13 presents a sample of the Patient Strengths section of a BPS.

Mental Status Exam

The **Mental Status Exam** (MSE) is a unique part of the BPS, as it solely features your clinical observations rather than a compilation of your patient's reported information. The MSE is a structured way to describe your patient's mental state at the time of your clinical interview. Some clinicians do not include an MSE in their BPS; however, you should become familiar with this aspect of clinical writing, as it is a helpful way to convey your patient's cognitive status at the intake. Moreover, MSEs can assist in guiding your diagnostic process.

MSEs can be conducted formally, with a list of predetermined questions to ask. One of the most commonly used MSEs is the Mini Mental Status Exam (MMSE; Folstein et al., 1975), which is typically found in psychiatric and medical settings such as hospitals, inpatient units, and nursing homes. Oftentimes, therapists utilize a more loosely structured approach that might include some particular questions but is heavily guided by clinical observation. The written document is concise, direct, and hits on a number of specific domains, including a review of the following five areas: (1) General Description, (2) Emotions, (3) Thoughts, (4) Cognition, (5) Judgment and Insight.

General Description

Included in General Description are your observations of your patient's appearance, motor behaviors, speech, and attitudes. Questions to consider and document an answer to are as follows:

- Does your patient present as their stated age?
- What are your patient's weight and height relevant to the general population?
- What did your patient wear to the appointment? Is it appropriate for the context? Are they clean (e.g., stained or disheveled clothing, limited clothing in cold winter months)?
- Are there any noticeable oversights in your patient's grooming and hygiene (e.g., dirty nails, greasy or disheveled hair, scabs from skin picking)?
- Are there any noticeable motor concerns (e.g., abnormal movements, tics, tremors, fidgeting, agitation)?
- What is your patient's speech like (not the language or content, rather the behavioral/mechanical aspect of speech)? What is their rate and volume of speech, range of intonation, and any observable impairments (i.e., stammering or stuttering)?
- What is your patient's general attitude toward you and the intake process? Are they cooperative, or resistant?

Emotions

You will then comment on aspects of your patient's emotions, including their mood and affect. **Mood** is thought of as the ongoing feeling tone that is prominent in the patient's daily experience. You might gather information about your patient's mood from their report and your observations of the quality of their mood (i.e., the depth of the mood, how long it lasts, and the degree of variation). Mood descriptors commonly include terms like low, depressed or sad, anxious or nervous, panicky, angry, and euphoric. Avoid using less specific descriptors, such as "distressed" or "agitated."

Affect, on the other hand, describes the behavioral/observable expression of your patient's mood. Typically, you will want to comment on whether your patient's affect aligns with their purported mood (e.g., a patient who is reporting suicidal ideation while laughing is presenting with a low mood and incongruent and inappropriate affect). You will also want to evaluate the mobility and range of your patient's affect (i.e., how much variability or change is observed and how broad or restricted the affect presents, respectively). For example, patients experiencing mania might present to intake with a labile affect (i.e., high variability), while depressed patients might present with little variation (i.e., fixed) and a blunted or flat affect (i.e., little to no emotions).

Thought

In this section, you will record your observations of your patient's thought processes and the content of their thoughts. Evaluation of these areas can often be done simply through the general interaction that you have with the patient throughout the intake. This is also the section in which you will comment on any concerns regarding the elicitation of delusional content or your patient's report of hallucinations. Questions that you can ask yourself include the following:

- Is the patient's thought process organized and coherent (i.e., clear, logical, easy to follow)?
- Is there continuity in the patient's thought process (i.e., goal directedness)? Do their thoughts follow the logical progression from an initial point to the conclusion/goal of the thought?
  - Does the patient incorporate unnecessary details? Do they have difficulties arriving at the final point of the response (i.e., circumstantial thoughts)?
  - Do they digress from the topic? Incorporate unrelated information (i.e., tangential thoughts)?
  - Do they jump from one topic to another without clear associations between the topics (i.e., loose associations)?
- Is the patient reporting that they are hearing or seeing things that others cannot hear/see?
- Is the patient discussing grandiose or paranoid ideas?

Cognitions

In a more formal MSE, cognitions are typically tested with a set of questions that target specific cognitive abilities. In this section, you will want to comment on the following domains:

- Consciousness: alertness vs. unconscious (i.e., coma)?
- Orientation: to time, place, circumstances (i.e., what day/year is it? Where is the patient located? Who is the current president?).
- Attention and Concentration: can the patient direct their attention, and do they have the ability to maintain it for a set amount of time?
- Memory: how accurate of a self-reporter is the patient? Comment on short-term and long-term memory, often observed during recalling historical details.
- Expressive and Receptive Language: what is conversation like with the patient? Estimate the patient's language abilities and their mastery of the spoken language.

Insight and Judgment

The final domains to discuss are your patient's level of insight and whether their judgment is intact. Insight relates to your patient's ability to understand that they have a presenting concern and that they can review the

MSE Example

Mr. X 29-year-old male of above-average height and average weight. He presented as his stated age and was dressed in casual business attire, with no noticeable oversights in his hygiene or personal grooming. During the evaluation, Mr. X maintained appropriate eye contact. He displayed no psychomotor agitation or retardation. His gait and ambulation were unremarkable. Mr. X was oriented to the current time and circumstances of his environment. He exhibited coherent and rational thought processes, denied hallucinations, and no delusional content was elicited. Mr. X displayed some attentional and memory difficulties for immediate and recent information, consistently requiring the evaluator to repeat questions throughout the intake. Mr. X's expressive speech was slow at times, and he demonstrated some word finding difficulties. Receptive language abilities appeared intact. He expressed a fluent understanding of the English language, both written and spoken. Mr. X's range and intensity of emotional expression was somewhat blunted and generally congruent. His judgment and level of insight appeared to be appropriate. Mr. X denied any prior or current homicidal ideation, intent, or plan. He endorsed historical and recent passive suicidal, without a plan or intent.

Figure 3.14 Sample of the Mental Status Exam Section of a Biopsychosocial Report.

potential causes and solutions. Judgment encompasses your patient's ability to assess contexts (e.g., social situations) appropriately and make sound decisions. In your written record, you will want to comment on the quality of your patient's insight (i.e., limited, strong, impaired) and the appropriateness of their judgment.

While it is necessary to include the discussed sections, these can be recorded in a flexible manner within your MSE. Moreover, it is important to note that this MSE review is not exhaustive and should only act as a guide for your MSE writing. Figure 3.14 highlights a basic MSE that covers the general sections necessary to inform your reader of the patient's cognitive status at the time of the intake.

Clinical Summary/Conclusions

Consider this section as the final stop on your reader's narrative journey. The title of this section can vary, including Clinical Summary, Clinical Findings, Clinical Conclusions, or Clinical Impressions. Essentially, it is a succinct review of the significant aspects of your patient's presenting issues and history. It should include the important relevant information from the BPS interview, ultimately creating a clear and accurate clinical picture. Your formulation of the content should lead your reader to a sensible diagnostic conclusion. Figure 3.15 presents a sample of the Clinical Summary section of a BPS.

Clinical Summary/Conclusions Example

Mr. X cited a history of psychological distress related to ongoing issues with depressive and anxious symptoms, dating back to early adolescence. He cited ongoing self-esteem issues, negative thinking, and passive suicidal ideations. He is reportedly perpetually disconnected from others and is seeking closer relational contact. It is likely that Mr. X's adverse childhood experiences of verbal and emotional abuse have contributed to the development of a negative self-perception, poor self-esteem, and low self-worth. Such aspects have greatly influenced Mr. X's interpersonal style, resulting in limited close relationships, despite his reported desire for increased social contact. Based on Mr. X's self-report, it is clear that he continues to experience depressive and anxious symptoms on a daily basis that negatively impact his functioning.

Figure 3.15 Sample of the Clinical Summary Section of a Biopsychosocial Report.

Diagnostic Impressions (if appropriate)

Depending on your approach, the patient's needs, and the setting in which you are providing therapeutic services, you may offer a diagnostic conclusion. Should it be appropriate to offer a diagnosis, it is recommended that you simply list the formal procedural codes found in the *Diagnostical Statistical Manual* Fifth Edition (DSM-5; American Psychiatric Association, 2013) and the *International Classification of Diseases* 10th Revision (ICD-10; World Health Organization [WHO], 2012). Specify that it is an admitting diagnosis, as there is a possibility that your impression may change throughout the therapeutic process. The following example demonstrates the appropriate documentation for this section.

Admitting Diagnosis

296.31 (F33.0) Major Depressive Disorder, Recurrent, with Anxious Distress, Mild
   The above-listed diagnoses are in accordance with DSM-5 and ICD-10.

Treatment Goals and Strategies

A review of treatment goals and therapeutic approaches/interventions and strategies is not required and should only be included when you have had the chance to engage in formal treatment planning with the patient. Treatment goals will be recorded in a structured, more detailed manner, in another document called the Treatment Summary (to be reviewed further). The goal of this section is to concisely document your patient's initial treatment goals, a rationale for treatment, and the interventions/strategies that you are planning to utilize. Figure 3.16 presents a sample of the Treatment Goals and Strategies section of a BPS.

Treatment Goals and Strategies Example

Treatment goals and approach were collaboratively developed by Mr. X and this therapist. It was determined that this therapist would utilize a cognitive behavioral approach to address Mr. X's negative cognitions and schemas about himself, others, and the world. Targeting such aspects will aid in increasing self-esteem and enhancing interpersonal relationships, which will aid in reducing reported depression and anxiety. It is recommended that Mr. X attend weekly individual therapy sessions to achieve these treatment goals.

Figure 3.16 Sample of the Treatment Goals and Strategies Section of a Biopsychosocial Report.

The final part of your BPS should include a place for your signature, along with your full name, degrees, and title. If you are a licensed provider, you must include your license number.

Risk Assessments

It is important that you query about past and current suicidal and homicidal ideation in the initial intake session. Many clinics include these questions in their intake paperwork and if this is the case, you can review the patient's responses, confirm verbally, and document the interaction in your intake notes. As discussed, this information should be included in either the patient's BPS psychiatric history or the MSE sections. It is particularly important to complete a formal assessment of active suicidal ideation when warning signs and risk factors are present (e.g., your patient reports loss of hope and indicates that they are isolated and depressed).

Formal risk assessment documentation typically comes in a template format. I recommend the use of the free screener, the Columbia Suicide Severity Rating Scale (C-SSRS; The Columbia Lighthouse Project, 2016), as it is evidenced-based and recommended by the U.S. Department of Health and Human Service's Substance Abuse and Mental Health Services Administration (SAMHSA; n.d.). However, it can be appropriate to develop your own template with differing stylistic preferences, albeit following the guidelines of the C-SSRS. The main goal of the assessment is to determine the presence of suicidal ideation, intent, and plan and their severity and frequency. The responses then guide your immediate intervention. The following key questions and their answers should be recorded:

1   In the past few weeks, have you wished you were dead or not wanted to wake up in the morning? **Y or N**
2   In the past week, have you had thoughts about killing yourself? **Y or N**
3   Are you having thoughts of killing yourself right now? **Y or N**
    If yes, please describe _____
4   Have you developed a plan for how you would kill yourself? **Y or N**
    If yes, please describe _____
5   Do you have intentions to act on these thoughts or carry out a plan? **Y or N**
6   Do you have access to any lethal means in your home? **Y or N**
    If yes, please describe _____
7   Have you ever tried to kill yourself in the past? **Y or N**
    If yes how and when? _____

Risk assessment documentation should be clear and concise. It should reflect your patient's *exact* responses to the questions asked. For example,

Risk Assessment Note Example

Mr. X endorsed passive suicidal ideation during the intake. Given this endorsement and his

report of depressive symptoms, this therapist completed a comprehensive risk assessment (see

copy of document attached to note). The risk assessment revealed that Mr. X has experienced

thoughts of death in the last few weeks, with the most recent time being one week prior to the

intake. He described this experience as wishing that he could go to sleep and not wake up. Mr. X

denied ever developing a plan to die by suicide and denied maintaining any intentions to act on

his thoughts of death. Given the endorsement of some suicidal ideation, this therapist and Mr. X

engaged in safety planning in order to best prepare him to deal with these thoughts in times of

distress and to ensure that he is equipped with appropriate resources when in need.

Figure 3.17 Sample of a Risk Assessment Note.

if your patient endorses "Y" for number four, record their exact words regarding the plan they have made. Risk assessment writing is an important part of assessment documentation, as it serves as a record of your ethical practices in the face of suicide risk. In addition to the risk assessment document, you will want to write a thorough note that reflects the actions taken throughout the risk assessment. Attach the risk assessment documentation to the completed note. Figure 3.17 presents a sample of a Risk Assessment note.

Any time you encounter a positive risk assessment, your next step will be safety planning. This also involves another important document that you will develop. The next section will review your safety plan development in more detail.

Safety Plans

Safety plans are a critical document that you should become familiar with prior to providing any therapeutic services. These plans are created when there are indications that a patient is at-risk for suicide and/or self-harm and are typically completed after a risk assessment. Essentially, safety plans are a written commitment for what your patient will do to prevent suicidal behavior. The plan answers the question: *"What would you do later tonight or tomorrow if you begin to have suicidal thoughts?"* Safety plans are written documents that detail the steps that the patient will take in times that they experience suicidal ideation or desires to self-harm.

These steps should include a prioritized list of coping strategies and sources of support.

The foundational concept behind a safety plan is that in times of crisis, patients can experience feelings of confusion, impulsivity, and despair. They are often unable to access or effectively implement their previously learned coping skills. Moreover, the idea of trying to find appropriate resources in a time of crisis can be daunting. Safety plans act as a go-to for patients and a written guide on the tools and necessary information to utilize during times of distress. The content of safety plans is partially collected during your risk assessment, although additional information will need to be gathered from your patient.

It is important to clarify that a safety plan is *not* a no-suicide/self-harm contract. Safety plans provide guidance on staying safe in times of distress; no-suicide/self-harm contracts simply obtain an agreement with the patient that they will not engage in such behaviors. These contracts have come under critique over time, and best practices have shifted to the use of safety plans (Jobs & Chalker, 2019).

Once you are alerted to the concerns regarding at-risk behaviors, it is your duty to collaboratively develop a safety plan with the patient. Some therapists utilize a template for their safety plans, while others choose to customize their own. The Stanley-Brown Safety Plan (2021) is a formal plan that comes highly recommended by many organizations and can be found online. You will want to consider these options and determine your approach prior to the administration of therapeutic services. Regardless of your choice, there are key points that you must include in your safety plans, including the following:

- Triggers and warning signs
- Internal coping strategies
- External coping strategies
  - Identified sources of support, formal and informal
- Emergency services
- Restriction of access to means
- Reasons for living

Your safety plans should include sections for each of these points and must be collaboratively completed with your patient. Safety plans should be specific and realistic and must include the identification of safety people that your patient can turn to in times of crisis. As the mental health professional, you should take the lead in recording the content of the plan. By acting as the scribe, you allow your patient to be present in the moment and think more freely; it also promotes collaboration.

In all cases, you should make efforts to record written information in the patient's language. Avoid using psychological jargon or therapy speak and keep the content direct, concise, and easily accessible. If you decide to have a template designed, be sure to have pre-printed copies that are ready to use. Another option is to record the plan in a less structured format on lined paper with a pen/pencil. If you have a laptop accessible, the plan can also be typed. Regardless of the approach, it must be legible for you, the patient, and any other relevant individuals whom you might share a copy with.

Triggers and Warning Signs

Begin by recording the relevant triggers that your patient has identified. These likely include specific environments, situations, or people that prompt distress. Listing out these triggers creates a mindful consideration of the things that may push your patient to a point of crisis. Examples might include specific holidays, toxic relationships, or potentially risky settings, such as a bar or club. You should also spend time recording your patient's identified warning signs for crisis. These can be a range of signs, such as desires to self-isolate, low mood, increased impulsivity, or stomach aches. Utilize your patient's language and record the triggers and warning signs in a concise list format. Figure 3.18 presents a sample of the Triggers and Warning Signs section of a Safety Plan.

Internal Coping Strategies

Upon completing the Triggers and Warning Signs section, you will move on to record several ideas for **internal coping strategies** that the patient can employ in times of crisis. Internal coping strategies can be thought of as resources that the patient has within themselves to cope with and distract from distressing emotions. These are strategies that the patient has cited as being helpful in past times of distress. They can assist your patient in taking their mind off of suicidal thoughts without having to contact another person. These strategies are typically things that provide distractions and mood and environmental changes.

Section 1: Triggers and Warning Signs

What might prompt distress? What are signs that I'm going into crisis?

1. High-stress periods at work. I become tense and want to drink alcohol more often.
2. Bar settings. I tend to overdrink and engage in risky behaviors and feel regretful and sad afterward.
3. Mood changes. Low moods and feelings of being overwhelmed often lead to wanting to escape life.

Figure 3.18 Sample of the Triggers and Warning Signs Section of a Safety Plan.

Examples of internal coping strategies include exercising, practicing mindfulness, and watching or listening to uplifting content. These ideas should be recorded in a list format, with your patient's phrasing, e.g., "I will look at cute baby animals on YouTube." Additionally, the patient must voice a confirmation that they will use the agreed upon resources. Figure 3.19 presents a sample of the Internal Coping Strategies section of a Safety Plan.

External Coping Strategies

Next, you will record a list of potential **external coping strategies**; that is, resources that your patient can utilize that are outside of themselves. These include sources of support and settings that can provide a positive distraction. Sources of support often relate to important individuals in your patient's life. When constructing this list, ensure that your patient identifies a number of people and entities that they can reach out to when in times of distress, including both formal (i.e., relevant professionals) and informal supports (i.e., loved ones).

Examples of professionals include the patient's psychiatrist, a beloved teacher or mentor, and suicide/crisis hotlines. One important consideration is the inclusion of your contact information, and it is an important boundary to consider in the development of your safety plans. Informal supports include family members and close friends whom your patient feels comfortable being vulnerable with. It can be helpful to include contact numbers so that all the pertinent information is at your patient's fingertips.

External coping strategies might include reaching out to the identified sources of support, making a safe connection with someone online, going to visit a neighbor, taking a walk at the mall, or calling the suicide prevention lifeline. *It is imperative that you document the suicide prevention lifeline and the crisis text lines in all safety plans.* Record the external resources in the same list format as you did with the internal coping strategies, integrating your patient's language as much as possible. Remember, it is imperative that you confirm that the patient will in fact reach out

Section 2: Internal Coping Strategies

How can I distract myself? What can I do to relax or calm down?

1. Go for a brisk walk, at least 15 minutes
2. Engage in a mindfulness eating activity
3. Watch YouTube videos of cute baby animals
4. Take a bubble bath
5. Listen to my positive music playlist

Figure 3.19 Sample of the Internal Coping Strategies Section of a Safety Plan.

Section 3: External Coping Strategies

Who can I reach out to for help? Where can I go for a positive distraction?

Sources of Support: these are people who I will contact when I'm in crisis:

Informal (loved ones)

1. Sister, Jennifer. Phone number: 555-555-555.
2. Aunt, Jill. Phone number: 666-666-666.
3. Best friend, Stacey. Phone number: 777-777-777.

Formal (professionals)

1. Your name. Your Phone number.
2. Treating Psychiatrist. Phone number: 888-888-888.
3. Coach Randy, tennis instructor. Phone number: 999-999-999.
4. National Suicide Prevention Lifeline: 988
5. Crisis Text Line:

Places to go

1. Bookstore
2. Mall
3. Local coffee shop
4. Religious institute

Figure 3.20 Sample of the External Coping Strategies Section of a Safety Plan.

Section 4: Emergency Services

Who can I call when I am in imminent danger?

1. 911; local police and emergency response services. Contact if you are in imminent danger of suicide.
2. Local Crisis Response Unit. Phone number and address.
3. Closest Emergency Room. Phone number and address.

Figure 3.21 Sample of the Emergency Services Section of a Safety Plan.

to these external resources. Figure 3.20 presents a sample of the External Coping Strategies section of a Safety Plan.

Emergency Services

After documenting external coping strategies, you will record the contact information for relevant **emergency services**. These are professional entities that your patient can contact in times of crisis. You should always list 911 first, as this is the most immediate way to obtain intervention in a time of crisis. Additional suggestions include local crisis response units and the closest emergency room. You must be sure to document these resources in *every* safety plan. Figure 3.21 presents a sample of the Emergency Services section of a Safety Plan.

Restriction to Access of Means

Part of safety planning includes ensuring that your patient does not have access to any lethal means. Record the ways in which your patient will maintain a safe environment. Ideas include removing weapons from the home (e.g., having a friend hold a firearm) or bringing prescription medications to the therapist. Be specific in your documentation and be sure to think of all possible ways to keep your patient's environment safe. Figure 3.22 presents a sample of the Restriction to Means section of a Safety Plan.

Reasons to Live

The last part of the safety plan includes your patient's reasons to live. For some patients, this may be difficult to identify. Your validation of this experience is important. In a case like that, you might record your wish for the patient to live. Other examples include your patient's loved ones, the hope for changes in the future, or beloved pets that are in need of your patient's care. Figure 3.23 presents a sample of the Reasons to Live section of a Safety Plan.

Once you have completed each section of the safety plan, your patient and you will each sign and date the plan, as documentation of your collaborative completion. Then, you will make a copy for yourself and for your patient. If your patient is seeing other health professionals (e.g., psychiatrist, nutritionist), consider whether this plan should be shared with them, as well. If your patient is over the age of 18 years, try to include

Section 5: Restriction to Means

How will I keep my environment safe?

1. I will remove all potentially lethal pills from my home. I will give them to my aunt Jill to keep.
2. I will keep alcohol out of the house since it acts as a trigger to me.
3. I will stay away from bars.

Figure 3.22 Sample of the Restriction to Means Section of a Safety Plan.

Section 6: Reasons for Living

What are my reasons to not die by suicide?

1. My parents would miss me.
2. My therapist wants me to live and has hope for the future for me.
3. My dog would have no one to care for him and he needs me.

Figure 3.23 Sample of the Reasons for Living Section of a Safety Plan.

someone else in their life who can be aware of the safety plan (e.g., parents, significant other, and/or close friend). Try to determine if this additional person is capable of supporting the patient and connecting them to the appropriate professional, if needed. Share copies of the plan with these individuals, with your patient's permission, of course. If your patient is a minor, their parents must be included in the process and should have a copy of the plan as well.

The last step is to complete a safety planning note that documents the completion of the safety plan, including the participants and individuals who received a copy. This is often done in conjunction with your risk assessment note. Specify that crisis contact lines were provided and appropriate individuals were notified (i.e., in the case of a minor). Attach your copy of the safety plan to this note for your records.

Treatment Plan

Upon completing the BPS, you will collaboratively develop a treatment plan with your patient. A **treatment plan** is a guiding document for the therapeutic process that is individualized to your patient's needs. The primary purpose of a treatment plan is to outline your patient's agreed upon goals for therapy and the ways in which your patient will meet them. Structure the plan to answer the following questions: (1) *What should we change?* and (2) *How should we make the changes?* Treatment plans must address a number of key components, including the following:

- Patient Name and Date of Plan
- Patient Current Diagnosis (DSM-5 and ICD-10 codes)
- Patient Strengths/Protective Factors: relevant factors that are a buffer to risk and signal a positive prognosis for treatment (e.g., strong social support, openness to treatment)
- Patient Challenges/Risk Factors: pertinent factors that are of difficulty to your patient, negatively impact their functioning, and potentially put them at risk (e.g., significant mood variability, prior suicide attempt)
- Impacted Domains of Functioning: areas in the patient's life that have been impacted by the presenting concerns and/or are relevant to the treatment goal (e.g., interpersonal, psychological, occupational)
- Behaviors and Symptoms: these serve as a rationale for a treatment goal; each goal should make sense according to the recorded behaviors and symptoms (e.g., increased social withdrawal + goal to develop more social connections)
- Treatment Goals: measurable, specific, and individualized (e.g., decrease anxiety symptoms)
- Objectives: the way in which you and your patient will work to achieve their goals (e.g., engage in therapy, learn and implement coping skills)

Patient Name: Mr. X

Date of Plan: 12/2/2022

DSM-5 & ICD-10: 296.31 (F33.0) Major Depressive Disorder, Recurrent, with Anxious Distress, Mild

Patient's Protective/Risk Factors:

Strengths: Insightful, open minded, motivated for treatment, employed

Challenges: Low mood, limited support system, variable engagement in psychiatric care in the past, financial stressors, passive suicidal ideation

Impacted Domains of Functioning	Behavior & Symptoms	Therapeutic Goals	Objectives	Intervention	Frequency & Duration	Target Date
-Psychological -Intrapersonal	-Chronic low mood -Feelings of sadness and hopelessness -Low motivation -Desire to improve functioning	1. Decrease symptoms of depression	-Engage in consistent therapy -Gain and implement new coping and positive psychological skills -Learn to challenge and reframe faulty cognitions -Complete weekly BDI-II -Complete assigned homework -Utilize Safety Plan as needed	1. Individual Therapy 2. Narrow Band Assessment: BDI-II	3. Once weekly for 45 mins 4. Once weekly	6 months review: 6/22/2022
-Interpersonal -Leisure	-Limited close relationships -Feelings of loneliness -Desire to create deeper interpersonal connections	2. Increase social connectedness	-Engage in consistent therapy -Gain and implement new interpersonal skills -Learn to reframe negative schemas about others -Complete assigned homework	Individual Therapy	Once weekly for 45 mins	6 months review: 6/22/2022

Criteria for Discharge: Patient will report decreased depressive symptoms and increased social connections; BDI-II scores will reduce below clinical levels of severity.

Patient Signature and Date: _____

Provider Signature and Date: _____

Figure 3.24 Sample of a Treatment Plan.

- Intervention: how you and your patient are working toward this goal (e.g., individual psychotherapy, psychiatric consult)
- Frequency and Duration: how often and for how long will you engage in the intervention (e.g., once weekly for 45 minutes)
- Target Date: the agreed-upon date at which you and your patient will review their treatment goals
- Criteria for Discharge: the agreed-upon indicators that would signal that your patient has met their goals and that they can terminate therapy services

As with a BPS, you will want to determine ahead of time how you would like to record your treatment plan. Treatment plans can be more comprehensive, including a written report, or more concise, in a table with bullet points. If you are working for a clinic or private practice, they may have a template that you can use. Otherwise, you might want to construct your own copy of a fillable treatment plan template (see Figure 3.24), as it is the most time-efficient approach. Regardless of your choice, it is important to be prepared prior to the development of a treatment plan. While the content can be collected in a more flexible format (e.g., free-handwritten notes), the information gathered should be recorded in a structured manner (e.g., written report or table).

One important aspect of your treatment plan is the assessment of treatment effectiveness. This answers the question: *Is my patient making progress toward their goals?* Best practices include the use of (1) a broad-band measure that assesses multiple disorders, (2) narrow-band measures that are specific to the presenting problem(s), and (3) weekly or bi-weekly assessments of how your patient is doing. You should also assess the risk and protective factors that you are targeting in treatment (e.g., cognitive distortions) and obtain data from a variety of sources.

Upon identifying how you will assess progress, you will then record the criterion that you will use to determine whether a treatment goal has been met and/or what will signal the termination of services. The treatment plan should have a place for both you and your patient to sign and date.

Treatment Summary

Treatment summaries are the final assessment document to review, and they provide information on the entirety of the treatment process. These summaries are completed at the end of your therapeutic relationship with a patient, whether services have been terminated or the patient is being transferred. The purpose of the document is to record a written snapshot of the therapeutic journey, beginning with the patient's initial presenting problem and treatment goals, along with their participation in services (i.e., the format of therapy and how many sessions the patient attended and no showed to) and reason for discharge.

Treatment Summary Example

Mr. X attended 25, once weekly, individual psychotherapy therapy sessions with this therapist between 12/22/2022 and 9/1/2023. Mr. X presented to treatment to target issues related to experiences of depression, anxiety, low self-worth, and interpersonal difficulties. Treatment goals included the following: 1) decrease depressive and anxious symptoms, 2) increase self-esteem and self-worth, 3) increase relational connections. Prior to beginning treatment, the patient was provided a Beck's Depression Inventory-II (BDI-II) and a Beck's Anxiety Inventory (BAI) in order to obtain a baseline of Mr. X's symptoms. These measures were administered bi-weekly throughout treatment to assess Mr. X's progress toward his goals.

The first phase of therapy centered around building rapport and creating a trusted and safe place for the patient. This shifted into a deeper review of Mr. X's depressive and anxious experiences. Exploration and identification of his automatic thoughts and behavioral reactions lead to the identification of his core and intermediate beliefs, ultimately generating the conceptualization of major depressive disorder, with anxious distress.

Upon establishing a solid understanding of Mr. X's maladaptive belief system, he and this therapist moved into the middle phase of treatment in which Mr. X's cognitions were targeted. Psychoeducation was provided regarding the cognitive triad and Mr. X's tendency to engage in maladaptive thinking patterns. Mr. X worked to gain awareness regarding the thinking traps he engaged in and collaborated with this therapist on ways to challenge these negatively skewed thoughts and come to alternative, balanced thoughts. Weekly homework assignments were provided, including the consistent use of thought logs. These thought logs were reviewed regularly in session and modeling of challenging and reframing was provided.

Mr. X reported difficulty completing his homework and often was unable to do so prior to session. As a result, this therapist incorporated Motivational Interviewing (MI) strategies, e.g., decisional balancing exercises, in order to engage Mr. X regarding his ambivalence about change. Through this, it was determined that he was experiencing high levels of fear regarding change. This therapist and Mr. X worked to challenge his cognitive distortions about the potential changes to come and to reframe them with more balanced approaches of thinking. In the final phase of treatment, Mr. X began to engage in regular homework completion and demonstrated the skills to independently challenge his maladaptive thinking styles. This skill proved to be helpful in reshaping Mr. X's self-esteem, as he was able to better assess his perception of himself (e.g., I always mess up and am a worthless vs. Sometimes I make mistakes, just like all humans, and that doesn't define my worth). Mr. X reported a decrease in depressive and anxious symptoms, and this was confirmed in the observed decline of BDI-II and BAI scores over time. Moreover, Mr. X shared that his relationships had improved and that he was beginning to build more deeper connections with those in his life. Mr. X and this therapist reviewed Mr. X's treatment plan and agreed that Mr. X had met his goals, thereby prompting a mutual termination of services.

Admitting Diagnosis:
296.31 (F33.0) *Major Depressive Disorder, Recurrent, with Anxious Distress, Mild*
Discharge Diagnosis:
296.31 (F33.0) *Major Depressive Disorder, Recurrent, with Anxious Distress, Mild*

Figure 3.25 Sample of a Treatment Summary.

The bulk of the treatment summary contains a review of what took place in therapy. This includes the interventions implemented, skills learned, and work completed toward treatment goals. Oftentimes, this section is broken into phases, including a beginning, middle, and end phase of treatment. Phase One typically includes what took place in the initial sessions, including your efforts to build rapport, establish a therapeutic alliance, and your patient's socialization to the therapeutic process and your approach. Phase Two outlines the intervention process and is where the majority of the content is recorded. Phase Three emphasizes the end of treatment, including the final progress made and the decisions that led to termination. Lastly, you will want to include the patient's admitting diagnosis and diagnosis at termination (see Figure 3.25).

The treatment summary content is a balance between a broad review of the therapeutic process with the inclusion of specific details. It should convey the general progression of therapeutic contact and work toward achieving treatment goals. Treatment challenges should be discussed throughout the report (often in Phase Two), including any relevant barriers that you and the patient encountered, along with the steps taken to mitigate these issues (e.g., patient recurrently struggled to complete the homework, prompting this therapist to engage in motivational interviewing to target the patient's ambivalence about the therapeutic process).

Summary

Assessment writing requires dedicated time, effort, and thought. It encompasses critical documents for your patient's treatment and should be completed with care. While there is flexibility in the approach, assessment documents should always reflect a somewhat structured and highly professional manner. The guidance provided in this chapter should be a helpful reference in your evaluation of patient needs, strengths, and challenges.

References

American Psychiatric Association. (2013). *Diagnostic and statistical manual of mental disorders* (5th ed., text rev.).

Columbia Lighthouse Project. (2016). Retrieved October 12, 2022, from https://cssrs.columbia.edu/.

Folstein, M. F., Folstein, S. E., & McHugh, P. R. (1975). Mini-Mental State Examination (MMS, MMSE).

Jobes, D. A., & Chalker, S. A. (2019). One size does not fit all: A comprehensive clinical approach to reducing suicidal ideation, attempts, and deaths. *International Journal of Environmental Research and Public Health, 16*(19), 3606–3620.

Stanley, B., & Brown, G. (2021). *Stanley-Brown safety plan.* Retrieved November 10, 2022, from https://bgg.11b.myftpupload.com/wp-content/uploads/2021/08/Stanley-Brown-Safety-Plan-8-6-21.pdf.

Substance Abuse and Mental Health Services Administration. (n.d.). Retrieved October 12, 2022, from https://www.samhsa.gov/resource/dbhis/columbia-suicide-severity-rating-scale-c-ssrs.

U.S. Department of Health and Human Services. Retrieved October 1, 2022, from https://www.hhs.gov/hipaa/index.html.

World Health Organization. (2012). Retrieved October 1, 2022, from https://www.who.int/publications/m/item/errata-for-publishing-icd-10-2010.

Chapter 4

Forms and Pragmatic Letters

Michael D. Reiter, Myron Burns, & Kayleigh Sabo

As a therapist, you come in contact with clients before, during, and after the actual therapy session(s). These contacts outside of the therapy room usually happen through written documents which may be used as invitations to clients to attend sessions or as explanations of the contract of therapy. This chapter provides an overview of some of the common contracts and pragmatic letters that therapists write and use.

The therapy relationship is based upon a contract between therapist and client. This contract generally defines what the roles of each person are and what they can expect from the other. Some of the contracts in therapy are straightforward (see below for the Informed Consent form and the Release of Information form). Other contracts are covert, where you and the client have agreements about how to engage one another and you never explicitly discuss the rules. For instance, you might have as part of your therapy contract a statement about outside-of-session contact. Many therapists put a statement like, "In case of emergency, please contact 911 immediately." But what constitutes an emergency? Can a client call you? Email you? Will they know, based on the information you have put in your various forms and contracts, what they can expect of you? Of what you expect of them? The answer to these last two questions should be "yes." Thus, your therapeutic contracts should detail this information.

As a therapist, you must engage the client in an ethical manner. Most organizational ethical codes provide an overview of the importance of proper record-keeping. For instance, Section 6 of the American Psychological Association's code of ethics is fully about record-keeping and fees. As an example, code 6.01 Documentation of Professional and Scientific Work and Maintenance of Records states:

> Psychologists create, and to the extent the records are under their control, maintain, disseminate, store, retain, and dispose of records and data relating to their professional and scientific work in order to (1) facilitate provision of services later by them or by other professionals, (2) allow for replication of research design and analyses,

DOI: 10.4324/9781003294702-4

(3) meet institutional requirements, (4) ensure accuracy of billing and payments, and (5) ensure compliance with law.

Further, there are certain standards and expectations for you to follow so that you adhere to the Health Insurance Portability and Accountability Act, 45 C.F.R. (HIPAA). The following section describes some of these forms that are mainstays in every psychotherapist's practice.

Contracts/Forms

The Intake Form

The **intake form** is used to accomplish a variety of goals. Professionals from diverse fields have different agendas; however, all must obtain the same basic information:

1 Obtain the greatest amount of accurate information relevant to treatment.
2 Conduct it in the shortest period of time.
3 Do it in a consistent manner creating and maintaining a good working relationship with the client.

Point numbers 1 and 2 above are essential as point number 2 (i.e., doing it in the shortest period of time) may not always happen and is dependent on a number of factors (e.g., cognitive functioning of the client, presenting issues/problems). Therapists working in private practice may not have an intake form and instead may schedule a 10- to 15-minute meet-and-greet where they talk through the information. However, almost every agency and organization will have an intake form.

You can fill out the intake form in one of three ways. First, you can have the client fill it out. This may be by sending it to them, having them download it (or fill it out on your website), or asking them to come some minutes early to the session and fill it out in the waiting room. The benefit of having the client fill out the intake form before the session is that you can use the time in the session for purposes other than basic information gathering. This provides a more cost-effective experience for the client. However, therapy is usually a process about relationships and connections. When a client is filling out the intake form, especially when it is asking sensitive questions (e.g., about suicidal ideation, drug use, or past mental hospitalizations), they may feel embarrassed or put off reporting this information to a cold piece of paper instead of a warm-blooded human being who is empathetic.

Second, you can fill out the intake form with the client. In many community agencies, the intake form may be quite lengthy. It may also need to be filled out electronically where you are sitting in front of the computer asking the preset questions and typing in the client's responses. The benefit of this method is that you will be able to use vocalics along with active listening skills to let the client know they are being listened to and understood by a fellow human being. You can also ask for clarification, or the client can ask you for clarification. However, in our experience, clients tend to attempt to move the conversation to be therapeutic rather than sticking to the information gathering. Therefore, it is very important to frame the process of filling out the form:

> Thank you for coming in today. I just want to be clear that this is not a therapy session. This is an intake session. I will be asking you a lot of questions to get a lot of information. This will help us best figure out what services you need. Once we complete this form then we can begin the therapy process.

The last way to fill out the intake form is for you to fill it out after you have talked with the client. This may be after you have talked on the phone with a client and then you fill out whatever intake form you or your agency use. We do not recommend filling out an intake form in this manner. It is best to have the client fill it out using their language or to be present so that they can provide further clarification if needed. Thus, it is important to use the client's language on the intake form as much as possible to most accurately capture what the client discussed.

Many times, clients will be asked to fill out other forms (such as Informed Consent and Release of Information forms) and then attend an intake interview before their first official therapy session. This more in-depth intake might be considered a **Biopsychosocial**. There are typically three main areas of the biopsychosocial intake interview:

- Psychological—A client uses drugs and alcohol because their overbearing spouse reminds them of their parent. They associate substance use with relief from stress produced by this relationship.
- Biological/Medical—Both parents are alcoholics; in fact, there is a genetic link to alcoholism on their father's side of the family.
- Social—Several friends drink and use drugs; these behaviors are accepted, even encouraged, in their social circle.

Presenting problems are not the result of only one area above; they interact with one another. Past experiences contribute to current problems, and only a complete intake interview can satisfactorily give you this information.

When initiating the interview, you should greet the client and maintain eye contact. Introduce yourself and explain your educational background, training, and areas of specialization. Next, explain the purpose of the interview and be sure to mention confidentiality and time involved in the interview process. Depending on one's setting, the nature of the problem, and the cognitive level/functioning of the client, intake interviews can take between 45 minutes and more than one hour. Other special considerations include building rapport or a good working relationship at the beginning. Icebreakers or asking the client about transportation/ parking, weather, etc. can help begin this process. Later in the interview, you may be asking some very sensitive questions, and you may also have a reluctant or guarded client entering therapy. As a result, you do not want to rush into the interview. You should also avoid the use of jargon, technical terms, and repeating questions. Show genuine interest in your client rather than trying to rush through the interview process.

Some agencies/organizations have specific people (such as interns) who complete the intake interviews so they can more easily match the client to the appropriate therapist based on the presenting problem. Thus, you may not be the one completing the intake interview at all. If this is the case, it is important that you read the intake forms completed from the interview so you have some background of your client before the first therapy session.

Standard intake interview forms tend to include the following information:

- Identifying information about the client (name—note nickname if applicable; address, contact number; sex—note gender identify/ preferred pronouns; date of birth/age; marital status; children; occupation; ethnicity).
- History of present illness (main complaint(s); onset of problems; stressors; key events; effects on work/family; client perceptions about the problems—note clients may lack an awareness of the magnitude of how some stressors are impacting their current state).
- Psychological information (depression; anxiety; psychosis; history of being abused; alcohol/drug abuse; suicidal ideation/attempts; family history of mental disorder; history of violence toward others; previous psychological treatment; outcome of treatment—note client's satisfaction with services received, as this can help provide insight on their perceptions of the therapeutic process).
- Past medical history (illnesses or diseases, past hospitalizations, medications currently taken, sleep patterns).
- Personal/social history (details of the family of origin, marital satisfaction, and work satisfaction [all three can help provide a narrative on the client]; education; sexual orientation [some clients may have identity issues or face discrimination/abuse from one's family and community surrounding sexual orientation]; legal/criminal issues; leisure activities; and social support network—can help with recovery planning).

At the end of the intake interview, the therapist or intake person should make a concluding statement of interest and appreciation for taking the time to answer some very sensitive and potentially painful questions. Therapists should also give feedback on their assessment, ideas to the client, and how issues/problems can be treated.

Informed Consent Forms

The variety of ethical codes for the range of psychotherapy organizations all hold to the notion of respecting people's rights and ensuring their autonomy. One of these areas is self-determination. Clients should make the choice as to whether they engage in therapy or not. Further, this should be an informed decision. They should know what they are agreeing to. Similar to the business statement of "caveat emptor"—let the buyer beware—your therapy clients should have an understanding of what the therapeutic relationship and process should entail. To do so, you should have a form that explains the therapeutic process in enough detail that they can make an informed decision as to whether to agree to this relationship or not. This is where the informed consent form comes into play.

The **informed consent form** provides the client with enough information about engaging in therapy with you so that they are not later shocked or surprised about an aspect of therapy. While you are likely not able to provide all specifics for what will happen in therapy (i.e., at some point if it is clinically implicated, utilizing the empty chair technique), the informed consent form provides a general overview of the rules and guidelines of the therapeutic encounter.

Every psychotherapy oversight committee has some statement in their ethical codes about informed consent. For instance, in the American Psychological Association's code of ethics, Section 10: Therapy, the first code focuses specifically on informed consent:

> 10.01 Informed Consent to Therapy
> (a) When obtaining informed consent to therapy as required in Standard 3.10, Informed Consent, psychologists inform clients/ patients as early as is feasible in the therapeutic relationship about the nature and anticipated course of therapy, fees, involvement of third parties, and limits of confidentiality and provide sufficient opportunity for the client/patient to ask questions and receive answers.

All individuals 18 and over who have the capacity to give **consent** need to do so, in writing, before you meet with them in therapy (individuals under 18 can sign the informed consent—what we call giving **assent**). Usually, therapists provide a series of documents to clients before they meet with them in the first session. These documents can either be a packet of physical documents or an electronic version of these documents, depending on what medium the practice/facility uses. Regardless of the format of the documents, one of these forms will be the **Informed Consent form**. The form should be written in simple language, so most individuals will be able to read and understand it. However, just because the client signs the form, do not assume that they comprehended everything. You should verbally go over the form with them, providing them a space to follow up and ask any questions they may have about it. The American Association of Marriage and Family Therapy ethical code highlights how your informed consent document should be worded in a way that people can understand:

1.2 Informed Consent

Marriage and family therapists obtain appropriate informed consent to therapy or related procedures and use language that is reasonably understandable to clients. When persons, due to age or mental status, are legally incapable of giving informed consent, marriage and family therapists obtain informed permission from a legally authorized person, if such substitute consent is legally permissible. The content of informed consent may vary depending upon the client and treatment plan; however, informed consent generally necessitates that the client: (a) has the capacity to consent; (b) has been adequately informed of significant information concerning treatment processes and procedures; (c) has been adequately informed of potential risks and benefits of treatments for which generally recognized standards do not yet exist; (d) has freely and without undue influence expressed consent; and (e) has provided consent that is appropriately documented.

Once the client signs the Informed Consent form, it should be placed in the client's official file if it is a physical form. With the increase in the use of technology in the therapy world, HIPAA-compliant electronic documentation is common as well. If the Informed Consent form is filled out and signed electronically, the form is usually stored in the client's profile in the HIPAA-compliant platform that the practice uses.

While your Informed Consent form will likely differ from other therapists', there will also likely be many similarities between them. Standard informed consent forms tend to include the following information:

- Information about the therapist
- Explanation of the therapy services
- Fees and charging policies (i.e., arriving late or missed appointments)
- Expected number and duration of sessions
- Details regarding setting and canceling appointments

Informed Consent Form

Welcome to _____ (name of practice). This document contains important information about the practice's policies, such as billing and scheduling, and therapeutic services. Before beginning services, it is important that this information is reviewed and signed to establish an agreement and understanding of the practice. If you have any questions after reading this document in its entirety, please feel free to reach out to the office or your individual therapist.

Therapeutic Services

Psychotherapy services can vary between therapists, but there are general aspects of psychotherapy that are important to note. First, there can be both risks and benefits to therapy. Risks may include but are not limited to the experience of negative emotions, such as sadness, anxiety, anger, and discomfort due to the discussion of personal concerns that are often distressing. However, the benefits of therapy come from the open discussion of these aspects of life which can lead to healing and growth. There are no guarantees of what will take place during therapy or what will result from it, and therapy requires active and purposeful participation from both client and therapist.

The first few sessions of therapy will be geared toward getting to know you, your background, and your reasons for coming to therapy to determine treatment goals and expectations of therapy. Your therapist will also share with you their background and general therapeutic approach. If at any point you feel that your therapist is not a good match for your needs, please don't hesitate to let your therapist or the office know.

Appointments/Cancelation Policy

All appointments are 50 minutes. Your initial intake appointment will be scheduled when you call the office to set up therapy. During your intake appointment, you will discuss your availability/preferred days/times to match you with a best-fitting therapist both based on presenting concerns and schedules. Once scheduled for your first session, you may either call the office or email your therapist to cancel or reschedule appointments.

We have a 24-hour cancelation policy. Thus, to avoid a late cancelation fee, you must give the office or your therapist 24 hours' notice. If you do not show up to a session or cancel within one hour of the appointment, you will be charged a No-Show fee (the full cost of the session). Please refer to our Fees/Billing form for additional information on fees and cancelation policies.

Fees

The standard fee for a 50-minute appointment is $150. Fees are due at the time of the session unless special arrangements have been made with the office. Some of our therapists operate on a sliding scale. There will be a separate form to be signed regarding specific fees if you are seeing your therapist on a sliding scale basis.

Insurance

While our practice does not accept insurance, we do have therapists that operate on a sliding scale fee. See our Fees section above for additional information on sliding scale.

Confidentiality

Our practice abides by all laws concerning confidentiality in the State of Florida. Four exceptions to confidentiality include: (1) threat to harm self, (2) threat to harm others, (3) abuse of a minor or elder, and (4) court-mandated scenarios. For more details on confidentiality, please refer to the Notice of Privacy Practices form.

Contacting the Practice/Therapist

Please feel free to call the office (xxx-xxx-xxxx) at any time for any questions or concerns. If you call outside of our business hours, please leave a voicemail on our confidential voicemail box, and we will get back to you within 24 hours. Your individual therapist will also provide you with their email. Please allow up to 48 hours (two business days) for your therapist to respond to your email. If you are experiencing an emergency and are unable to keep yourself safe, call 911 immediately.

Termination of Therapy

You have the right to terminate therapy whenever you believe it is in your best interest. If you believe that therapy is not progressing, please reach out to me and let me know so that we can try to make alterations or provide you with alternative services.

Client's Name (printed): _____
Client's Signature (or authorized representative): _____
Date: _____

Figure 4.1 Sample of Informed Consent Form.

- Rules regarding the therapist-client relationship
- Limits of confidentiality
- Potential risks and benefits of treatment
- Procedures for when a crisis occurs
- Potential aspects surrounding the termination

It will be up to you, if you are creating your own informed consent form, to determine how detailed you want to be in each section. If your informed consent form is too long, you risk clients not taking the time to read it. On the other hand, if you are too brief, clients may not have enough information to make an informed decision to enter treatment. During the course of therapy, it will also be important to review informed consent topics as clients may forget and need to be reminded. Figure 4.1 is just one example of a potential informed consent form. This sample form is a shorter version of what a full Informed Consent form would typically look like, as they are usually more detailed. We recommend that you have a legal representative review the form to ensure that you have the accurate and necessary information.

Release of Information

Clients have the right to confidentiality. That is, just about everything that they say in session is privileged information. You should not tell anybody what the client said in the session, let alone that that person is even a client of yours. However, there are limits to confidentiality. As a therapist, you are obligated to break confidentiality when necessary, such as in cases of abuse or potential harm. Every ethical code has some statement (and usually multiple codes) that refers to confidentiality. For instance, the American Association of Marriage and Therapy code 2.2 Written Authorization to Release Client Information states:

> Marriage and family therapists do not disclose client confidences except by written authorization or waiver, or where mandated or permitted by law. Verbal authorization will not be sufficient except in emergency situations, unless prohibited by law. When providing couple, family or group treatment, the therapist does not disclose information outside the treatment context without a written authorization from each individual competent to execute a waiver. In the context of couple, family or group treatment, the therapist may not reveal any individual's confidences to others in the client unit without the prior written permission of that individual.

However, there are also times that you will talk to other people about your client when you are not mandated. This usually happens when you are trying to gain information about your client from a third party or when your client would like for you to provide information about them to someone else. Most likely, the person you are wanting to speak to or are being asked to speak to is another medical professional so that you can either coordinate services or that one or both of you gain more information about the client so that you can provide better services. Other times it could involve speaking to the courts on behalf of the client (e.g., a parent may want to demonstrate or show gains made in therapy for child visitation). In order for you and the third party to speak to one another, the client will need to agree to this. While they may do so verbally, you will want (and legally need) this agreement to be in writing. This is where a **Release of Information form** comes into play (sometimes referred to as an ROI). Clients should be made aware that if they agree to allow you to speak on their behalf, all information obtained in therapy may be made available (i.e., if asked, the therapist cannot just highlight all the positive gains made in therapy; they may also be asked to disclose what led to past problems). This is a difficult decision that clients may sometimes have to make.

On many release of information forms, clients may even select the elements of treatment (e.g., financials, medications, progress in therapy, presence in therapy) that they want to be disclosed. Thus, if a client leaves something unchecked, that means they did not give the therapist permission to discuss that particular element with the third party. For example, a 23-year-old adult client may be receiving therapy that is paid for by their parent. Because they are an adult, the client would need to sign a release of information form for their parent to pay for sessions. If this client does not want their parent to have access to any information other than financials, the client could simply select "presence in therapy" and "financials" on the release of information form so the parent could simply pay for sessions. The therapist would be able to acknowledge the client's presence in treatment and any relevant finances with the parent, but they would not be able to discuss other aspects of therapy. In court-mandated cases, it is usually required that all elements on a release of information form are checked off, as the therapist would need to address multiple elements of the case with the relevant parties.

Before speaking to someone else about your client, make sure you have signed a HIPAA release form. If you do not and you still share their protected health information, you are opening yourself up to potential litigation and licensure sanctions. The release form should have, at a minimum, the following information:

- A description of what information will be disclosed
- The purpose of disclosing the information
- The name of the person (or organization) that the information will be disclosed

- An expiration date (or event) when consent for disclosure will no longer be valid
- The client's (or authorized individual's) signature

Besides these basic elements, the release form should also inform the client as to how to revoke their authorization, exceptions to their rights to revoke the authorization, an explanation of how the authorization can be revoked, and that there are no conditions for them to sign the release (that they are signing it of their own free will).

If you are working in private practice, you will need to develop your own release of information form, or you can buy or utilize one that other people have developed. If you are working in an agency, that organization most likely has a standard release of information that you will use. In either case, the release of information should be written in such a way that it is understandable by most people. Thus, the more you use straightforward and plain language, the better. Once you and the

---

Release of Information Form

Effective Date: _____

Authorization for Use or Disclosure of Protected Health Information (Required by the Health Insurance Portability and Accountability Act, 45 C.F.R. Parts 160 and 164)

1. **Authorization**. I authorize _____ to use and disclose the protected health information described below to _____.
2. **Effective Period**. This authorization for release of information covers the period of health care from _____ to _____.
3. **Extent of Authorization**. I authorize the release of my psychotherapy treatment and progress notes.
4. **Use**. This medical information may be used by the person I authorize to receive this information for medical treatment.
5. **Termination**. This authorization shall be in force and effect until _____, at which time this authorization form expires.
6. **Revocation Rights**. I understand that I have the right to revoke this authorization, in writing, at any time. I understand that a revocation is not effective to the extent that any person or entity has already acted in reliance on my authorization or if my authorization was obtained as a condition of obtaining insurance coverage and the insurer has a legal right to contest a claim.
7. **Benefits**. I understand that my treatment, payment, enrollment, or eligibility for benefits will not be conditioned on whether I sign this authorization.
8. **Disclosure**. I understand that information used or disclosed pursuant to this authorization may be disclosed by the recipient and may no longer be protected by federal or state law.

Client's Name (printed): _____
Client's Signature (or authorized representative): _____
Date: _____

Figure 4.2 Sample of Release of Information Form.

client sign the release of information, you should give the client a copy of it and place the original in the client's official record/chart. In many cases, when you are reaching out to other professionals (e.g., primary care physician, psychiatrist), they will require a release of information form to be signed on their end as well allowing them to talk to you. Your client will thus likely need to fill out a release of information form for you to speak to the other professional and another form for the other professional to speak to you.

Figure 4.2 presents a sample of a Release of Information form.

Permission to Record Sessions/Use Case Material

Most therapy sessions are not audio- or video-recorded. If you are currently training as a psychotherapist, you are likely required by your university or training site to record one or more sessions so that you can review them with your supervisor to enhance your continued growth as a therapist. If you are past your training days, you can probably remember having to record your sessions. Viewing recorded sessions is an excellent means of reviewing your cases, either alone or with a supervisor, to allow you to see areas of professional growth. But hopefully, you don't think that recording sessions is only for therapists-in-training. Our field is predicated on continued life-long learning. Reviewing our sessions, preferably through video recording, can help us understand and learn more about our own practice as a therapist.

Regardless of when in your career you record sessions or the purpose of recording them, you cannot do so without the client's consent. They must be informed as to when you will record, how you will record, and what you will do with the recordings. Ethical codes all have a standard for recording sessions. For instance, the AMHCA code of ethics standard 2j states:

> Sessions with clients may be taped or otherwise recorded only with written permission of the client or guardian. Even with a guardian's written consent, CMHCs should not record a session against the expressed wishes of a client. Such tapes should be destroyed after the timeframe specified by state regulations.

Most training programs will have a standard form that they use for permission to record sessions and to use the case materials. When working in private practice, if you were to record, you would need to develop your own form. Figure 4.3 presents a sample **Permission to Record form**.

Permission to Record the Session Form

_____ (name of agency/business) provides therapeutic services for individuals, couples, and families in the community. In addition to these services, _____ (name of agency/business) also promotes and supports the professional development of its therapists. Audio taping and video recording of the therapy sessions are a vital tool that aids therapists in their continued development and growth. No audio taping or video recording is conducted without the permission of the client.

I _____ (name of client) authorize _____ (name of agency/business) to (check all that apply): ____ audio tape ____ video record the duration of our therapy sessions. I understand that these recordings will be listened to/viewed by my therapist, their supervisor, and other therapists on the consulting team for learning and case conceptualization purposes. I understand that I have the option to request that these recordings be destroyed at any point.

Client's Name (printed): _____
Client's Signature (or authorized representative): _____
Date: _____

Figure 4.3 Sample of Permission to Record the Session Form.

Pragmatic Letters

Welcome Letter

Besides the informed consent and intake forms (and potentially a release of information form if the client knows from the get-go that they want you to talk to someone, such as the courts or a primary care physician), most first sessions occur without the need for any paperwork occurring before the client gets to the office. There are some therapists who might have clients fill out questionnaires beforehand, but overall, therapists tend to not send clients documents before the first contact. In this section, we want to present a possibility that can be useful on multiple levels, what we will call in this chapter a **welcome letter**, which becomes the first intervention in the therapeutic process.

A welcome letter to clients before you have the first session prepares them for what they might expect from the therapy process and informs them of their potential role in this process (Graham, 2003). One of the reasons for the welcome letter is that it increases client satisfaction since the client and therapist have a mutual understanding of the process of therapy. In essence, the welcome letter provides clients with a role preparation opportunity.

One problematic occurrence that most therapists deal with is clients no-showing. This can be especially problematic in private practice as

Welcome to _____ (name of practice)

Dear _____ (client's name),

   This is just a friendly reminder for your appointment at _____ (name and address of practice) this Thursday, _____ (date), at 11 am. This will be an initial intake appointment in order to gather the necessary information and sign the appropriate documentation to begin therapy sessions thereafter. The intake session usually takes around 45-60 minutes.
   If you have any questions before your appointment, please don't hesitate to give us a call at _____ (phone number) or email us at _____ (email). We look forward to seeing you!

Figure 4.4 Sample of Welcome Letter.

your income is predicated on whether the client comes to the session or not. While you might have a no-show policy—if a client is allowed any and if not, how much they will be charged for missing the session— enforcing the policy can be quite difficult, especially with clients who come to therapy for the first session.

Receiving a letter that provides both a reminder of the day, time, and location of the first session and an orientation to what will occur during the first session (e.g., the conducting of an intake session) helps to improve the rate of showing for the first session (Swenson & Pekarik, 1988). These authors found that there was a lower no-show rate for those who received this orientation letter prompt one day before the session than for those who received it three days before. This suggests that you might consider developing an orientation letter that you send to all new clients. You might then send this letter out in hopes that it arrives one to two days before the scheduled session. You might send the letter by regular mail or electronically. Figure 4.4 presents a sample of Welcome Letter.

Letters to Maintain Engagement

While some clients may no-show for a first session, leading to the usefulness of the welcome letter, clients will also continue to no-show throughout the course of the therapeutic process. On average, clients will miss one session per month (Defife et al., 2010). Some clients will either cancel or no-show for quite a few sessions, but luckily not that many people do this. Either way, any missed appointment leads to potential lost revenue for you, increased frustration, and a likely decrease in therapeutic gains. As such, it might be useful for you to periodically send letters to your clients to maintain their engagement in therapy.

Throughout the course of psychotherapy, there may be times when the therapeutic alliance is not that strong. This is likely to occur at the beginning of therapy or possibly after a rupture has occurred. At these times, you can write a **letter of alliance** to your client. These types of letters are designed to either establish or strengthen the therapeutic relationship (Kindsvatter et al., 2009). By taking the time to write a letter to the client, you demonstrate your interest in the client as a person. These letters are usually encouraging and hopeful, providing the client to experience your desire for their positive well-being.

Two subsets of letters of engagement are formulation letters and supplementary letters. Allen et al. (2016) found that **Formulation Letters** (which are case formulations about the etiology of the presenting problem) predicted higher treatment acceptability (especially those that focused on the development of anorexia nervosa). Further, letters that were respectful and reflective led to higher reductions in eating disorder symptoms.

Nunnally and Lipchik (1990) utilized **Supplementary Letters**. These letters are given periodically between sessions, specifically when the therapist realizes after the session that they did not convey certain information that was important to help the client to move toward change. This letter would be used as a quick boost when the therapist thought that waiting to deliver the message in the subsequent session would not be as timely or beneficial as providing that information more immediately.

While most letters written to help maintain the client's engagement in therapy are straightforward in trying to connect the client to therapy, the process of letter writing with clients in a session can enhance engagement.

Dear _____ (client's name),

    I wanted to reach out to you and reflect on our session this past week. There were several important topics we discussed, and there were a few themes that I found particularly significant to make special note of before our next session. This past week, we talked about your relationship with your husband and some of the quarrels you two have been having recently. We reflected on how this has understandably been extremely frustrating for you since you care about your relationship so much, yet it feels like you both are against each other right now.

    However, I wanted to emphasize something else that I heard you mention. While there have been a lot of struggles recently, you still talked about how you and your husband are a team. Above all, I got the sense that you see your relationship as a partnership where it is you two against the world. The way you talk about the issues you are facing is from the perspective that it is something you both will solve together rather than you are facing alone while fighting against him. When I asked you about what you think his experience of all of this is, you confidently stated that it hurts him because he sees you both as a unit as well. I thought it would be important to point this out before going into our next session, as we didn't explicitly note this innate strength within your relationship. I wonder if it would be helpful to explore this foundation of your relationship during our next session.

Sincerely,

Therapist Name/Signature: _____

Figure 4.5 Sample of Letter to Maintain Engagement.

For instance, White and Murray (2002) used therapeutic letter writing when working with adolescents since it is an indirect form of communication. Many adolescents may have a hard time sitting face-to-face with a therapist and orally communicating for the whole of a session. Writing a letter together shifts the therapist and client from facing one another to doing a joint activity. This is similar to adolescent males shifting from facing one another and talking to both facing a television screen or playing a video game while they also might be talking, which will tend to be more comfortable for both of them. There is a fine line between letters designed to maintain engagement and those that are intended to be truly therapeutic (see Chapters 5 and 6). These two intentions overlap. In this chapter, we are presenting these letters as a means of keeping the client engaged in treatment. The next two chapters go into much greater depth explaining how you can write therapeutic letters. Figure 4.5 presents a sample of letter designed to maintain engagement.

Recruiting Non-attending Family Members

Many times, a client will come, and you will only meet with that one client. Although they may at times discuss conflicts they are having with others—such as a spouse, parent, or child—you are likely to only talk with your client. However, depending on the setting you are working in and the type of therapist you are (e.g., if you are a couples/family therapist), you may want to invite other family members into the session. This could be done in one of two ways. First, you might ask the client to invite other family members to come. However, they have likely tried in the past to no avail. Probably, their attempts at conjoint therapy led to fights and conflict and they decided that at least one of them had to go to therapy, so they took it upon themselves to do so.

If the client's request for their family member to attend sessions doesn't pan out, then you might consider writing a letter to recruit a non-attending family member to join the therapy. There are many different ways that you can take to offer the space for the family member to come. For example, in marital therapy, one possibility is to provide research data in your communication as to how one-spouse marital therapy is not as effective as both spouses participating (Wilcoxon & Fenell, 1983). Another example is in the field of substance abuse where a client may deny or minimize the extent of their substance use. While the client's behaviors may influence the family, family members' behaviors may also influence the client. Family members can be encouraged to provide valuable insight into the origins of the client's substance use.

When introducing the idea of an **invitation letter to non-attending family members**, you should talk this through with your client, as they must be comfortable with the communication that you are sending out. This is where getting them to sign a release of information form for you to contact other people for the purpose of therapy invitation is extremely important.

After writing the letter, you then have a couple of options for delivery methods. You might physically print out the letter and mail it to the person, email it to them, or print it out and have your client hand-deliver the letter. There is no one better method; rather, it depends on the situation, your judgment, and the client's judgment on which delivery method will have the greatest likelihood of gaining the other person's agreement to come to therapy.

As you know, clients have autonomy in consenting to therapy. Given this, you might include in the letter a statement about your willingness to provide a space for both your client and the other person to be able to discuss their situation and utilize therapy as a place to shift their relationship. You might encourage them to have a discussion outside of therapy about their thoughts about the usefulness of therapy in their relationship. Conversely, you might offer up a therapy session for them to come together and talk about where they want their relationship to go. Figure 4.6 presents a sample of letter designed to recruit a family member to join the current sessions.

Dear _____ (family member's name),

  I am reaching out to you because, as you know, I have been seeing your partner, _____ (client's name), for individual therapy sessions over the past few months. We have talked about a variety of topics, including your partner's job, parents, and personal goals. Naturally, we have also touched on your relationship, and _____ (client's name) gave me a background of how you both met, how long you have been together, what you two do for fun, etc.

  _____ (client's name) has also talked about some newer challenges you two have been facing together recently. I have heard a lot from your partner about these concerns and potential solutions; however, there are obviously two people in the relationship, so we thought it might be even more helpful if you joined us for a session. This would provide me with the opportunity to get your perspective and gain additional insight into the relationship. I think this could be incredibly helpful for the therapy process, as having both partners in a therapy session about relationship topics winds up being much more beneficial than having just one.

  I also want to emphasize that this would be a space for you to open up about anything important to you and your relationship as well, as _____ (client's name) mentioned how they are hoping to use this space for you both to share each other's perspectives and then, as a team, figure out where you both want the relationship to go moving forward. If you two find this session helpful, you both are more than welcome to utilize the sessions as joint sessions moving forward. If you have any questions or further curiosities about the process, please feel free to reach out to me by phone or email. If you are wanting to attend the next session, just let _____ (client's name) know, and they can give me a heads-up before the session. I look forward to potentially meeting/speaking with you!

Sincerely,

Therapist Name/Signature: _____

Figure 4.6 Sample of Letter of Recruitment.

Referral Letters

In the stage play *Hamlet*, William Shakespeare coined the famous line "Know thyself and to thine self be true." The ethical codes for many different psychotherapy organizations all adhere to this notion. One of these areas is through competence and responsibility. That is, therapists should recognize the boundaries of their competence and the limitations of their techniques. They should only provide services and use techniques for which they are qualified by education and training. If a therapist is uncomfortable with a particular area, they can refuse to engage in treatment and should refer people. All ethical codes have some provision about referring clients. For instance, the National Association of Social Workers code of ethics standard 1.16 Referral for Services (a) states:

> Social workers should refer clients to other professionals when the other professionals' specialized knowledge or expertise is needed to serve clients fully or when social workers believe that they are not being effective or making reasonable progress with clients and that other services are required.

Lack of competence in a particular area is not the only reason why a therapist may need to refer. There are other times a therapist may be totally competent in the client's area of need, but sometimes it is still necessary to help the client find additional sources of support where needed. The following are potential reasons for making referrals:

- The therapist has close ties to the client either directly or indirectly.
- The therapist lacks competence in this area.
- The client requires a specialist in an outside area (e.g., could be a biological medical issue).
- No progress is made in therapy (could be due to resistant clients, personality issues, or differences between client and therapist).
- The client may be a danger to themselves or others.
- Countertransference issues disrupt the therapeutic process.
- The client has another need (e.g., let's say you have a minority client you are treating for depression and anxiety. One of the factors contributing to their current state deals with housing discrimination. While therapists should never tell a client what decisions to make, if a client asked for resources in this area, we should point them in the right direction for advice and assistance).

Sometimes beginning-level therapists and counselors may view referrals as a sign of weakness or lack of skill. Knowing one's limitations is a sign of strength. Being aware of the different referral agencies puts the client in the best position to make the right choice for themselves. Remember your two most important ethical principles: (1) do no harm to the client and (2) do what is in the best interest and welfare of the client.

One of the primary people psychotherapists write a referral letter to is a psychiatrist so that their client can get evaluated for the potential benefits of psychotropic medications. When writing a referral letter, there are some general areas to cover (these might change based on your therapeutic orientation and how much information you have about the client). These areas are an introduction identifying yourself and the client, presenting problem, history of the problem, client history, clinical assessment, medical history, and differential diagnosis.

Coordination of Care Letters

Just as it is important for therapists to refer their clients out to other professionals when appropriate, it is equally as significant that therapists are in contact with their clients' other relevant professionals to coordinate care. It is thus common for therapists to communicate with other relevant figures in the client's life. Many individuals see multiple healthcare professionals—a therapist, a psychiatrist, a primary care physician, a gynecologist, etc. Clients also have other individuals (e.g., bosses, school counselors) who play important roles in other contexts of clients' lives. Oftentimes, the concerns that clients are coming to you with overlap with what they may be discussing with their other healthcare providers and/or important figures. While it may not always be necessary to be in communication with these other people, there are times when this communication would benefit the client.

Sometimes, the client may come to you asking for you to reach out to another professional. For example, a teenage client may start seeing you for anxiety issues, manifesting as frequent panic attacks at school. This client also has meetings with their guidance counselor in order to assist the client in coordinating their academics with their recent bouts of panic attacks during classes. The client and their parent may ask you to keep in touch with the guidance counselor to convey any relevant developments and collaboratively discuss solutions that could be implemented in the client's school.

Other times, you may suggest to your client that it could be beneficial for you to speak with another professional whom they see. For instance, you may think that it would be helpful for you to discuss your client's medication with their psychiatrist. If your client agrees for you to reach out to someone else who aids in their care, it is important that you fully go over what you are hoping to discuss with the other professional. Your client should be aware of the purpose and parameters of the conversation. Regardless of whether your client requests coordination of care

Dear _____ (professional's name),

    I am _____ (your name and credentials), and I am seeing _____ (client's name) for therapy services at _____ (name of practice) for some depression and anxiety concerns. My client mentioned that they also started utilizing your psychiatry services in order to see what medication would be beneficial for them. During our most recent session, _____ (client's name) and I were talking about how we could coordinate what we are working on in therapy with other important aspects of their care. We collaboratively determined that it would be incredibly helpful for me to be in contact with you, their psychiatrist, about their medication in relation to how their treatment is progressing and what their primary needs are.

    Attached in this email is a release of information form signed by my client giving me permission to speak with you. They had let me know that they were contacting your office to sign the same form on your end. As soon as you get that form, I'd love to hear back from you either via email or a telephone call. If you'd like to schedule a call, please feel free to email me back or you can reach me at (xxx) xxx-xxxx. I look forward to hearing from you.

Sincerely,

Therapist Name/Signature: _____

Figure 4.7 Sample of Coordination of Care Letter.

themselves or agrees to it at your suggestion, you will need the client (or their legal guardian/authorized representative) to sign the appropriate release of information form.

    Your coordination of care letter will look different depending on why you are contacting another professional about your client. Figure 4.7 provides an example of what a **Coordination of Care Letter** could look like.

No Contact Letters

You will find in your practice, like so many of us do, that some clients will stop coming without letting you know. This can happen for a variety of reasons, including the client getting all they wanted from therapy but not knowing how to have an overt conversation with you about stopping, a rupture in the therapeutic relationship, the client moving away, or other reasons.

    Some therapists will not reach out to the client if the client does not reach out to them. Others, however, will document that they tried to reach out to ensure that they could provide services if needed. We suggest that if a client continues to no-show, you document that you reached out to them. Sometimes, therapists may send an email and/or give the client a call (and potentially need to leave a voicemail) in order to try and contact

Date: _____

Dear _____,

It has been a while since we were able to meet. Our records indicate that you were last seen for a therapy appointment on _____. I have not heard from you since then. I wanted you to know that you are welcome to come back and resume our meetings. If you are still interested in therapeutic services, please contact me at your earliest convenience.

If you are no longer interested in receiving therapeutic services through our agency or are interested in receiving a referral to another counseling agency, again, please let us know at your earliest convenience. We can be reached by phone at (xxx) xxx-xxxx or by mail at _____ (address).

Please be advised that if we do not hear from you by _____, your case/file will be closed. Should this occur and you decide to contact us for therapeutic services after this date, we cannot guarantee that we would have an immediate opening for you and you would be placed at the bottom of our waiting list.

Should you have concerns about your discharge, please feel free to contact our office at (xxx) xxx-xxxx.

Sincerely,

Therapist Name/Signature: _____

Figure 4.8 Sample of No Contact Letter.

a client they have not heard from. However, the **No Contact letter** can also be utilized to reach out to clients whom we haven't heard from in a while. This letter is used for several purposes, including trying to encourage the client to re-engage in therapy as well as a form of protection for you, documenting that you did not abandon the client. Figure 4.8 provides a sample of No Contact Letter.

Closing/Termination Letters

An imperative aspect of any psychotherapy is ending the relationship at some point (Joyce et al., 2007). This is known as termination. Terminations may be well planned or happen abruptly (Barnett, 2016). For example, sometimes there are not enough sessions left, insurance coverage has stopped, or the client no longer wishes to continue therapy. Termination may also convey a sense of loss for some clients. Abrupt terminations can bring about feelings of sadness, anger, and despair, whereas well-planned terminations may be seen as valuable, healthy, and productive (Fragkiadaki & Strauss, 2012). Termination is not something that should happen at the end of therapy. It should be mentioned at the beginning and throughout therapy so that it is well planned out. The following are recommendations for well-planned and thought-out terminations (the first three points are modified from Barnett, 2016):

- Agree on how therapy will end from the beginning (e.g., is it based solely on progress made, client insurance, or other factors).
- Agree on therapy goals and what meeting these goals should be.
- Prepare for client interruptions (e.g., illness, financial changes, insurance coverage, job loss, or relocation).
- See therapist reasons for referral in the previous section.

Therapists may use a letter at the end of therapy as a way to terminate the therapeutic process/relationship. These letters might be called closing letters, farewell letters, or case summary letters. These letters tend to summarize the therapy process, focusing particularly on the client's attained goals and steps made toward progress. Simmonds et al. (2020) held that, based on positive research, results of goodbye letters, and treatment outcomes, the time spent by the therapist in writing them is worth the effort. Figure 4.9 provides a sample of **Termination Letter**.

Date: _____

Dear _____,

     Thank you for allowing me to work with you. When we first met you presented with_____. The focus of our time together was on addressing_____, and I approached your issues and concerns by engaging in_____.

     Throughout our time together I have seen you [note behaviors, feelings, and thoughts seen in therapy]. I have seen growth and improvement in_____. You have displayed coping skills learned in therapy by making them applicable to your personal life. I have seen firsthand how you were able to_____.

     You should be proud of the work you have done and the accomplishments you have made in therapy. Remember, even though our journey is ending together the work you have put in, the progress you have made, and the knowledge and skills gained never stops.

     Should you need further assistance in the future or have any questions or concerns, please feel free to contact our office at (xxx) xxx-xxxx.

Sincerely,

Therapist Name/Signature: _____

Figure 4.9 Sample of Termination Letter.

Comments on Writing Style

Regardless of the type of contract or pragmatic letter you write, there are some general guidelines that you should consider using. We will talk about them here in hopes that they help whenever you conceptualize and construct your written communication with clients and others.

All the documents that we've presented in this chapter are professional documents that need to be written with the understanding that how you come across in the letter potentially impacts the therapeutic relationship or the interaction with other professionals. Given this, it is extremely important that you proofread every written item that comes out of your office. The more errors that people read in your contracts, reports, and letters, the less likely they will believe in what you are writing and your overall treatment. Your writing should be clear and well written. Feel free to have a colleague read through your contracts/letters as well (making sure confidentiality is maintained when appropriate) for a double check of understanding, spelling, etc. We also recommend having a legal representative review all your forms and contracts to assure that they adhere to the legal components of your locale.

Once you get one version written for each type of document/letter, you can use it as a template for future ones. Most of your release of information forms, for example, should have the same format. The only thing that will likely change is the information of the client and the information of the person to whom they are giving you permission to speak. Other letters, such as coordination of care and recruitment letters, may look slightly different in format, as what you are trying to convey to the receiver of the letter may change. However, you will find that the template can still be used as a helpful base to structure the rest of your content.

When composing a written communication, you will also need to think about who your audience is, as that will slightly impact how you write. We will talk about a few of these differences here. When communicating with clients, avoid jargon. Technical language can be confusing to them and leave them feeling like an object rather than a person. However, when writing to other psychotherapy professionals, it is appropriate to use the lingo apropos for the field. When writing to a client, you generally would want to avoid saying something like, "We have recently been discussing the ways that the symptoms of your unspecified anxiety disorder have increased due to the use of unhealthy coping mechanisms such as substance abuse." While there is nothing inherently incorrect about this statement, it uses more therapist lingo that might make your client feel like a clinical case instead of a person. Instead, you could note, "We have recently been reflecting on how anxiety seems to be connected to behaviors that you aren't finding to be beneficial to your growth, such as smoking marijuana." This sentence essentially gives the same information, but it does so in a way that is more colloquial and most likely mirrors how these topics were discussed in the therapy room between therapist and client.

In contrast, if you were writing to another therapist who is seeing your client's partner, for example, you might discuss your client's diagnosis, their prognosis, what therapeutic techniques you are using, how that might help with couples sessions, etc.:

> With my client's diagnosis of unspecified anxiety disorder, we have been working on coping mechanism development through a solution-focused lens in order to help them work through the challenges that they are facing with their partner. I believe these techniques may be helpful to use in joint sessions...

Just to note, this would all need to be done with the appropriate release of authorization forms signed. The information included in the letter should also always be clinically relevant to the purpose of the letter, so there is no need to include any clinical information that isn't pertinent.

The contracts and letters should also be free of biased language. All ethical guidelines hold that therapists must be non-discriminatory where you provide services for people regardless of their age, race, gender, sexual orientation, ethnicity, socioeconomic status, and national identity. This belief in the equality of all people should come across in your writing as well. For example, if you are seeing a couple who are in their 70s, you should not refer to them as "seniors" or "elderly." The seventh edition of the *Publication Manual of the American Psychological Association* (American Psychological Association, 2020) has a whole chapter on the use of bias-free language, which includes examples of biased language and non-biased language than can be used as a replacement.

Summary

Therapy is a contractual endeavor. While this contract should be verbally agreed upon, it is imperative to have it in a written format and signed and acknowledged by the client. To do so, therapists use many different forms and contracts which help them adhere to the various ethical codes that we operate by as well as to assist in treatment by welcoming clients into therapy, encouraging people in the client's relational field to join the therapy session, to maintain the client's engagement in therapy, or as a means of terminating therapy. Further, depending on the client and therapeutic situation, you may have the client fill out Release of Information forms or send out a Coordination of Care form. Please proofread every form and contract you have, as these are both indicative of your professionalism and are legal forms. In total, your forms and contracts serve the purpose of educating the client on services, providing them or others pertinent information about the treatment, and providing a medium to enhance participation in therapy.

References

Allen, K. L., O'Hara, C. B., Bartholdy, S., Renwick, B., Keyes, A., Lose, A., Kenyon, M., DeJong, H., Broadbent, H., Loomes, R., McClelland, J., Serpell, L., Richards, L., Johnson-Sabine, E., Boughton, N., Whitehead, L., Treasure, J., Wade, T., & Schmidt, U. (2016). Written case formulations in the treatment of anorexia nervosa: Evidence for therapeutic benefits. *International Journal of Eating Disorders, 49*(9), 874–882.

American Psychological Association. (2020). *Publication manual of the American psychological association* (7th ed.).

Barnett, J. (2016, October 6). *6 strategies for ethical termination of psychotherapy: And for avoiding abandonment.* Society for the Advancement of Psychotherapy. Retrieved July 29, 2022, from https://societyforpsychotherapy. org/6-strategies-for-ethical-termination-of-psychotherapy/.

Defife, J. A., Conklin, C. Z., Smith, J. M., & Poole, J. (2010). Psychotherapy appointment no-shows: Rates and reasons. *Psychotherapy Theory, Research, Practice, Training, 47*(3), 413–417.

Fragkiadaki, E., & Strauss, S. M. (2012). Termination of psychotherapy: The journey of 10 psychoanalytic and psychodynamic therapists. *Psychology and Psychotherapy: Theory, Research and Practice, 85*(3), 335–350.

Graham, G. H. (2003). Role preparation in brief strategic therapy: The welcome letter. *Journal of Systemic Therapies, 22*(1), 3–14.

Joyce, A. S., Piper, W. E., Ogrodniczuk, J. S., & Klein, R. H. (2007). *Termination in psychotherapy: A psychodynamic model of processes and outcomes.* American Psychological Association.

Kindsvatter, A., Nelson, J. R., & Desmond, K. J. (2009). An invitation to between-session change: The use of therapeutic letters in couples and family counseling. *The Family Journal, 17*(1), 32–38.

Nunnally, E., & Lipchik, E. (1990). Some uses of writing in solution focused brief therapy. *Journal of Independent Social Work, 4*(2), 5–19.

Simmonds, J., Allen, K. L., O'Hara, C. B., Bartholdy, S., Renwick, B., et al. (2020). Therapist written goodbye letters: Evidence for therapeutic benefits in the treatment of anorexia nervosa. *Behavioural and Cognitive Psychotherapy, 48*(4), 419–431.

Swenson, T. R., & Pekarik, G. (1988). Interventions for reducing missed initial appointments at a community mental health center. *Community Mental Health Journal, 24*(3), 205–218.

White, V. E., & Murray, M. A. (2002). Passing notes: The use of therapeutic letter writing in counseling adolescents. *Journal of Mental Health Counseling, 24*(2), 166–176.

Wilcoxon, A., & Fennell, D. (1983). Engaging the non-attending spouse in marital therapy through the use of therapist-initiated written communication. *Journal of Marita land Family Therapy, 9*(2), 199–203.

Chapter 5

Therapeutic Letters to Clients

Michael D. Reiter

So far in this book, we have discussed how therapists write for official documentation purposes, such as progress notes, informed consent, therapeutic contracts, assessments, and treatment plans. These documents inform people as to the parameters of the therapeutic relationship or provide an overview of the difficulties a client is dealing with at that time. However, these types of writing are not intended to be interventive—while a treatment plan discusses what *will* happen in therapy, it is not usually seen as *creating* change but rather as documenting any change that has occurred. In this chapter, we focus on interventive letters. We will explore some general guidelines when writing therapeutic letters to clients, their importance, several different types of letters, letters from different theoretical modalities, clients' reactions to receiving a therapeutic letter, and the ethical implications of writing and giving your client a therapeutic letter.

Therapeutic Letters

Periodically throughout the course of treatment, therapists may write letters to clients. These letters may be more formal, such as those inviting people into therapy via a welcome letter or perhaps at the end of treatment via a closing letter (see Chapter 4). Letters written by therapists may also be more interventive, what we will call **therapeutic letters**. This chapter, and Chapter 6, presents those therapeutic letters that you might write to your client that are designed to help them change—to move them closer to their therapeutic goals. These may be some of the most impactful interventions that you engage in with your client. I hope by the end of this chapter that you are so invigorated and enthusiastic that you begin (if you haven't already) to incorporate therapeutic letters into your therapeutic practice!

Therapist letters to clients have been a part of psychotherapy for most of its history. Freud, the founder of our field, was known to write letters to clients. Perhaps one of the most famous of this was his letter

DOI: 10.4324/9781003294702-5

correspondence with the father of "Little Hans" (a five-year-old boy who had a fear of horses). Freud wrote letters to the father—and received letters from the father—that helped him to conceptualize the etiology of Hans' fear. Through the letters, he directed the father on how to help Hans. Freud only met with Hans once, mainly talking with the father, and mainly through a letter exchange where the father reported on Hans' behavior, interactions, and dreams. Freud claimed that after the father had a conversation with Hans about concepts discussed in the correspondence between Freud and the father, Hans' phobia of horses disappeared.

If you haven't yet written a therapeutic letter, you might question their benefit. In essence, what is the use of therapeutic letters? In general, therapists' use of writing tends to send messages, focus clients' attention in certain areas, heighten the dramatic impact of therapy, clarify directives, and act as interventions (Nunnally & Lipchik, 1990). A letter you send a client provides a novelty in therapy where the clients may be more primed to think about the content in the letter. Based upon how many sessions you have had with clients, you verbally saying something to a client may merge into the other 55 minutes of that conversation. However, slowing down and reading an idea that is set on paper (or in an email) may provide sufficient weight that it stimulates the client to think about the situation or themselves in a different manner that opens new possibilities.

If you have never written a therapeutic letter, it is not the same as letters you may have written to loved ones, family, or friends. They are interventions and should be given the respect they deserve as they can be quite impactful. Moules (2003) explained that therapeutic letters differ from social letters in their context, content, intent, and effect. Social letters tend to inform and be informal. Therapeutic letters are purposely used, purposely worded, and purposely purposeful. You are likely to spend a greater amount of time wordsmithing your therapeutic letter than one you would write a personal acquaintance. This is important since the therapeutic letter occurs in the context of a therapeutic contract—one where the person you are writing the letter to is paying you to provide a service and the letter you are writing is one of the outputs of that service.

Most therapy occurs face-to-face (and we can include videoconferencing here) where the bulk of the interactions happen via the spoken word. Therapists might use a variety of techniques, some of which are not verbal, such as sculpting, art, music, or dance. Therapy letters are another type of intervention where the words being conveyed shift from the mouth and air to the pen and paper. Therapeutic letters tend to be in addition to the main work that happens within the session. However, they have a significant impact in helping to increase clients' motivation for coming to sessions, implementing the therapeutic interventions, and transitioning to life without therapy. Letters to clients tend to increase clients' sense of agency by helping them contact and utilize both internal and external relationships (Jolly, 2011).

Some therapists have conducted therapy solely through letters; however, this process is not standard. There are many concerns about never meeting face-to-face with your client (via teleconferencing is included here), given that you are taking the client's word (literally!) for what they are experiencing, without having visual and auditory support and assessment. Some therapists have even explored conducting therapy with suicidal clients only with letters (Schustov & Lester, 1999). Before doing this, consider the ethical and safety implications. One of the concerns is that there is not a strong therapeutic relationship developed between therapist and client. However you decide to use therapeutic letters in your practice, be sure that they are housed within a strong therapeutic alliance.

Therapy does not happen outside of context. Letters written by therapists to clients always involve the therapeutic relationship. The purpose of the letter may be trying to initiate, maintain, or end the relationship. Whatever the purpose of the letter, you should write it in a relationally responsive manner. Pyle (2009) explained that "letter writing provides a unique opportunity to be attuned to the therapeutic relationship and responsive to the 'goings-on' of the therapeutic conversation" (p. 66). The letter serves as addition and perpetuation of the positive therapeutic alliance that you've developed with your client. One of the benefits of therapeutic letters is that they tend to lead to greater relational connectedness between therapist and client (Rodgers, 2009). In almost all the cases I've worked with, as therapist or supervisor, the client has expressed appreciation to the therapist on receiving the letter, feeling like the therapist really understood them.

For most of the 20th century, people primarily communicated to one another, in written form, through letters. Letters were written when we were away from loved ones and wanted to let them know how we were doing. Letters were written to a paramour, where we looked forward to receiving a love letter back from them. Letters were written to people after they interviewed us for a job, to thank them for taking the time to meet with us. We became excited when we went to the mailbox and saw that we received a handwritten letter. Today, our residential mailbox primarily contains junk mail and bills. The mailbox we think about today is electronic. Emails and text messages have replaced letters. However, receiving a letter, particularly one that focuses on our strengths and growth, has significant implications. More than a message read on an iPhone, a personal letter on a piece of paper provides a modicum of importance that is unrivaled. This is not to say that you cannot write and send a letter through email, as this practice has become more common (Epston, 2009). However, I believe there is still something magical about holding a piece of paper and reading from it—there is weight to it (even if only in ounces). This chapter introduces the process of therapists writing therapeutic letters to their clients. Hopefully, by the end of this chapter, you will have many ideas of how you can incorporate therapeutic letters into your practice.

The Importance of Letters

Perhaps the first hand-written letter was written by Queen Atossa of Persia in around 500 BC. This was a start of how letters have become ubiquitous for human communication. Throughout much of the last several centuries, letters have served an integral role in how people convey information to one another. You are likely to have received many of these (whether they were printed and mailed or typed and emailed). Think about your letter of acceptance into college, a love letter from a paramour, a letter of resignation, or a letter of recommendation. Whether you wrote it, or it was written to you, it was written with certain intents to convey specific information.

Whatever type of letter, they have a theme to them where there is a purpose. They provide a glimpse into one or more aspects of the person's life. The content of the letter is a snapshot and a piece of the client's life story. This is significant since people story their lives (White & Epston, 1990). We give meaning to our experiences through the stories we tell ourselves. In essence, the stories we tell about ourselves shape our lives. When these stories, especially the positive ones, are documented in a letter, they have a significant influence on continuing and enhancing that story.

The words and concepts written in letters help to confirm the various stories that we and others hold of us. The acceptance letter opens space for the story of our academic success. The Dear John letter presents part of a story of lost love and heartbreak. The employment letter helps construct a story of who we are as a worker. These stories are connected to our past and our identities. They also may foretell our future and the identities we want to walk into. This is important since therapy is usually a process of helping people shift from limiting identities to identifying and implementing more resourceful identities (Reiter et al., 2020). Therapeutic letters usually focus on uncovering and promoting these resourceful identities.

Whereas traditional therapy is a talk-oriented endeavor, letters use words more tangibly. The words we use are put down on paper and can be accessed anytime the recipient wants. Spoken words are at greater risk of fading into the ether. Written words are more permanent. Letters also help organize our words, placing them into a context where they present a theme, a partial story for the recipient. While you want your words to go with your clients, when they are in the form of a letter, they are more mobile. The client can fold the letter up and put it in their pocket, having your words travel with them no matter where they may go. They can take out the letter, read it, and re-experience their therapeutic growth. As we know, the more that clients make active change efforts the greater the likelihood is that they will make changes. Thus, having a therapeutic letter that they can frequently access increases the possibility that the letter will function as a prompt for continued movement toward their goals.

General Guidelines

This chapter provides you with an overview of a few of the main types of therapeutic letters that you will likely give and send to clients. While we can't know exactly how to word these letters, there are a few general guidelines that should help you when you construct your own. This section presents some of these general guidelines. Please keep in mind that this is a guide rather than a prescription. It will be up to you, based on your therapeutic orientation, the context in which you are practicing, the type of client you are working with, and the quality of the therapeutic relationship to determine which of these guidelines may need to be altered or adapted to better serve your purposes with the letter.

The first guideline, and perhaps most important, is that the letter should be indicative of a strong therapeutic alliance. The more the client appreciates the connection between you and them, the more import they will give to the intent and the content of the letter. Moules (2003) explained the significance of the alliance when giving a therapeutic letter, "I suggest that without relationship, the words, the content, would have been interpreted as irrelevant or disregarded as insignificant to one's life" (p. 42). Letters from people we do not know or do not like are usually placed to the side, unread or skimmed. Letters from important people in our lives are provided a space of reverence, where the words and ideas begin to shine. While you should not try to make yourself meaningful to the client—as we always want to ensure the client's personal agency and limit the possibility of dependence—you should try to create a positive working alliance.

For beginning therapists, the thought of writing a therapeutic letter may be a bit daunting. This was the case for one of my supervisees this past week. She was nervous about writing a therapeutic letter to her client. She had been trained in certain verbal and nonverbal skills and therapy theory, but no one had ever talked to or taught her how to compose a therapeutic letter. No previous professor had even talked about why a therapeutic letter can be quite beneficial for her client(s). I had her read an article I wrote on creating temporal therapeutic letters (see Chapter 6), and she drafted her first therapeutic letter. I helped edit it and at the end of her session with that client, she read the letter to the client and gave it to her. The client had a smile on her face the whole time she was listening. After the therapist finished reading the letter, the client told her that during their sessions she knew the therapist was listening to her but didn't realize how deeply she understood her situation—*and* understood *her*. It was an extremely positive, intimate, and beneficial moment for the therapist (who was positively reinforced in writing and giving her first therapeutic letter!), the client (who felt fully heard and was able to engage in introspection), and the therapeutic alliance (which was significantly bolstered).

This positive experience may not be the same for all people taking on the endeavor of writing their first therapeutic letter. However, you won't know until you try (as they say, you miss 100% of the shots that you don't take). I encourage you to use some of the tips and ideas presented in this and the next chapter and write a draft of a letter. Then review it with either a supervisor or a colleague and give it to a client to see what impact it might have. Basing your letter on the guidelines presented in this chapter should help you keep it focused and useful. Here are a few more tips. Freed et al. (2010) provided guidelines for beginning therapists when writing a therapeutic letter. These directions include, in any order:

1   Your appreciation for their willingness to work with you.
2   Notation of changes you have observed.
3   Positive statements affirming the client's efforts and accomplishments that you have noticed.
4   Encouragement for the future.
5   Notation of what you learned in meeting them.
6   Do NOT reveal anything private, that would normally be kept confidential or that could be embarrassing.

(p. 269)

Davidson and Birmingham (2001) recommended highlighting only three or four main ideas that were discussed in the session. Like Freed et al., they encourage therapists to focus on the positive aspects of client experiences where there is a focus on change rather than on problems. The letter does not have to be an essay like you might turn in to class. Sometimes, less is more. Figure 5.1 presents a sample of therapeutic letter that is quite short.

Another guideline is for you to not use any jargon. Jargon is the use of professional terms. In psychotherapy, these would probably come in the form of specific psychiatric diagnoses, theoretical model concepts and interventions, and other terms that are not commonplace. For instance, don't use terms such as "corrective emotional experience," "Oedipal complex," or "non-differentiated." One of the problems with jargon is that the recipient is likely not going to understand what you are trying to say. This will lead to what you write being meaningless to the person and perhaps lead you to come across as pretentious (Steinberg, 2000).

November 13, 2023

Dear Piper,

I wanted to take a moment to express my appreciation for the level of energy and motivation that you have when you come to therapy. You clearly want to grow and live a happier life. Over the last few sessions, you've made quite amazing progress. Initially, you were hesitant to stand up for yourself. You felt guilty for having a voice. This week you did not want to go out with your friends, and you let them know that you preferred not to. Hopefully, you can acknowledge what a difference that is from just a few weeks ago. You are now prizing and appreciating yourself. In the session, you even said, "I realize now that I really am worthy." You are right. You really are worthy!! I look forward to our next meeting to hear about whatever further growth you continue to make and how you continue to value yourself.

Sincerely,

Jimena Garcia

Jimena Garcia, LMHC

Figure 5.1 Sample Brief Therapeutic Letter.

The language of therapeutic letters should achieve three things (Blanton, 2006). First, you should write in a way that is speculative and tentative. To do so, you might use phrases such as "I am curious...," "I am wondering whether....," and "Might it be...." You might use these types of phrases in questions, where the client is invited to become aware of their viewpoint. Further, tentative language provides space for the client to agree or disagree with what you have written, allowing them to have more autonomy and personal agency in the therapeutic process.

Second, therapeutic letters should be written in a way that makes sense for the client. Your words should be relevant and familiar to the client. The more that you use their terms, or even quote from what they've said in the session, the more the client can relate to the letter and put themselves into it. People know when they are reading a form letter—a letter that is written for multiple people rather than personalized. When you use the client's words and language, you better match their understanding of self and the therapy.

Lastly, you should write respectfully. Because the therapeutic letters you write are supposed to capture the client's experience, you might work with them to ensure that the language you use fits for them. If they do not, the client will likely not place much importance on what you have written.

One way of bridging what you want to get across with the client's reception of the letter is to write authentically (Moules, 2003). Moules explained this concept,

> Perhaps our authenticity lies in the intent of the letter, and in the effort to write from the heart with sincerity. Authenticity might be

about the openness to writing hearts and lives into the letter, not in an effort to make the letter *about* me, but *of* me.

(p. 41)

Authenticity comes through in the tone of the letter, where it is written in your voice. This is similar to Rogers' (1989) belief that one of the core conditions of change was the therapist being genuine. This genuineness, otherwise known as authenticity, should also come through when you communicate with the client outside of the session, including through your therapeutic letters.

When you are authentic, you appreciate the context of the relationship. You don't write whatever comes to the top of your head. Therapeutic letters are for the client, as you must always operate from the ethical principle of beneficence. Thus, when writing a letter to a client, keep in mind how the client will receive it. Will they be negatively impacted by any words, phrases, or implications that you make? How might they potentially misinterpret something that you write? How do you take ownership of everything you write, so that if the client questions you about something you can clearly explain your thought processes?

As you decide whether to write a letter and, perhaps even more, whether to give or send the letter to the client, you should consider the quality of the therapeutic relationship. While you can give a letter to a client in the first session, they usually have more resonance when they are tied to a positive therapeutic relationship. Moules (2003) explained,

Out of the context of relationships, words can be read more gently, motivations assigned more benevolently, and interpretations freed in the trust of the relationship to coddle the words tenderly, rectify them at a later point, and even obscure them if inapplicable.

(p. 44)

Depending on the type of letter, they may differ in length. However, most therapeutic letters tend to be brief, perhaps not more than three or four paragraphs (Kindsvatter et al., 2009). Given the recency and latency effects, your clients will most likely remember most of the material that is presented at the beginning of the letter and the end of the letter. However, that doesn't mean that what is in the middle is unimportant. If we think about a sandwich, the bun would be the first and third paragraph and the meat (or faux meat if you are vegan like me) is in the middle. The meat, toppings, sauce, and bread should all work together. Thus, your therapeutic letter should flow where paragraphs are not separate entities but rather connect to and build on one another. Figure 5.2 presents a three-paragraph therapeutic letter that is designed to be cohesive between all paragraphs.

December 4, 2023

Dear Koji,

Today, as you expressed, was an eventful session. You came to some realizations that you had not previously had. These included your relationship with your mother and how you feel that she still has a significant influence in your life even though you are an adult. As you stated, "There are times that I think she never cut the umbilical cord." This was quite a powerful statement that you made.

I was wondering what your life would look like if the umbilical cord was cut. Might you have a different relationship with your mother? How would you be different in that interaction? I am curious how your love life, which you say you have put on hold, would be when you have the mindset of being (in your words) "a real adult."

While you expressed frustration about the current relationship with your mother, might it be that there is something about that closeness that you like? In what ways is it useful for you, right now? I am wondering whether you will know when it is time for *you* to cut the cord, rather than waiting on your mother to do so. I know these are difficult questions. I am looking forward to talking with you in more depth in our future sessions.

Sincerely,

Tyrone Tulio, Psy.D.

Figure 5.2 Sample of Three-Paragraph Brief Therapeutic Letter.

Regardless of what content you write in the letter, you will have a choice of when to write the letter. Some therapists (see Shilts & Ray, 1991) write the letter during the session, perhaps when they take a consultation break. This provides immediate feedback for the clients. Other therapists (see Davidson & Birmingham, 2001) prefer to write it after the session so that they have a few hours where they have been able to think and process what occurred. However, you shouldn't wait longer than 24 hours to write it so that you do not forget important information. There is no right or wrong time to give the letter. It will depend on the situation. There are times I provide the letter during the session because I want to be able to discuss it with the client. There are other times that I think it will be more useful for the client to not read the letter until they get home. Further, for most of my clinical practice, I have been afforded the luxury of working in a university clinic where I spend six hours a day with students seeing clients and engaging in pre- and post-session conversations. Sometimes we write the letter together. Other times I will have the students write the letter at home and we will edit it together. When working with my own clients, I tend to write the letter outside of session and edit it during a mid-session break to include whatever new information was included in the therapeutic conversation. You will find what works for you (and what works for you may be many different things).

Therapeutic Letters

For many clients, their only contact with the therapist is for one hour one time per week. They will likely realize that they are not the only client on your caseload, which may lead them to think they are just another payer—someone that is meaningless to you outside of the money you get for that hour. However, knowing that you took time, outside of the session, to think about them and prepare a letter tends to convey a sense of respect from you to the client.

Letters convey information in a way that is different from the spoken word. Similar to how therapists may utilize experiential activities in therapy (such as music, dance, sculpting, or art), letters are an additional pathway of understanding for clients. Further, having the ideas that were talked about in the session in the written word gives them more gravitas. Paré and Rombach (2003) explained that "therapeutic letters provide a powerful means of committing preferred stories to paper and rendering them more concrete or real by drawing on the special legitimacy we often grant to the printed word" (p. 200).

Letters may be written on the therapist's own or in collaboration with the client. For instance, Shilts and Ray (1991) recommended that therapists ask clients' permission first before writing the letter. Coming from a solution-focused modality, these authors then outlined their therapeutic letters by using compliments, presupposing that the client's life will improve, encouraging the client to notice small changes, and then providing a task for the client. Having a structure for what to have in a therapeutic letter can help therapists focus during a session on what to pay attention to and privilege (Alexander et al., 2008). Burns (2015) posed several questions that therapists might ask themselves before writing a therapeutic letter:

- How do we make decisions about what is and is not recorded?
- How do we use creativity and personal flair while being true to those with whom we meet?
- How do we consult those we meet with to ensure we are appropriately representing them and their stories?
- What kind of document do we create, and what will be most resonant for those with whom we meet?

(p. 27)

The answers to these questions can help you decide whether to, what type, and what to include in the letters you write your clients.

Once you've spent time deciding what to put in the letter (as well as what to exclude), you then have more decisions to make. You have a choice to read it to the client in session, to read it to the client in session and give it to them so they can read it in the future, or to give it to them in session (or mail it to them) for them to read on their own. This decision is based on several factors, including context, relationship, and intent. In my experience, I find that reading it to the client and then giving them a copy is the most impactful. Clients appreciate receiving the letter and keeping it so they can go back and read it later when they can take their time and appreciate the implications of the content. Reading the letter to clients also puts them in a receptive position where they don't have to think about responding but can just sit and listen.

The process of reading a letter slows down people's contact with the information. This provides them an opportunity for heightened levels of introspection and contemplation (Fishel et al., 2001). When reading a letter, clients don't use their normal thought processes. Instead, they engage in a new type of communicational process where they access different senses as well as emotional states (Lown & Britton, 1991). This provides a unique space for clients to integrate the new meanings presented in the letter. Since letters have become an increasing rarity in people's lives, receiving a letter provides a sense of respect to clients that they may not normally encounter.

Further, most sessions tend to have a lot of information and ideas exchanged between therapist and client. Just a few hours after the session, many therapists will forget many of the primary facts, themes, and interventions from a session. The same is likely to occur for clients. Having the therapist write a letter about what occurred in therapy will help to enhance clients' memories, giving them multiple opportunities to contact and take in the information. This is extremely beneficial since one of the most important skills and processes in therapy is repetition.

There are several possibilities for the delivery of a letter. Most therapists prefer to read it to the client in session and then give them the letter. Others give the letter and ask that it be read later. Paré and Rombach (2003) believed that letters are homework; that is, outside of the session the letter encourages the client to continue to engage in useful behaviors and think about what benefits will come if they do more of what has been working. Another benefit of having the client read the letter at a later point than in the session is to increase the client's sense of expectancy. They are likely to leave the session wondering what is in the letter. They may be more receptively primed to give attention to the content of the letter when they delay reading it.

Letters to Couples and Families

Most therapists will primarily work with individual clients. Writing a letter for a specific client is self-intuitive; you write the letter for that one person. But what happens if you are working with a couple or a family? Can you still utilize therapeutic letters? If so, who do you write them to? The good news is that therapeutic letters are not only useful when working with individuals but are also important to use when working with couples and families. This next section presents three modalities of therapy and how they use therapeutic letters with individuals, couples, and families.

Narrative Therapy Letters

Narrative therapy has fully embraced the use of therapeutic letters. This section will give a brief overview of how narrative therapists utilize letters. This section should be not taken as prescriptive but inspirational, where the ideas present can be replicated, augmented, changed, or discarded. What is important is that the letter helps the client better appreciate their own personal agency and the ways that they have protested the problem's influence in their lives. As one example, Rombach (2003), a narrative therapist, begins her letters with an introductory paragraph describing the purpose of the letter. One of the main aspects of this introduction is an attempt to recruit the client into the role of editor-in-chief. Rather than being a passive recipient of the information in the letter, she encourages them to be active when reading it. Since clients are the ultimate authors of their stories, this push is to get clients to change anything in the letter that needs changing. They can read the letter with a pen in their hand and cross off, add, or alter anything that doesn't fit their lived experience.

The letter then includes thanks from the therapist to the client. These thanks are about the courage the client had in coming to therapy and the trust that they are putting into the therapist. The next section involves highlighting the client's strengths and resources. These are aspects of the client that help them to have more personal agency over the problem. Further, these strengths reflect the client's positive identity. While there are likely many strengths and resources that can be discussed in the letter, which you should acknowledge, you can also select and focus on a star resource. The star resource has immense potential in helping the client achieve their goals. The letter ends by explaining that the ideas are preliminary and not set in stone. Figure 5.3 presents a therapeutic letter from a narrative therapy perspective.

Letters to clients can take many shapes and sizes. White and Epston (1990), the originators of narrative therapy, utilized a variety of letter types to help them in their work with clients. These letters attempt to bring the client's voice and story to the forefront of the therapeutic conversation. Here is a listing of a few types of narrative therapy letters. You are encouraged to review their groundbreaking book, *Narrative Means to Therapeutic Ends*, for a more in-depth exploration and examples of these letters.

Dear Sonny and Cher,

I wanted to take a moment to write to you a summary of what we discussed yesterday to ensure that I correctly understood what you both were saying and what is important for you. What happens in therapy is a two-way process, so please check my understanding here and change anything that you think should be changed.

I should start by congratulating you. It is an important thing that you both did; searching for someone to talk to when your relationship was at an impasse. You knew that things were not going as you wanted them to and were wise enough to reach out. Many people are unaware of how courageous an action that is. How were you each able to recognize this and begin to do something about it? How did you decide together that now was the time for change and action?

Throughout our conversation today, I heard about some of the concerns that you are currently having. These included feeling upset at where your relationship currently is and that you do not think your relationship is in the place that you would like it to be. I also heard some other things that I think are extremely important. These were your strengths and resources. I will list a few of them here:
- Your desire to live a meaningful life.
- Your want to start a family.
- Your ability to occasionally laugh during times of pain.
- Your knowledge that there is more to your relationship than the hurt you currently feel.
- Your frequent camping trips together.

One thing that seemed to stand out in our conversation was the talk about absurdity. This seemed to be a value that you both hold extremely close to your hearts. You mentioned that in the past you were able to see the absurdity of various situations, which brought a smile and giggle into your lives.

After our meeting, I continued to think about the continued role of absurdity in your lives. Could you bring absurdity with you when you think about the various stressors that you are dealing with? Could absurdity help you bring a smile when life tries to get you to frown? Could absurdity help you to see yourself in a new way, one that is more positive and hopeful than you currently hold? How might absurdity play an integral role in your relationship? I am providing these thoughts after our first meeting, knowing that this initial way of hearing what you were both saying may or may not fit for one or both of you. Either way, I am interested in hearing your thoughts, as ultimately, you are the author of your story.

Sincerely,

Skylar Echols

Skylar Echols, MSW, LCSW

Figure 5.3 Sample of Narrative Therapeutic Letter Focusing on a Star Resource.

- **Letters of Invitation**: Used to invite people who may be reluctant to attend sessions.
- **Redundancy Letters**: Used when people find themselves stuck in a role that is not useful for them (e.g., "overprotective mother," "overbearing father," or "mischief-maker"). These letters show how redundant and unnecessary this role is.
- **Letters of Prediction**: Used at the end of therapy to predict the person's, relationship's, or family's future. You can use any timeframe you find useful, though six months seems to be a standard. You might put the letter in an envelope and write a date in the future for them to open it (i.e., a date six months from when you give it to them).
- **Letters of Reference**: Used to help people other than the client to gain a view of the alternate story that was developed in therapy. The letter of reference highlights the client's preferred identity. You can give the client copies of the letter for them to give to whomever they deem it is important (e.g., the school principal, lawyer, or case manager).
- **Brief Letters**: These are usually one-off letters helping the client shift their relationship to the problem. The themes of brief letters include post-session thoughts, help for the therapist (an invitation to provide the therapist with information about their lives and relationships), nonattendance, recruiting an audience (asking the client who in their relational field might be useful in the therapeutic process), mapping of influence (descriptions of how the client has taken personal agency over the problem), historicizing (bringing forth the identification of alternative knowledges), challenging the techniques of power (bolstering the client's sense of protesting against the problem), and challenging specifications for personhood and for relationships (bringing forth the client's views of self that may not align with societal or familial expectations).

Solution-Focused Letters

While narrative therapy practitioners have perhaps utilized therapeutic letters more than those from other models, solution-focused therapists have also found them to be quite influential. In brief, solution-focused therapy is predicated on uncovering clients' solutions—those ways of thinking, being, or relating that have been useful for them in the past—and getting them to do more of that. Solution-focused letters are designed to bring forth these past actions, what are called **exceptions**. Some additional uses of solution-focused letter writing are to focus on strengths, work toward positive change, and serve as a means of connecting sessions (Alexander et al., 2008). Other solution-focused therapists use letters to help focus clients' attention, clarify directives, send messages to non-attending family members, and increase the dramatic impact of the therapeutic process (Nunnally & Lipchik, 1990).

While a solution-focused letter will look different depending on the therapist who writes it, they will all have a focus on the client's strengths and resources. There are a few general tips you can use when writing a solution-focused letter, including the use of compliments, presupposing positive change, highlighting small changes, and potentially offering tasks (Shilts & Ray, 1991). After reading the letter, clients should have a greater sense of personal agency. As Alexander et al. (2008) stated, "Letter writing offers a practical method of obtaining therapeutic goals and helps clients to become relieved and empowered" (p. 65). In the letter, rather than focusing on the client's impediments and mistakes, you will highlight their strengths and accomplishment. This goes to the solution-focused rule that once you find out what works, do more of it.

Traditional solution-focused therapy tended to end with a homework assignment, a task given to clients. Many solution-focused therapists would use an end-of-session letter to highlight what the homework assignment was to ensure the client remembered it accurately (Nunnally & Lipchik, 1990). As I'm sure you've experienced, during a session you created and assigned a client a homework assignment knowing that this will be useful for the client if they completed it. Nonetheless, you begin the next session by asking about the outcome of the homework only to find that the client either totally forgot about it or when they tried to do it didn't remember correctly what it was. Writing it down in a letter, even if the letter is only a paragraph and only focuses on the directions for the assignment, can be useful as a reminder to the client to attempt the assignment as well as to help them know the specific steps to take.

Solution-focused letters are usually delivered at the end of the session; however, there are times when the therapist comes to some realization or understanding after the session has ended. At these times, you can write a **supplementary letter** or an afterthought letter (Nunnally & Lipchik, 1990). Figure 5.4 provides an example of a supplementary letter.

Letters from the Team

Usually, the client's therapist will write the letter. However, depending on the context in which you are providing services, you might play with who the author of the letter will be. This alteration of authorship will potentially occur in training locations. In private practice, you are likely to only work with the client and not with other professionals. There is a greater chance of multiple individuals taking part in the client's treatment in a university training program. For instance, I supervise in a university therapy clinic where we work on teams of four to six student therapists

Dear Anthony and Patricia,

After you left our last session, I realized that I had not told you how impressed I was with what you did during the session. You both came to therapy frustrated with your relationship where there were a lot of frequent conflicts. In the session, I saw that you were talking about an issue (finances) that you did not agree with each other on what to do. Instead of making it an argument, you listened to what each other had to say and then thoughtfully and calmly explained your positions. While this may not seem like a huge event, it truly was. It shows that you are taking your happiness and relationship into your own hands and doing so respectfully. So, I just wanted to congratulate you on that.

Also, I just wanted to remind you of the homework assignment we had talked about and agreed upon. You were going to, each day this week, pay attention to those times that were happening between the two of you that you thought were useful for your relationship and that you wanted more of. If you could each please write down at the end of each day what these occurrences were, we will start our session next week focusing on these because they are the foundation of your future relationship!

I look forward to seeing you both next week.

Sincerely,
Hiro Okumoto
Hiro Okumoto, MS, LCSW

Figure 5.4 Sample of a Solution-Focused Supplementary Letter.

and watch cases from behind a one-way mirror. When we write letters to clients, we usually end them from the therapist and the team.

An alternative to this is when there is a reflecting team. **Reflecting teams** occur when a group of therapists watches a session, eventually switching places with the therapist and client. The team then talks with each other about significant aspects of the session, noting aspects of the client's story and bringing a variety of different perceptions into the therapy room. When finished, the therapist and client switch places again with the team and discuss aspects of the team's conversation that they paid particular attention to. One of the benefits of the reflecting team is that it allows space for the client to not have to think about what they want to say. Rather, they are given the space needed to listen, providing an opportunity to develop new ideas and perspectives.

Because there are many different voices to listen to, there is a chance that the client—and the therapist—can experience the conversation as a cacophony. To offset this, the reflecting team could write a letter as an addition to the reflecting process (Fishel et al., 2001). This letter is a verbatim account of what the reflecting team said during their discussion with one another. Since spoken accounts may not always flow, the letter can be edited for readability. Further, to help offset the nonhierarchical intent of reflecting teams, the letter can contain what the client(s) said to

Dear Cheyenne and Lindsey,

The team wanted to present this letter to you summarizing what we said to each other while you were listening to our conversation. We were impressed by the concern that you both shared toward each other. While it is clear there are aspects of your life that you each want different, the love and affection in your marriage shine through. We wondered how you were able to do this. What is it about the other person that leads you to keep at it and try? We heard how meaningful this marriage is to you. What are the aspects of it that you value so much? We also paid particular attention to some of the ways you described each other: "She's the love of my life," "I haven't felt anything like this before," and "I want a future with her." How are these statements indicative of the relationship? How do you keep them in the foreground even when there is a pothole on your joint journey?

When we went back behind the mirror after our discussion, we listened as the two of you turned to each other and expressed your desires for the future of your marriage. We were moved by the way that you touched each other, held each other's hand, and described how important it is that you work things out. We laughed when you both described your relationship as "like a rollercoaster, with ups and downs, but with excitement, and our hands held hi."

Sincerely,

The Team

Figure 5.5 Sample of Letter from a Reflecting Team.

the therapist after the reflecting team. You can get the client's consent to audio-record so that someone can go back to the recording to transcribe it. If you cannot get consent for recording, someone might be able to type what is being said by the team so that all their comments are contained in the letter as close to how it was said during the reflecting team discussion. Another possibility is to paraphrase the discussion.

The reflecting team letter provides clients an opportunity to reengage with the many ideas they found significant during the initial reflecting team process. Thus, they have a document that serves as a reminder of what they had learned during the initial encounter. Since clients are processing a lot of information during the reflecting team, receiving the letter of that conversation provides them a space to contact the ideas when they are better able to be reflective. The reflecting team letter is also useful for the therapist as a reminder of key ideas and potential therapeutic pathways. Figure 5.5 presents a sample of reflecting team letter.

Clients' Reactions to Receiving Letters

How clients receive letters is dependent on many different factors. For instance, if the client reads the letter outside of the therapy session, the therapist cannot be certain about the client's mental and emotional space at that time. Perhaps the client is mentally in a very bad place and is not quite able to appreciate the material in the letter at that moment. Or the client might be in a hurry and quickly reads through the letter while thinking about something else.

The impact of the therapeutic letter is based on the meaning the client attaches to it (Moules, 2003). While you will write the letter to provide certain meanings that you think will be beneficial for the client, you cannot assure that the client will receive, understand, and accept your meanings. Further, therapy, in whatever format, is always a process of mutual meanings interacting with one another. During face-to-face interactions, it is much easier for you to be able to pay attention to the client's nonverbals to determine the level of synergy happening between you. This does not occur when clients read therapeutic letters outside of the actual session. Therefore, it is important for you to think about how you have worded the letter.

The letters that clients receive from therapists, and more specifically therapeutic letters, tend to focus on the strengths and resources of the client. As such, they tend to paint the client within a positive and resourceful context, highlighting what clients have done to move toward their goals. Seeing their desires and efforts illuminated in writing makes clients feel validated and acknowledged (Lamprecht, 2015; Pyle, 2006). This then leads to clients feeling a greater sense of confidence, encouragement, and self-esteem. They also are more likely to open up and be less reserved in future sessions.

One of the primary reactions from clients to therapeutic letters is their appreciation of having something tangible from therapy that, upon successive readings, becomes a resource for them (Lamprecht, 2015). These letters allow clients time to assimilate the information from sessions and develop a new perspective about themselves (Hamill et al., 2008). Most clients tend to keep the therapeutic letters sent to them by their therapists. This helps to enable the therapy to continue in perpetuity (Pyle, 2006). The therapeutic ideas can last longer, with clients recontacting the letter to help continue to mark their personal growth.

Receiving a therapeutic letter does not end at that reading. It usually occurs in a relationally responsive process (Pyle, 2006). Clients tend to take in the information from the letter and then respond to the therapist. This may be verbally in session or with a written letter of their own. Throughout the course of therapy, clients tend to refer to the letter(s) and the information discussed within it. This helps to shift the letter from potentially being a monologue to creating a dialogue between client and therapist. Moules (2003) explained that one way to help develop a more dialogic type of letter is to use language that is tentative and speculative, leading to speculation and interpretation, further stating,

> The workings, therefore, of therapeutic letters lie in the ways that the recipients allow the letters to enter, inform, invoke, influence, and change them in some way. The meanings attached to the letter, the

place that the letter finds in the context of the clinical relationship and in the life of the recipient, is the heart of the influence and workings of this intervention.

(p. 45)

The greater the therapist's certainty in the letter, via the language they use, the less clients might see themselves in what is written in the letter.

Clients tend to experience receipt of letters to signify that the therapist cared about them and was concerned about their well-being (Freed et al., 2010). Clients can see that the therapist is committed to their growth (Hamill et al., 2008). In giving out many letters to clients, one of the common comments I receive is how appreciative the client is that I took the time to write the letter in such a thoughtful way. Further, the letter demonstrated something about the positive therapeutic alliance, where the client felt both closeness and collaboration with the therapist.

Not all clients will react the same way to a letter. Those who are more customers for change—where they believe there is an issue that they can positively influence—tend to find letters from therapists more useful (Graham, 2003). Clients who are visitors—who do not believe there is a problem—may not even read the letter. While you might write a letter to someone who is a visitor to therapy (in the precontemplation or contemplation stage of readiness), there will likely be a greater impact when the client is in the preparation, action, or maintenance stage.

One of the benefits of a therapeutic letter, particularly one that is either handwritten or printed out, is that this is a modality that people do not receive much anymore (Freed et al., 2010). Before the development of the internet, most people corresponded either through the telephone or by written letter. The more computer technology became a mainstay, the more communication moved online. This is where many job applicants have shifted from writing thank you letters to those they interview with to perhaps a thank you email. Thus, giving a letter to someone might be a semi-novel event. The good news for therapists is that novelty can be a very useful aspect of information intake.

Receiving the therapeutic letter helps to document what the client is working on in therapy as well as their growth. Since most therapeutic letters are written from a strength-based perspective, clients are more likely to want to circulate the knowledge presented in the letter. Thus, clients are likely to show family members and friends the therapeutic letter to help the other understand their experience in therapy and what they are working on (Lamprecht, 2015).

It is important to keep in mind that no matter how careful you are in crafting the letter, using specific words for specific desired intent, you cannot control how the client receives the information. All communication happens through a process of coding and decoding information.

Along the way, there is the possibility of noise and interference. You can have errors happen when you try to put your thoughts down on paper yet use words that don't quite describe what you were hoping. The client can read what you wrote and put their own meaning to it. For instance, a client I was working with showed me a text from his ex-wife who wrote, "Last night Jud [their son] was at your house. This morning he is out of control." My client read the message and ascribed a certain meaning to it—the ex-wife was accusing him of having done something problematic to trigger the son. When he confronted her about this, she explained that she wasn't, but instead was just trying to convey information.

While we want our words to be important, they are not as important as the client's meanings. There is a connection between the influence of the therapeutic letter and the meaning the client attaches to it (Moules, 2003). Client meanings are not isolated from the therapist's intended meanings. However, you need to gauge how the client has received the therapeutic letter. If it is not how you have intended, and not useful for the client, you should consider how to rectify the situation. This might be by writing a new letter that better incorporates the client's understanding of self and situation. Or you can have the client write a letter to you explaining what they have gotten out of therapy (see Chapter 7).

Ethical Issues in the use of Letter Writing to Clients

The use of therapeutic letters is an extremely beneficial potentiality in psychotherapy. The letter may even be more significant than a session as it is tangible and mobile, being able to be read when, where, and how the client wants outside of the therapy session. As with any psychotherapy intervention, therapeutic letters are not without concern. However, there are many more indications for use than contraindications. A few times when a letter may not be useful are when the client has severe language difficulties, including writing or reading learning disabilities, may not be able to keep the letter in a secure location, or is struggling with psychotic symptoms.

Steinberg (2000) provided the two following lists; the first providing the benefits when writing letters to clients and the second list the risks:

1   The letter helps train thinking.
2   It helps train writing.
3   It provides a concise written guide to assessment and treatments.
4   The letter survives the session physically, and renders substantial and permanent feelings and relationships which were transitory. It is a solid symbol of something which might be helpful. It can

capture and "hold" something safely which is troubling, confusing, elusive, or ambiguous until it can be dealt with. It contributes to continuity.

5   It is a record of a significant piece of work; it can be reread outside the session. It is a reminder.

6   More than a record, it can be a contract. In some cases, perhaps increasingly, it may be reread whether the writer wishes it. For this reason alone, it's worth gaining experience at getting it right.

7   It might make you more efficient at planning care; it can even be interesting.

Risks and side effects

1   Litigation.
2   Problems with confidentiality.
3   Getting it wrong in black and white.
4   Loss of control of the circumstances—perhaps time, place, situation and mood—in which the letter's message is read.
5   Misunderstandings and unintended messages.
6   The letter as a substitute for the session instead of a supplement for therapeutic work, or dominating it.
7   The letter as a substitute for writing proper notes.
8   The letter as something to make the therapist feel better.

(pp. 16–17)

One of the primary ethical considerations when writing—and perhaps more importantly, sending—a letter to a client is that of privacy. Given that there is likely to be some type of personal information in the letter, such as the client's presenting problem or their reactions and actions during therapy, it is important to ensure that no one sees the letter that the client does not want to read it. Any time the letter is in transit poses a potential point in which other people may have access to it. This includes if the letter is mailed or emailed to the client. Some therapists try to get around this by giving the client the letter in the session. While this does minimize the risk of someone accessing the letter while in transit, there is also the potential that someone could come across the letter while it is in the client's possession. Once the client has the letter, it is for them to either put the letter in a trusted location, throw it away, or shred it. One way you can assess the safety of the client's information that is in the letter is to ask the client's permission to write and give them the letter (Kindsvatter et al., 2009). Further, you could also remind them that they might consider where to keep the letter to try to ensure that only those people they want to see it see it.

Summary

Letters have been a primary modality of conveying information between people. In the 21st century, there has been a move away from letters to more text messaging and electronic communication. Writing a letter to your client puts more gravitas to what is on paper, where the client can appreciate the time and energy that you took in thinking about and constructing the letter. This appreciation both signifies the importance of the therapeutic relationship and strengthens it. Your therapeutic letters, coming from a place of authenticity, translate what occurred in the session, providing a space for you and the client to put meaning to the therapeutic process.

References

Alexander, S., Shilts, L., Liscio, M., & Rambo, A. (2008). Return to sender: Letter writing to bring hope to both client and team. *Journal of Systemic Therapies, 27*(1), 59–66.

Blanton, P. G. (2006). Introducing letter writing into Christian psychotherapy. *Journal of Psychology and Christianity, 25*(1), 77–86.

Burns, C. (2015). 'My story to be told': Explorations in narrative documentation with people from refugee backgrounds. *The International Journal of Narrative Therapy and Community Work, 4*, 26–38.

Davidson, H., & Birmingham, C. L. (2001). Letter writing as a therapeutic tool. *Eating and Weight Disorders-Studies on Anorexia, Bulimia and Obesity, 6*, 40–44.

Epston, D. (2009). The legacy of letter writing as a clinical practice. *Journal of Family Nursing, 15*(1), 3–5.

Fishel, A. K., Buchs, T., McSheffrey, C., & Murphy, C. (2001). Adding written reflections to the reflecting team. *Journal of Family Psychotherapy, 12*(3), 81–88.

Freed, P. E., McLaughlin, D. E., SmithBattle, L., Leanders, S., & Westhus, N. (2010). "It's the little things that count": The value in receiving therapeutic letters. *Issues in Mental Health Nursing, 31*(4), 265–272.

Graham, G. H. (2003). Role preparation in brief strategic therapy: The welcome letter. *Journal of Systemic Therapies, 22*(1), 3–14.

Hamill, M., Reid, M., & Reynolds, S. (2008). Letters in cognitive analytic therapy: The patient's experience. *Psychotherapy Research 18*(5), 573–583.

Kindsvatter, A., Nelson, J. R., & Desmond, K. J. (2009). An invitation to between-session change: The use of therapeutic letters in couples and family counseling. *The Family Journal, 17*(1), 32–38.

Lamprecht, L. M. (2015). A phenomenological inquiry of clients' experiences of receiving a humanistically oriented therapeutic letter from their counselor between counseling sessions. *Journal of Humanistic Counseling, 54*, 187–202.

Lown, N., & Britton, B. (1991). Engaging families through the letter writing technique. *Journal of Strategic and Systemic Therapies, 10*(2), 43–48.

Moules, N. J. (2003). Therapy on paper: Therapeutic letters and the tone of relationship. *Journal of Systemic Therapies, 22*(1), 33–49.

Nunnally, E., & Lipchik, E. (1990). Some uses of writing in solution focused brief therapy. *Journal of Independent Social Work, 4*(2), 5–19.

Paré, D., & Rombach, M. A. M. (2003). Therapeutic letters to young persons. In C. F. Sori, L. L. Hecker, & M. E. Bachenberg (Eds.), *The therapist's notebook for children and adolescents* (pp. 199–203). Routledge.

Pyle, N. R. (2006). Therapeutic letters in counselling practice: Client and counsellor experiences. *Canadian Journal of Counselling, 40*(1), 17–31.

Pyle, N. R. (2009). Therapeutic letters as relationally responsive practice. *Journal of Family Nursing*, 15(1), 65–82.

Reiter, M. D., Jung, W. F., Popham, J., Fitzgerald, C., Garcia, E., de Perez, M. G., Lockhart, T., & Villanueva, N. (2020). Training through naming: A process of psychotherapist skill developing utilizing recursive frame analysis. *The Qualitative Report, 25*(8), 2085–2099.

Rogers, C. R. (1989). The necessary and sufficient conditions of therapeutic personality change. In H. Kirschenbaum & V. L. Henderson (Eds.), *The Carl Rogers reader* (pp. 219–235). Houghton Mifflin.

Rombach, M. A. M. (2003). An invitation to therapeutic letter writing. *Journal of Systemic Therapies, 22*(1), 15–32.

Schustov, D., & Lester, D. (1999). Counseling the suicidal client by letter. *Crisis Intervention and Suicide Prevention, 20*(3), 127–131.

Schustov, D., & Lester, D. (1999). Counseling the suicidal client by letter. *Crisis Intervention and Suicide Prevention, 20*(3), 127–131.

Shilts, L., & Ray, W. (1991). Therapeutic letters: Pacing with the system. *Journal of Strategic and Systemic Family Therapies, 10*(3 & 4), 92–99.

Steinberg, D. (2000). *Letters from the clinic.* Routledge.

White, M., & Epston, D. (1990). *Narrative means to therapeutic ends.* Norton.

Chapter 6

Temporal Therapeutic Letters[1]

Michael D. Reiter and April Brown

Most psychotherapy occurs through verbal dialogue between therapist and client. However, the adjunctive use of the written word has been a part of psychotherapy for over half a century (Pearson, 1965). Therapists from a wide range of therapeutic models, working with clients from various cultural groups, with a wide variety of presenting problems, have successfully incorporated letter writing into their practice. The addition of therapeutic letters, with the inclusion of the written word, provides added opportunities for both clients and therapists.

This chapter describes a way of structuring therapeutic letters utilizing temporality to guide the construction and flow of the letter. We present an overview of the use of therapeutic letters in psychotherapy, especially in narrative therapy where they have been primarily utilized. We will then discuss our use of what we call temporal therapeutic letters—those letters that are based upon temporality that is common in most stories and are structured from the past, to the present, and then to the future. We provide two temporal therapeutic letters as examples of the construction of this type of letter. We then discuss some ideas regarding the use of temporal therapeutic letters and how they might be used and/or adapted by other clinicians.

Therapeutic Letters

One of the benefits of utilizing therapeutic letters is that clients can take the therapy home with them. That is, clients can read the therapeutic letter as often and wherever they would like. This sends a message to the client that their life in the world, rather than in the therapy office, is more important (Nylund & Thomas, 1994). The use of therapeutic letters adds further opportunity outside of the actual therapy session for client self-exploration and change (White & Murray, 2002). France et al. (1995) utilized therapeutic letters to provide a space for clients to reassess their strengths, focus on positives, and promote personal agency. Bacigalupe (1996) stated, "Writing in systemic therapy can help clients to distance

DOI: 10.4324/9781003294702-6

themselves from problem-saturated descriptions, mobilize multiple meanings and voices and facilitate the re-storying of their dilemmas" (p. 372). Thus, therapeutic letters tend to help clients to harness and appreciate their own knowledge of self and move toward more desired future possibilities.

Therapeutic letters are also beneficial for the therapists who write them. Alexander et al. (2008) explained, "Through the use of letters, therapists can slow therapy down, reiterate points, and assist clients in exploring new solutions" (p. 60). The writing of therapeutic letters allows therapists to reflect upon what has occurred in therapy and utilize therapeutic ideas to be used as interventions (Rombach, 2003). Further, letters provide transparency into how the therapist thinks about and understands the client's situation as well as the process of therapy. Therapeutic letters can also be used to help reinforce therapeutic frames and interventions by emphasizing those aspects of the therapeutic dialogue therapists want clients to remember (Wojcik & Iverson, 1989).

Therapeutic letters seem to be of great worth to clients. Michael White and David Epston explored the value of letters and their role in a positive outcome in therapy with their clients and discovered that clients perceived that (1) one letter was equivalent to 4.5 sessions and (2) 40–90% of the positive outcomes in therapy could be attributed to therapeutic letters (Freeman et al., 1997). Nylund and Thomas (1994) had similar results where their clients rated the average worth of a therapeutic letter as being equivalent to 3.2 face-to-face interviews and accounting for 52.8% of the gains in therapy. Understanding this can be of great importance when the process of letter writing appears time-consuming and unnerving. The investment of time needed to compose a letter can have lasting effects on the therapeutic outcome and relationship.

Therapeutic letters enhance the growth and changes that have occurred during sessions. They provide an opportunity to acknowledge and augment interventions, leading to stronger and longer-lasting change and understanding for clients (Wojcik & Iverson, 1989). Kindsvatter et al. (2009) explained, "Therapeutic letters constitute a unique and helpful intervention in that they give life, credibility, and permanency to what occurs in counseling sessions" (p. 32). Besides the benefits to clients of receiving a therapeutic letter, the construction of them, particularly those focusing on clients' solutions, helps to promote a therapy filled with hope and energy (Nylund & Thomas, 1994).

Weeks and L'Abate (1982) classified therapeutic letters as being either paradoxical or linear. Paradoxical letters were associated with the strategic therapies (see Palazzoli et al., 1978; Weeks & L'Abate, 1982; Wojcik & Iverson, 1989). They tend to be cryptic and ambiguous, placing clients in a double bind and trying to interrupt dysfunctional interactional patterns. Weeks and L'Abate suggested using paradoxical letters as a last resort. Linear letters, on the other hand, are straightforward, providing direct feedback to the client about what has been discussed in therapy. Most therapists, especially in contemporary use, write therapeutic letters that are linear.

Therapists use letters for a variety of reasons, tailoring them to one or more individuals as well as those people's contexts. Therapeutic letters can be designed to fit with the client's current motivational level (Shilts & Ray, 1991). That is, based on a person's motivation for engagement in therapy, the therapeutic letter is written to coincide with that person's worldview of their connection to therapy. Thus, some therapists have used letters to try to promote attendance by a non-attending family member (Wilcoxon & Fenell, 1983), or they can be used to promote change for those clients who might be classified as customers (see de Shazer, 1988), or in the preparation, action, or maintenance stages of readiness for change (Prochaska et al., 2013).

Therapeutic letters may be used to explain what has happened in therapy or what might happen in a client's life. That is, letters may be used as an overview for what has occurred, promotion for the next step in the therapy process, or looking more long term in the future. Regardless of the purpose, therapeutic letters require some type of structure. Goldberg (2000) wrote therapeutic letters through the use of emplotment. As he described, emplotted letters allow clients to explain their current story while setting the stage for future transformation. Several of the characteristics of emplotment include personal agency, future orientation in time, overcoming adversity, having an unknown ending, and openness where the conclusion is not foregone.

Therapeutic letters can be given to clients anywhere along the therapeutic process. Letters can be sent to clients even before therapy starts, as in the case of encouraging non-attending members to come to therapy (Wilcoxon & Fenell, 1983). Shilts and Ray (1991) mainly wrote therapeutic letters during the first session they had with clients as they found that this enabled them to promote cooperation and engage with clients as well as connect the letter to the solution building process. Many therapists write letters during the middle portion of therapy. Used in this capacity, the letters tend to highlight client progress or act as interventions, such as the paradoxical letters of strategic therapists. Therapeutic letters can also be used during the termination process, either on their own (if a client does not come back to therapy and is not available by phone) or as an adjunctive to a termination session (Wojcik & Iverson, 1989).

Therapeutic letter writing has been used by clinicians in a wide variety of models, such as strategic, solution-focused, and narrative therapy. The next section describes the use of letter writing in narrative therapy, as clinicians in this model have utilized letters more than therapists from other theoretical orientations.

Narrative Therapeutic Letter Writing

Developed by Michael White and David Epston, narrative therapy is strongly influenced by the text analogy or narrative metaphor (White & Epston, 1990). The narrative metaphor highlights that stories can allow for events across time to ascribe meaning in people's lives. Creating narratives and stories in the therapeutic process allows for experiences to be temporalized (White & Epston, 1990). Stories offer a way to organize experiences relative to when they occurred and imagine about experiences of the future. Through this process of storying, some aspects are left untold, while other events are privileged. Narrative therapy aims to identify and co-create alternative stories in the lives of people that create new preferred meanings and ways of being.

Narrative practice offers different ways to develop, thicken, and enrich these preferred ways of being, one of which is therapeutic letter writing. Letters are then seen as an extension of the narrative metaphor and text analogy in the therapeutic realm (Madigan & Epston, 1995). Letters, just like stories, allow for the stories developed within the therapeutic process to be established within the context of time. From this perspective, letters are used for the purpose of translating the lived experiences of people into a story. They solidify the development of the story and allow for the continued interactive involvement of the client and therapist in the client's narrative (Freedman & Combs, 1996). Letters offer a bridge for the story between the client's world and the therapeutic room. Letters are the shared property of both the therapist and the client as they reflect the constructed reality developed through the therapeutic process (White & Epston, 1990). This echoes the theoretical assumptions of narrative therapy that there are multiple realities that are developed and co-constructed through language. Therapists working from this framework see themselves as co-authors, writing alternative and preferred realities together with the client. Letters are seen as a way to allow the therapist to think more critically about the language they are using, immersing the therapist into the co-authoring process (Freedman & Combs, 1996).

Since letters are seen as a medium, White and Epston (1990) believed that there was a myriad of ways that they could be used in the therapeutic process. Some of these include letters of invitation, brief letters, letters recruiting an audience, letters that map influence, letters that challenge the techniques of power, and letters that are offered on special occasions. Letters may assist people in reauthoring their lives, encourage them to recruit a wider audience to bear witness to their story, help people identify alternative knowledge and experiences not consistent with the dominant story, and explore how they can perform new meanings related to their desired alternative self and relationships (White & Epston, 1990).

Other therapists who identified with the narrative perspective, such as Freedman and Combs (1996), described the main purpose of letters to be threefold. They believed the purpose of letter writing in therapy to be to summarize sessions, encourage the development of stories that began in therapy, and involve people in the therapeutic process that did not attend therapy (Freedman & Combs, 1996). Summarizing sessions allows the therapist to highlight the development of the alternative stories and continue the line of questioning around the emerging narrative beyond the therapy room. If there were thoughts or ideas in the therapeutic conversation that stood out or echoed a unique outcome, an event or behavior that does not coincide with the dominant problem discourse, a letter may offer a way to amplify this idea. Letters may also allow a family member to stay up to date if they missed a therapeutic session or offer an avenue to invite voices and people into the therapeutic conversation. Letters in narrative practice are seen as natural extensions of a client's storied experience from languaged word to written word. It is often seen as an integral part of narrative therapy.

Rombach (2003) developed a way of writing therapeutic letters that integrated narrative therapy with a solution orientation. She starts her letters with an explanatory paragraph explaining the purpose of the letter. The next paragraph focuses on client strengths and wisdom. In this section she might select a "star" resource; that is, a client resource that seems to have potential of helping clients attain their goals. Next, she develops reflective questions that focus on problem resolution and the development of new realities. The temporal therapeutic letters described in this chapter are similar to Rombach's format in that they integrate ideas from narrative and solution-focused therapies but focus more on the temporal aspect of the past, present, and future. The next section describes the theoretical underpinning for the movement of change described in the temporal therapeutic letter.

Recursive Frame Analysis as a Template

Recursive frame analysis (RFA) was originally developed by Brad Keeney as a means of mapping the therapeutic discourse and has since been utilized as a qualitative research method as well as a clinical template to help therapists move the therapeutic conversation from initial problem discussion to conversation that focuses more on resourceful contexts (Chenail, 1995; Keeney & Keeney, 2012). RFA can be viewed as a three-act play that has a beginning, middle, and end (Keeney et al., 2012, 2015). Act one centers around the initial impoverished experience of the client, act two is a transition/bridge, while act three highlights the client's resourceful experience.

Reiter et al. (2020) have discussed implementing recursive frame analysis to shift clients from a problem- or deficit-based viewpoint to a resource focused perspective. This occurs in three acts: an initial focus on a limited problematic identity, movement to a more resourceful identity, and then implementation of that resourceful identity.

Having the framework of RFA as a guide during each session helps therapists to acknowledge the past limiting identities that clients initially bring to the therapy room while also having an ear toward more resourceful identities that have not been fully honored. Therapy becomes a process of identifying those resourceful identities in the present moment and challenging clients to hold that identity and expand it in the future. The temporal therapeutic letters that will be presented in the next section are based upon this current iteration of RFA that helps move the therapeutic conversation that initially focuses on a limiting identity, then identified more resourceful identities, and ultimately leads to an implementation of those resourceful identities. These acts are connected in a temporal manner that is isomorphic to the temporality involved in the temporal therapeutic letter.

Temporal Therapeutic Letters

This chapter describes the implementation of a specific format of writing therapeutic letters that focuses on temporality: past, present, and future. Most stories, whether in book, movie, or oral presentation, tend to have a linear temporality that has a coherent structure: beginning, middle, and end. White and Epston (1990) held that just about all conversations have a beginning, a turn of events, and an ending. Stories, presented in this format, have a completeness to them. They are based on a classic Aristotelian narrative that maintains the linear time structure. Stories may also be more uncertain where the future is not yet finalized (Dawson & Sykes, 2019). These authors call these stories "unfinalized prospective stories," stating, "These stories of the future are unfinalized...subjective and open to re-storying in seeking to make sense of ongoing and newly emerging occurrences as well as the uncertainties, threats and opportunities of a future that has yet to be" (p. 107).

Therapeutic letters help tell the story not just of clients' experiences but of the therapeutic process. While therapeutic letters can be written by either therapist or client and to a wide range of audiences (i.e., self, therapist, client, non-attending family member, referral source, etc.), this chapter will focus on therapist written letters directed to clients. These letters will be presented with the lens of temporality. White and Epston (1990) explained that

> ...temporality is a critical dimension in the narrative mode of thought where stories exist by virtue of the plotting of the unfolding of events through time. This sequencing of events in a linear fashion through

time is necessary to the derivation of any "storied sense." Stories have a beginning and an ending, and between these points there is the passage of time.

(p. 81)

We will now present our formatting of therapeutic letters that are based on temporality, what we call temporal therapeutic letters. They have a simple structure: past, present, and future. While they can be presented in any order, we recommend keeping them in the linear fashion that is known and expected by most people where the beginning is the past, the middle is the present, and the end is the future. As this translates into the letter, we typically construct temporal therapeutic letters into three paragraphs that embody standard story structure: paragraph one focusing on the past, paragraph two focusing on the present, and paragraph three focusing on the future. We now present each of these three parts and describe what we tend to include in each section and why we format the temporal therapeutic letter in this manner.

The Past

Clients come to therapy because they have concerns; either about themselves or someone else or someone else has concerns about them. This is where they start therapy from and is their focus. Many clients will have repeatedly thought about the story they will tell the therapist about why they are coming to therapy. This story tends to center around what has been and is currently going wrong in their lives.

While there are some therapists who do not want to talk about "the problem," this ideology seems to discount the client's experience. Nylund and Corsiglia (1994) described this, when done by therapists attempting to practice solution-focused therapy (although it is applicable to therapists from any modality), as really engaging in solution-forced therapy. One of the primary means of being solution-forced is pushing the client only to engage in "solution talk" and not honoring talk about the problem. One of the primary means of ensuring that a therapist is being solution-focused rather than solution-forced is to be aware of the focus of the conversation (Reiter & Chenail, 2016). These authors explained that therapists should initially place their focus on the client's focus, which, at the beginning of therapy, is usually on the problems that brought the client to therapy. While acknowledging the client's focus, the therapist then also sees the unfocused focus—the exceptions to the client's problems. Focusing first on the client's initial problem allows clients to feel heard and acknowledged regarding their initial concerns, leading them to be more easily open to hearing about the exceptions to their problems.

Anderson (1997) expressed that clients want to be listened to, validated, and taken seriously. This is in line with one of Carl Rogers' core conditions—accurate empathic understanding (Rogers 1989). Empathy entails a therapist hearing, accepting, and honoring a client's story. A client's story is actually multistoried. It begins with their concerns about their problems, then includes the changes that they have made as well as the potentialities that have not yet occurred.

Therapeutic letters are not neutral—far from the case (Pyle, 2009). Rather, they are extremely significant since they pertain to the client's lived experience, and as such, become one of the most important documents that a client can read. Pyle (2009) found that clients felt acknowledged and validated upon receiving a therapeutic letter. Based on this understanding, they were then able to use the letter as a tool of remembrance.

The temporal therapeutic letters presented in this chapter utilize a first paragraph that explores the beginning of therapy. This beginning includes the initial therapeutic talk, what is considered problem talk (Berg, 1994). Having an opening paragraph that provides a foundation of the past provides a foil for the subsequent changes that have occurred in the client's life and the potential future changes that are likely to continue.

The Present

The section of the temporal therapeutic letter that addresses the present highlights what has occurred in psychotherapy, which is important as it provides a summary of the progress and change that have been present. This section is a-theoretical, allowing therapists from any modality to explain what has been discussed in therapy along with the client's progress. It will include aspects of one or more sessions and the ideas that were co-constructed as well as reiterate all of the changes and progress the client has made to date.

Based on our clinical orientation, during the present focused section of the temporal therapeutic letter, the client's resourceful identity(ies) is addressed. This allows clients to re-experience themselves in a context of strengths and possibilities. The reiteration of the personal agency the client has taken to view themselves and their situation differently and to make positive changes in their behavioral and/or affective functioning can be viewed as a form of complimenting the client. Compliments are when the therapist points out ways of thinking or actions that the client has engaged in that are beneficial for them (de Shazer, 1985). Further, the temporal therapeutic letter acts as a type of witnessing, where the therapist becomes an audience to the client's performance of their new story (White & Epston, 1990). This witnessing is of the client's performance of their acknowledging of one or more resourceful identities.

The Future

The last portion of the temporal therapeutic letter focuses on the future. The letter has so far acknowledged the client's initial state in therapy (their limited identity) as well as the changes made thus far in therapy (their resourceful identity). The last section discusses future possibilities (implementation of their resourceful identity).

This temporal template for structuring the therapeutic letter does not happen in isolation from what occurred content-wise and interpersonally during the therapeutic sessions. Rather, it is an outcome of a therapeutic relationship (Moules, 2002, 2003; Rodgers, 2009). As Moules (2003) explained, "The tones of therapeutic relationships are carried in the letters; they echo the affectual, contextual, and substantive pieces of the relationship" (p. 45). Rodgers (2009) held that therapeutic letter writing aids therapist and client to experience their relationship in a more intimate manner.

The paragraph on the future leads these temporal therapeutic letters to fall into the "unfinalized prospective stories" that Dawson and Sykes (2019) described. The client is asked about their future that has not yet been solidified. The therapist does not know what the final outcome will be but proposes questions that the client will need to answer through the implementation of aspects of their resourceful identity that were co-constructed during the therapeutic dialogue.

During the future paragraph of the temporal therapeutic letter, the therapist can ask a variety of questions leading the client to reflect and ponder what will happen when they engage life through utilization of their strengths and resources. Examples of questions that might be presented include fast-forward questions (O'Hanlon & Weiner-Davis, 1989). These questions help clients to shift from envisioning a hopeless future with the problem to a hopeful future with the solution. As these authors explained, "It appears that the mere act of constructing a vision of the solution acts as a catalyst for bringing it about" (p. 106). The remainder of this chapter will present two examples of temporal therapeutic letters written utilizing this three-part format.

Case Example I

Lucy,[2, 3] a 43-year-old female from Scotland, sought therapy because she viewed herself as a failure, overly emotional and co-dependent. Lucy was born in Scotland but has lived in the U.S. for 20 years. Therapy focused on the client being able to improve her perception of herself. The temporal therapeutic letter was provided on the sixth session.

> Dear Lucy,
>   We wanted to take a few minutes to summarize our meetings together. When we first met, you shared how you felt crushed by life

because of your accident and current relationship. You were at such a low point in your life that you felt you had no one to talk to. You were overwhelmed by tears and didn't feel like yourself. You found yourself operating from a position of either being a victim or being a "straight up bitch." You were disappointed in both.

However, we heard quite a different story as well: a story of a woman who didn't realize that she was shifting from a caterpillar to a butterfly. During our time together, you described yourself as being in a chrysalis. You started to see how your love for farming butterflies was a true reflection of your life. A big part of you moving out of this caterpillar stage was for you to give voice to your tears or be able to identify the reasons behind it. As sessions continued you recognized and owned the chrysalis stage. During this stage you were no longer running from your challenges. You were developing inside the chrysalis and encouraged yourself to not be a victim and became more of a social butterfly where you went out to social gatherings, traveled with a friend, and worked your business. You started to unfold your wings so that you could fly.

In this growth process, what type of butterfly will you be? How will you see yourself as a social butterfly? What will it look like when you put wings out and take the first flight? How can you continue to be a social butterfly and still maintain barriers for protection? How will these barriers be useful for you as a social butterfly? What are the various ways you can continue to feel empowered and encourage yourself?

Sincerely,

Your Therapist and the Team

This letter begins with a focus on the past, which is exceedingly important because the client came to therapy in an extremely desperate state. She cried throughout the first several sessions because she was feeling hopeless in her situation: living with a partner who she despised and who was treating her extremely poorly, having severe medical issues after an accident, and having serious financial issues. To leave these aspects of her experience out of the letter would have been disrespectful to the client's story and would have left the letter missing an important piece: a baseline of where the client had come from which can be used to measure progress.

The second paragraph focuses on the current; what has occurred throughout the therapeutic endeavor. During the course of therapy, the client explained that she took great joy in keeping a small butterfly farm. She spent many hours in her backyard helping caterpillars become butterflies. This then became a primary theme of therapy—how the client was not a victim (a limited identity) but rather going through a metamorphosis into something that has wings and can fly (a resourceful identity).

The last paragraph explores the future and what will happen when the client enacts the resourceful identity. Since the therapist and client cannot see into the future, questions are asked for the client to be reflective and to begin to shift expectations from potential problems (as she did when she first came in and viewed herself in the limited identities of either victim or bitch) to potential solutions (by implementing her resourceful identity).

Therapy lasted for three more sessions. Lucy continued to take personal agency to be more the person she desired to be. She described herself as a butterfly and bought a butterfly necklace charm that she wore to remind herself that she did not need to be tethered to her past and problems. Lucy ended the relationship with her abusive boyfriend and sought medical treatment for the symptoms from her accident.

Case Example 2

Hector and Shamika, a husband and wife in their 60s, came to therapy because they were both unhappy in their marriage and each was considering the possibility of a divorce. At the beginning of therapy, they both expressed how they felt a lack of support and intimacy in the relationship. Both partners were previously married and have children from a previous marriage, but never lived with each other's children. They have been married 24 years. Treatment focused on being able to increase satisfaction in their marriage, be more supportive to one another, and improve positive communication. The temporal therapeutic letter was provided in the eighth session.

> Dear Hector and Shamika,
>
> We wanted to take a few minutes to summarize our time together to this point. We met you two a couple of months ago. Entering therapy, you each had many concerns. You were both frustrated in the marriage. There was a lack of support on both sides and communication was definitely not where you wanted it to be. There were also difficulties in putting yourselves in each other's shoes, and therefore you each were having trouble considering the other person's perspective. This made it difficult for you both to enjoy each other's company and work through arguments.
>
> However, there was also a different story that came to the forefront of our sessions. There were times, even before coming to therapy, where the two of you really enjoyed each other—especially when the two of you traveled together. You have built the foundation of what works for you—dancing, miniature golf, traveling together, being touch-feely, etc. You both were able to come to agreements about what needs to be fixed and where change is necessary. In session we discussed how the two of you could breathe support into the marriage. This would include acknowledging one another, laughing together, and providing service together. One session we had talked about how you provide service together for others, but more importantly, how you provide service to your partner. What seems to be

the biggest change in your relationship over these last few months is that fun has been brought back into your marriage. You have shifted your relationship from foreman/worker to colleagues and partners. Support is now reciprocated and each partner is being listened to. You have shifted from looking for faults and blame to care and connection.

The two of you have come a long way, where each of you has done a lot of hard work because your marriage is very important to each other. What will your relationship look like as you continue to put fun and intimacy as the cornerstone of the relationship? How can you continue to show support at various levels of life, from the mundane of taking care of the house to the intimate of looking into the other person's eyes and knowing that the two of you are connected? What other ways of listening to the other might you pour as the future foundation of your marriage? How else might you show service to yourself and to your partner? What things will you do when you view the other and yourself as a colleague and partner? We wish you well in your continued travels together.

Sincerely,
Therapist and the Team

Paragraph one acknowledges the low point the couple was in when they first came to therapy. This was very important, especially for this couple, as Shamika had expressed concern in session that she didn't want her worries to be overlooked, as she thought there were potential serious issues in the marriage. By writing about their initial positions, the clients were able to be heard and validated.

The second paragraph describes the course of therapy, where we focused on the couple's strengths and resources. One aspect that the team found particularly important was the couple's desire for providing service to others. They were both retired from jobs in the social service arena and did not want to be isolated inside their house and not contribute to society. In session we complimented them on their desire for service to others and talked about how they might view themselves as providing service to their partner. This included having a more egalitarian relationship that was based on viewing self and other as colleague/partner rather than foreman/worker.

The last paragraph focused on the future and what their relationship might look like when they are implementing the identity of providing service to the other and being a colleague/partner. This coincided with them applying some of the techniques that we had discussed in therapy that focused on positive communication.

After receiving the temporal therapeutic letter, the couple started to come to therapy every other week. While they had occasional flare-ups, they were able to dedicate themselves more to the other person and move their relationship forward.

Discussion

Temporal therapeutic letters may be an extremely useful adjunct in the therapeutic process. They are written after there has been some movement within the therapy process—the client has acknowledged that they see themselves as having resourceful identities. We have written these letters at various points during the therapy process: sometimes during the first session (when shift in client experience has occurred), sometimes somewhere in the middle, and at other times as a summary when we know we are ending the therapeutic relationship. In many ways, these temporal therapeutic letters become a counter-document to the problem-saturated experience clients had when they first entered therapy (White & Epston, 1990).

Moules (2003) cautioned that there may be ethical dilemmas of giving therapeutic letters (i.e., what information to put in them and to whom they are given). Further, she surmised that not all clients who receive therapeutic letters will find them useful. Steinberg (2000) also provided some risks of therapy letters: potential litigation issues, problems regarding confidentiality, not being accurate in what is written, not being able to control the context in which the letter is read outside of the therapy office, and potential misunderstandings due to how ideas are worded. While the temporally structured letters cannot control for all of these concerns, some of them are reduced as the letters are designed to connect clients to their initial complaints, the current status, and lead them to reflect on possible resourceful futures. Reading the letter first to the client within the therapy session helps us to gauge how the letter is coming across and whether there are any initial misunderstandings. Since we give the letter directly to the client, it is the client's purview of who to show the letter to and where to keep it. However, given that there is a document, there is potential for it to be viewed somehow by people the client did not want to view it. Therapists have an ethical obligation to respect the client's rights as it relates to their confidentiality and their protected health information. For this reason, therapists who use therapeutic letters in their practice should follow and adopt standardized ethical practices to protect the confidentiality of their client. This may include therapists explaining what a therapeutic letter is and what it might contain, as well as requesting the permission of the client to write a therapeutic letter (Kindsvatter et al., 2009). Such conversation might include the therapist discussing if the client will feel safe to receive a therapeutic letter and if they are concerned about it accidently being read by someone else other than the client or intended audience. A discussion around how letters are written and where they are kept may also be helpful to ensure the client feels that necessary confidentiality protocols are in place.

One of the major benefits of temporal therapeutic letters is that they extend the contact that clients have with the therapeutic discourse. Clients, and even therapists, may not be able to remember several days (or weeks, months, or years) what was specifically said in therapy. Temporal therapeutic letters help to alleviate this possibility. Clients may frequently return to the letter to re-experience the framing of their situation. Clients may also show the therapeutic letter to a wider audience, recruiting others in support of the performance of the new story and resourceful identities (White & Epston, 1990).

Given the advent of technology in psychotherapy, written communication is becoming even more prevalent. More therapists are utilizing e-mail and/or texts as an adjunct or critical component of psychotherapy. Moules (2009) cautioned that communication through e-mail may not promote client reflection as much as occurs in therapeutic letters. However, other therapists, such as Epston (2009), have been increasing their incorporation of e-mail as a writing medium when working with clients, doing so in a way that honors the use of letter writing in therapy while adapting it to the current technological medium. We have not yet engaged clients with the temporal therapeutic letter in an e-mail fashion. We prefer to present the letter at the end of the session to the client with the therapist first reading the letter out loud to the client and then giving the client a copy of the letter. This allows us to observe the initial reaction of the client to the letter to gauge what aspects of the letter seem to be endorsed by the client. Further, this bridges the oral component of therapy with the written. Clients have verbally expressed their thanks and appreciation for us taking the time to craft the letter as well as feeling supported in their process of change as the letter acknowledges their struggles but more importantly their accomplishments.

The structure of temporal therapeutic letters has been a clear and efficient guide for student therapists during their initial forays into developing therapeutic letters. As supervisors of various live supervision practicum teams, we have found that explanation of the three-part temporal letter (past, present, and future) has provided student therapists, as well as more seasoned therapists, with a framework that has easily enabled them to construct their own temporal therapeutic letters. Given that temporal therapeutic letters are a-theoretical, they can be used by clinicians from a variety of therapeutic modalities who work in varied settings with clients from diverse backgrounds. Temporal therapeutic letters are also an easily understood format for clients, as the letters follow a very familiar story format—past, present, and future.

Notes

1 This chapter was originally published in the *Journal of Systemic Therapies* and is reproduced with permission from Guilford. Reiter, M. D., & Brown, A. (2020). Temporal therapeutic letters: Using time as a structural guide. *Journal of Systemic Therapies, 39*(2), 1–16.
2 All identifying information has been changed to uphold anonymity.

3 The lead author was supervisor of a therapy team engaged in live supervision in which these cases were seen.

References

Alexander, S., Shilts, L., Liscio, M., & Rambo, A. (2008). Return to sender: Letter writing to bring hope to both client and team. *Journal of Systemic Therapies, 27*(1), 59–66.

Anderson, H. (1997). *Conversation, language, and possibilities*. BasicBooks.

Bacigalupe, G. (1996). Writing in therapy: A participatory approach. *Journal of Family Therapy, 18*, 361–373.

Berg, I. K. (1994). *Family based services: A solution-focused approach*. Norton.

Chenail, R. J., (1995). Recursive frame analysis. *The Qualitative Report, 2*(2), 1–14.

Dawson, P., & Sykes, C. (2019). Concepts of time and temporality in the storytelling and sensemaking literatures: A review and critique. *International Journal of Management Reviews, 21*, 97–114.

de Shazer, S. (1985). *Keys to solution in brief therapy*. Norton.

de Shazer, S. (1988). *Clues: Investigating solutions in brief therapy*. Norton.

Epston, D. (1994). Extending the conversation. *Family Therapy Networker, 18*(6), 31–37.

Epston, D. (2009). The legacy of letter writing as a clinical practice. *Journal of Family Nursing, 15*(1), 3–5.

France, M. H., Cadieax, J., & Allen, G. E. (1995). Letter therapy: A model for enhancing counseling intervention. *Journal of Counseling and Development, 73*(3), 317–318.

Freedman, J., & Combs, G. (1996). *Narrative therapy: The social construction of preferred realities*. Norton.

Freeman, J., Epston, D., & Lobovits, D. (1997). *Playful approaches to serious problems*. Norton.

Goldberg, D. (2000). "Emplotment": Letter writing with troubled adolescents. *Clinical Child Psychology and Psychiatry, 5*(1), 63–76.

Keeney, H., & Keeney, B. (2012). Recursive frame analysis: Reflections on the development of a qualitative research method. *The Qualitative Report, 17*(2), 514–524.

Keeney, H., Keeney, B., & Chenail. R. (2012). Recursive frame analysis: A practitioner's tool for mapping therapeutic conversation. *The Qualitative Report, 17*(38), 1–15.

Keeney, H., Keeney, B., & Chenail, R. (2015). *Recursive frame analysis: A qualitative research method for mapping change-oriented discourse*. TQR Books 1.

Kindsvatter, A., Nelson, J. R., & Desmond, K. J. (2009). An invitation to between-session change: The use of therapeutic letters in couples and family counseling. *The Family Journal: Counseling and Therapy for Couples and Families, 17*(1), 32–38.

Madigan, S., & Epston, D. (1995). From 'spy-chiatric' gaze to communities of concern: From professional monologue to dialogue. In D. Epston (Ed.), *Catching up with David Epston: A collection of narrative practice-based papers published between 1991 & 1996* (pp. 127–148). Dulwich Centre Publications.

Moules, N. J. (2002). Nursing on paper: Therapeutic letters in nursing practice. *Nursing Inquiry, 9*(2), 104–113.

Moules, N. J. (2003). Therapy on paper: Therapeutic letters and the tone of relationship. *Journal of Systemic Therapies, 22*(1), 33–49.

Moules, N. J. (2009). The past and future of therapeutic letters: Family suffering and healing words. *Journal of Family Nursing, 15*(1), 102–111.

Nylund, D., & Corsiglia, V. (1994). Being solution-focused forced in brief therapy: Remembering something important we already knew. *Journal of Systemic Therapies, 13*(1), 5–12. https://doi.org/10.1521/jsyt.1994.13.1.5

Nylund, D., & Thomas, J. (1994). The economics of narrative. *Family Therapy Networker, 18*(6), 38–39.

O'Hanlon, W. H., & Weiner-Davis, M. (1989). *In search of solutions.* Norton.

Palazzoli, M. S., Boscolo, L., Cecchin, G., & Prata, G. (1978). *Paradox and counterparadox.* Jason Aronson.

Pearson, L. (Ed.), (1965). *The use of written communication in psychotherapy.* Charles C. Thomas.

Prochaska, J. O., Norcross, J. C., & DiClemente, C. C. (2013). Applying the stages of change. In G. P. Koocher, J. C. Norcross, & B. A. Greene (Eds.), *Psychologists' desk reference* (3rd ed., pp. 176–181). Oxford University Press.

Pyle, N. R. (2009). Therapeutic letters as relationally responsive practice. *Journal of Family Nursing, 15*(1), 65–82.

Reiter, M. D., & Chenail, R. J. (2016). Defining the focus in solution-focused brief therapy. *International Journal of Solution-Focused Practices, 4*(1), 1–9.

Reiter, M. D., Jung, W. F., Popham, J., Fitzgerald, C., Garcia, E., de Perez, M. G., Lockhart, T., & Villanueva, N. (2020). Training through naming: A process of psychotherapist skill development utilizing recursive frame analysis. *The Qualitative Report, 25*(8), 2085–2099.

Rodgers, N. (2009). Therapeutic letters: A challenge to conventional notions of boundary. *Journal of Family Nursing, 15*(1), 50–64.

Rogers, C. R. (1989). The necessary and sufficient conditions of therapeutic personality change. In H. Kirschenbaum & V. L. Henderson (Eds.), *The Carl Rogers reader* (pp. 219–235). Houghton Mifflin.

Rombach, M. A. M. (2003). An invitation to therapeutic letter writing. *Journal of Systemic Therapies, 22*(1), 15–32.

Shilts, L. G., & Ray, W. A. (1991). Therapeutic letters: Pacing with the system. *Journal of Strategic and Systemic Therapies, 10*(3–4), 92–99.

Steinberg, D. (2000). *Letters from the clinic.* Routledge.

Weeks, G. R., & L'Abate, L. (1982). *Paradoxical psychotherapy: Theory and practice with individuals, couples, and families.* Brunner/Mazel.

White, M., & Epston, D. (1990). *Narrative means to therapeutic ends.* Norton.

White, V. E., & Murray, M. A. (2002). Passing notes: The use of therapeutic letter writing in counseling adolescents. *Journal of Mental Health Counseling, 24*(2), 166–176.

Wilcoxon, A., & Fenell, D. (1983). Engaging the non-attending spouse in marital therapy through the use of therapist-initiated written communication. *Journal of Marital and Family Therapy, 12*(2), 191–193.

Wojcik, J. V., & Iverson, E. R. (1989). Therapeutic letters: The power of the printed word. *The Journal of Strategic and Systemic Therapies, 8*(2–3), 77–81.

Chapter 7

Client-Written Letters

Michael D. Reiter

In the previous couple of chapters, we presented how therapists utilize both pragmatic and therapeutic letters to invite clients to therapy, summarize sessions, be used as an intervention, and as a summary of the whole of therapy. In this chapter, we explore how therapists might get clients to write letters of their own. Having clients take the time to think about their experiences, and put those down on paper, may produce changes in the ways that clients feel and think.

These letters are intended to help clients continue in their change process. Nau (1997) stated, "client-authored letters produce small changes in perspective, attitude, and vision" (p. 4). Clients can look at their situation and their internal experience in ways that they may not have previously. Client-written letters provide an alternative means for people to gain access to their personal narratives. While they may have a view of a specific instance, writing, in letter form, helps to story the person's experience. Viewing one's life in a story format is extremely significant, as people develop self-narratives which include the actions of one's life and the identities of who we are. White and Epston (1990) explained, "In striving to make sense of life, persons face the task of arranging their experiences of events in sequences across time in such a way as to arrive at a coherent account of themselves and the world around them" (p. 10). Having clients write a letter helps them to piece together aspects of their life into a coherent narrative.

There is also an aspect of novelty involved when clients are asked to write in the form of a letter rather than just being asked to verbally explain their thoughts and feelings. They have likely told their story to many people on many different occasions. They may use the same phrases, intonation, and even jokes when describing aspects of their life. However, by writing it down in a letter, perhaps addressed to a particular person, they may think about or internally experience differently what it is they are trying to communicate. This is similar to the process of sculpting, where expressing your ideas in a physical format through proximity and

DOI: 10.4324/9781003294702-7

positioning may lead to a different experience than when you verbally communicate the same information.

While client-written letters are extremely beneficial for clients, they are also quite useful, as information, for therapists. Reading a client's letter provides you with the client's conceptualization of their situation and their experience. The more that you can understand the way the client perceives the world, the more that you can frame your statements and interventions to better align with the client's position. This should enhance the therapeutic relationship and increase the chances that the client will utilize your suggestions and interventions.

This chapter explores the phenomenon of client-written letters where therapists get clients to write about their experiences. I introduce you to the purpose of having clients write letters and the variety of formats they might take, including writing the letter to oneself, others, the therapist, from the future, or in a group and family format.

The Basis of Client-Written Letters

For many people, letters of any kind provide a structure for communication and contain a level of gravitas. In the previous chapters, we discussed the importance people place when they receive letters from others (in this case a psychotherapist). In this chapter, we present how useful it is for clients when they are the ones to compose the letter. Letter composition is a skill that most people learn about during their primary or secondary schooling. Usually, formal and informal letters have a typical format:

- greeting
- introduction
- main body
- conclusion
- ending

The more formal the letter the more it tends to hold to this structure. Regardless of the purpose of why you would want the client to write the letter or the context in which to do so (individual, couple, family, or group therapy format), having these five sections can be a useful structure for your clients when they write their letters.

Ellis (1989) referred to the use of self-writing as epistotherapy. He believed they were useful for several reasons, including that the client did not have to worry about how much time was left in the session (and that those minutes had a monetary value to them). Rather, the client could take their time, in the comfort of their own home—or any other location that they happened to be in—and connect with themselves. Writing also provides the client with something to do, occupying their mind and giving them an emotional outlet. Given that the writing was something discussed with the therapist and likely to find itself back in the therapy session (either by the client bringing the writing in or talking about the content or the process of writing), these letters, written outside of the session, are a form of contact between client and therapist.

Having clients write letters provides them a context in which to bring out their creativity. They have the time to put their words together in a way that may better connect and describe their situation. Further, they can take time to sit with and process their ideas. However, the letters are not only about the actual words used. As we know with communication, there is both verbal and nonverbal communication and together they provide a richer context of interaction. Through letter writing clients can express themselves in multiple ways, including the type of paper they use, the color(s) of the paper, the color(s) of the writing implements, the type of writing implement (e.g., pencil, pen, crayon, marker), the type of font used, and perhaps the inclusion of images and pictures. If you take a second and think about some letters that you might write people, how would you do so differently? For what relationship would you use colored paper? Who might you use a blue pen for? Black pen? Red pen? Crayon? Who would you type the letter for? As you can envision, the impact of the visuals of the letter—regardless of the content—will have an impact on both you and who will be reading that letter.

We've just discussed the aesthetics of writing—in essence, the nonverbals. We can now talk about the content of what is written. This will depend on you, the client, and the situation they are dealing with. You might ask them to write only about positive aspects of their life or about troubling times. They could also write about a combination of these two. You will have to decide what you think is most useful for that particular client.

Clients writing, particularly about a personally traumatic life event, have differing impacts during the writing process and over a length of time (Pennebaker & Beall, 1986). These researchers found that when people wrote about the facts of a traumatic event as well as their emotions surrounding it, they experienced higher blood pressure and negative moods. However, six months afterward they had fewer health center visits than those who wrote about trivial topics. This suggests that when you have clients engage in therapeutic writing, you might prepare them beforehand. This may be through mindfulness work including deep breathing or other methods of stress reduction.

Some therapists might be concerned that having clients write about a negative life situation will only perpetuate that situation and the feelings surrounding it. What has been found is that the use of "negative" words in writing was based on the number of these words used (Pennebaker et al., 1997). When people use too many or too few negative words (e.g., sorrow, hatred, or frustration), they tend to have mediocre outcomes. Higher levels of positive words were associated with more beneficial outcomes. What this suggests is that when you have clients write it is important to have them address their concerns—utilizing negative words—while more so incorporating positive words into their narrative. These positive words will likely focus on how they have positively changed, where they want their life to go, and increasing their attention to hopeful expectations.

While there is not a specific amount of negative and positive words to be used, having clients write is beneficial. Writing about concerns and trauma is also beneficial. Watts (2011) explained "that the process of deep writing, in which a linguistic connection is made between traumatic event and emotional response, produces a healing effect" (p. 6). Over the course of many decades of having clients write, one thing has consistently come to the forefront: the process of writing is healing (see Anderson & MacCurdy, 2000; Borkin, 2014). As will be explained in this chapter and the next (see Chapter 8), there are many different forms of writing that clients can do throughout the course of therapy. Luckily, they are all beneficial.

Through writing, clients can express and explore themselves, providing a safe place for focusing on their lives, while having a cathartic experience (Phillips & Rolfe, 2016). For whatever reason, we may not be able to express ourselves in the ways that we would like. There is usually some type of blockage, more for some people and less for others. Writing about their own experiences allows clients to find a release valve, a way to communicate with others, or even self, that they may not have previously had. When people slow down and allow their experience to come to the forefront, they are likely to connect with aspects of self that they hadn't connected to in a while. These understandings help people have a better sense of their fuller sense. This process occurs because self-writing may be a safer place to hold and contain their stories—stories that are usually quite painful and disturbing. Just a word of caution here. Jolly (2011) holds that therapists should not promote clients writing letters from a stance of being isolated, confused, and wronged. The concern is that the person feels like a victim. Rather, Jolly encourages citizenship, where the letter writer may feel partly like a victim but perhaps, more importantly, they experience themselves as an active agent of change. Similarly, Voskanova (2015) believes that in-session writing provides an easier experience for some clients to express and process shame-related emotions. Having clients write, rather than verbally express themselves, around shame experiences affords a space where the client can stop concealing their shame while also being validated that their feelings are real and impactful.

Our field has explored the use of alternative approaches to helping people, including art, dance, and music therapy. One area that can be greatly enhanced is the extended use of writing—leading to a writing therapy. This chapter focuses on the therapeutic implications of having clients write, and more specifically, clients write letters to themselves, others, or even the problem. Therapists have successfully used client writings with a wide range of populations, be it culture, age, or presenting problem. I present here some ways that therapists have incorporated client letter writing into their practice. I will leave it to you to read and think about these ideas and how they might be pertinent for you and your clients, given the various social locations and contexts that are present.

Client Writing to Self

One of the primary individuals that therapists ask clients to write a letter to is themselves. This may seem odd. Why would a therapist want a client to write to themselves? Wouldn't they know everything they were writing? What benefit does it have when the client's letter is focused on self rather than being intended for someone else? Let's take a moment to answer these questions.

When clients write letters to themselves, they tend to encounter and realize the external and internal resources available to them (White & Murray, 2002). Given that the client knows quite well the facts of the story they want to tell, writing a letter to self may begin a process of looking at themselves from a unique position, one that is outside of self. Seeing themselves from this different viewpoint, they may be able to recognize possibilities and aspects of self that they might not have otherwise appreciated.

As we previously discussed, people put cogency to their lives by having a coherent story of what has happened to them and who they are as a person. Given this, some therapists (particularly narrative therapists) work with clients regarding their life being a story. How most people think about stories is through books. Even before we can read, most of us have read (or been read to) a ton of books. When we are younger, they are usually fairy tales. For my children, we read them books such as *The Very Hungry Caterpillar* or *Goodnight Moon* that took as little as five minutes. As we get older, the books we read or are read to lengthen and become what we call chapter books. As teens or adults, we then find which genres we like the best. Whichever book we read, it has a title, a beginning, a middle, and an end. Likely there are many chapters that cross this span. As therapists, we can use all these aspects when working with clients. For instance, you might have the client name the title of their life if their life was a book. Then they might name each chapter up to that point. You could then have them write a letter to themselves about what the next chapter of their life might be. In this way, the client is asked to write about future goals but perhaps in a more playful and fun manner.

With children, you can write a story in a book format—and even illustrate it with the client. Dolbin (2014) worked with children in this manner, helping them to become the authors of their life. Utilizing a narrative therapy framework, based upon externalization, Dolbin helps them write a book. She explained,

> When children reach a point where they have developed a positive and empowering alternative story and are nearing the end of therapy, it often is powerful to create a permanent record for celebrating and underscoring the child's progress in therapy and the changes that the child has made regarding the presenting problem.
>
> (p. 238)

In the session, the therapist and client write and illustrate the child's alternative story—a story about them having taken personal agency over the problem. Besides documenting the changes the client has already made, this activity also highlights the continued pathways to change. Further, the activity is fun for the client (especially child clients) and can be frequently read outside of the session by the client and potentially other important people in the client's relational field.

These client-written letters or stories help to bring forth an aspect of self that may have been underrepresented in the client's life—highlighting a more resourceful identity rather than the limiting identity that has perpetuated their problematic situation. So far, we have discussed the client writing from themselves to themselves. An alternative to having the client write a letter to themselves is to have them write a letter to themselves from the point of view of a lost loved one. When the client is having trouble dealing with the death of someone close to them, you might have them write a letter from the dead (Schlossberger, 1998). By getting the client to take on the point of view of the deceased, the client is better able to acknowledge and sit with their thoughts and emotions regarding their loss and grief. As Schlossberger explained, "Writing a letter helps focus thought, allows family members to share their feelings, and creates a permanent record that can be read again and again when feelings about the deceased resurface" (p. 299). To frame the development of the **Letter from the Grave**, you might explain to the client that some people find it quite beneficial to deal with the loss of a loved one when they attempt to see things from that person's perspective. You then ask the client to write a letter to themselves from the point of view of the deceased individual. Depending on their religious/spiritual beliefs, you might state that they can imagine they are that person looking down upon them from heaven. You might provide some question prompts such as "What do you think they are thinking about you?", "What do you think they would want you to know?", "How do you imagine they would tell you what they value in you?", or "What advice might they give you?"

Writing from the Future

A subset of client-written letters, when they are directing the letter to themselves, is having the clients do so from a future perspective. This is like a crystal ball technique or the miracle question (Berg, 1994) where the client imagines a future that is free of the problem and discusses what that future looks like, and then tells their current self about what occurred to get to this future. You could tell your client,

> Imagine that the problem is no longer a problem for you, and you are living a more enjoyable life. Looking back on this time in your life, what do you want to tell the current you? What is different in your life? How were you able to get there? What do you want to tell yourself about who you are and what it means to you that you've overcome this issue?

By writing from a place of an imagined future where there have been changes to the current life problems, new potential solutions can come into the therapeutic conversation.

This technique can be used with a variety of presenting problems. For instance, Kress et al. (2008) had clients who were dealing with sexual abuse write letters to themselves from the future. From what they call the **Older, Wiser Self Letter**, clients are directed to think about a future where they have overcome the problem and to write to their current self, providing suggestions on getting through their current life phase. Similarly, these clinicians utilize a **Rainy Day Letter** where the client is to write from a future perspective in which they are doing well to their current self, focusing on their strengths and resources. The letter highlights what a good day looks like. The client is then directed to read the letter on a "rainy day" (a day on which they are not feeling too well). This allows them to think about— both while writing the letter and then sometime in the future when they are reading the letter—possible actions they can take that can increase their personal agency in making their situation better.

Kress et al. (2008) also have clients write a couple of different completion letters. The first is the **Completion of Counseling Letter** where the client is directed to write from a future perspective to themselves when they just completed therapy. This letter is usually completed in the first or second session as it helps to shift the client's focus from the problems they are experiencing to what their hopes and goals are for therapy. The therapist holds on to the letter and then gives it back to the client— perhaps in session or through mail or email—close to termination. In the session, the processing of the letter can help assess whether the client's goals were fully met. In a related type of letter, the **Completion of Personal Accomplishment Letter**, clients write from the future perspective to themselves about the completion of the desired accomplishment, such as graduating from school or obtaining a job. Clients are asked to identify a personal goal and to then discuss in the letter, from their future self, how they were able to attain that goal. When reviewing the letter with the client, you should keep in mind the notion of equifinality—that there are multiple pathways to get to the same endpoint. Thus, how the client envisioned achieving their goal is just one way for them to do so. You should encourage them to write down a variety of paths. Perhaps the best way to get there is to use the most important therapeutic question and the simplest—what else. "Gregorio, in your letter, you mentioned that you were able to gain employment by sending out ten resumes a day. What else might you have done to get that job?" The more potential pathways clients have to reach their goals, the more likely they are to do so.

Writing Letters to Others

Many of the letters that therapists ask clients to write are done for only the client and/or client and therapist to view and read. These letters are extremely useful and help promote client growth within the therapy process. However, therapy is also enhanced when the ideas and changes experienced within therapy are circulated to others within the client's relational field. As such, there are times when you may want the client to write a letter to others. These letters are usually used when the client has been unsuccessful in face-to-face conversations with the person and is trying to find a different way of communicating that might help them to enhance the relationship. In this section, I provide a few examples of how therapists have had clients write letters to people in the client's relational field.

One of the primary areas of client-written letters is from one partner to another. For instance, Roberts (2009) had clients write letters to others, especially when there is a stuck conversation with a person in the client's relational field. The hope is that a new type of narrative for the client develops. This occurs via a four-stage process: conversation in a session about the possibility of writing a letter, the client writing the letter, the client reading the letter in session, therapist and client processing the writing of the letter. Jointly, the therapist and client decide on who the letter should be written to, based upon a stuck or un-voiced conversation. They also discuss what the tone and perspective of the letter should be. Two possibilities occur here; the client identifies new ways of understanding and voicing their perspective while also finding new voices and perspectives for the person they are writing the letter. The intent of the letter is not to give it to the other person. This is a possibility. However, the process of thinking about, writing, and then processing the letter construction with the therapist can be sufficient for therapeutic movement.

McCarthy and Wald (2013), when working with couples where there has been an extramarital affair, worked with the partner who had the affair to write a therapeutic letter to their spouse. The letter was to contain their feelings and behaviors before, during, and after the affair. The writer was encouraged to describe the positive and negative lessons they learned from the situation and to give a sincere apology to their partner for the hurt and pain they brought to the relationship and the partner. The letter ends with the writer discussing their hopes and goals for therapy and the marriage, focusing on their personal agency—the changes that they think they need to make for themselves, for the relationship, as well as sexually. This letter is then read in session to the partner where, with the therapist's facilitation, it is processed. The injured spouse will then likely be asked to write a therapeutic letter back to the offending spouse.

You might also have a couple that you are working with write letters to each other. These **interactional letters** could be used in a way similar to love letters (Rudes, 1992). In this format, the couple writes three letters to one another—each of the letters being of a romantic nature. In the first letter, they write a letter to their partner from their own point of view. In the second letter, they write a letter to themselves from their partner's point of view. In the third letter, they write a letter to their partner from a point of view that is difficult to identify.

The interactional letter is designed to help couples who have formed semi-rigid views of each other to bring in alternative points of view. This allows them to shift from a view of their relationship as unchangeable and unsatisfactory to increasing ambiguity and uncertainty. They are then able to change the meanings that they attribute to their partner and relationship and focus on each other in new and more resourceful ways. One of the primary aspects of these interactional letters is that partners had likely developed a view of what their partner perceived of them that might not have been accurate. They shifted from expecting their partner to have negative views of them to being surprised that the partner still felt optimistic about the relationship.

Couples who are distressed and write letters to each other significantly improve their marital adjustment and decrease their marital distress over distressed couples who are on a waiting list (Lange et al., 2000). In this study, during the first session, the therapist explained the purpose and procedure for the writing homework assignment. The couples in the interactional writing condition wrote letters to each other positively expressing their feelings. The therapist encouraged them to write about what the partner could do to make them feel better. The couple had to read each other's letters within 24 hours and not react immediately. Rather, they were to try to accommodate their partner's desires as best as they could. One of the benefits of this type of writing intervention is that it allows each member to reflect on what they want and engage in response prevention. Instead of quickly blaming and attacking the other, partners can explore their emotional wants and be overt in asking for them to be satisfied. People are better able to comply with their partner's demands when they know specifics of how the other person wants them to behave rather than being told how they should not behave.

Besides writing to actual people, clients may be encouraged to write to aspects of the problem. Based primarily on narrative therapy's process of externalization (White & Epston, 1990), where the problem (i.e., Anxiety, Depression, Alcohol) is separated from the person, writing to the problem can help the individual begin to see themselves as having more personal agency than they previously thought. **Externalization** objectifies the problem, moving it out of something internal to the person and personifies it so that the individual is in relation to the problem. White and Epston explained, "As persons become separated from their stories, they are able to experience a sense of personal agency; as they break from their performance of their stories, they experience a capacity to intervene in their own lives and relationships" (p. 16). Thus, you can get clients to write a letter to their problem as if it was another person. This may free them up to view themselves as more capable to initiate change rather than viewing themselves as fixed (i.e., "I am depressed," "I am anxious," or "I am an alcoholic"). Rather, they would express themselves as "in relationship to Depression," "being smothered by Anxiety," or "drowning by Alcohol."

Think for an instance about a problem that you are dealing with or have dealt with in the past. Perhaps it is imposter syndrome, shyness, or anger (or a plethora of other difficulties that we all deal with daily). You have likely internalized this problem: "I am an angry person" or "I am a shy person." On a scale of 1–10, how hopeful are you that you will move past this problem? Now, take a moment and think about this problem, not as something internal to you but as an external entity. Give it a name. It could be one word (e.g., Shyness or Anger—make sure that you capitalize the name like you would a person's name) or a phrase (e.g., The Empty Void or The Big Green Lump in My Stomach). Then, write a paragraph to that problem where you discuss how it has negatively influenced your life and the new type of relationship that you want with it. After doing so, go back to that scale of 1–10 and how hopeful you are that you will move past this problem. Where are you now on that scale? What impact do you think doing this would have on your clients?

You can also have clients write letters to aspects of themselves that are no longer present. For instance, Nau (1997) worked with an adult client whose leg was amputated after he was hit by a drunk driver. The client was dealing with this grief. The client was directed to write a letter to his amputated limb. After writing the letter and discussing it with the therapist and members of a grief support group, the client buried the letter and planted a small weeping willow tree on top of it. After several years of not coping with the loss of his leg, writing the letter to his leg allowed this client to enter a new relationship with it. He was able to move past a stuck point.

Many people find that they can take in information better when it is coming from someone who has been in their situation and is like them. This may be because of the phenomenon of universality where we tend to feel better knowing that others have experienced the same thing(s) that we have. Clients can be asked to write a letter to people they do not know but are dealing with the same difficulties. These letters might then be given to future clients as a form of support. This is reminiscent of narrative therapy's practice of outsider witness practices.

While this letter can be useful for other people, the client who writes it gains as well. Whatever thoughts and advice they write for others is advice for themselves. For instance, they might write:

> Hello,
>
> I hear that you are struggling with Depression. It is something that has also been a part of my life as well. I am still trying to find ways to let Depression know it can't get the best of me. This includes taking the medication my psychiatrist prescribed, coming to therapy, exercising, and engaging in a hobby. Mine is crocheting. What hobby do you have? Who do you talk to when you are feeling down and alone? Who do you talk to when you are feeling up? I'd say one of the most important things I've heard about Depression is that you are more than a diagnosis. You are a complete person. Don't let Depression limit you. Limit it!

In this letter, the client is providing support and inspiration for others. However, they are also bolstering their own growth and changes.

Writing Letters in a Group Format

Thus far we have talked about having individual clients and couples write letters to themselves, partners, others, or even the problem. In this section, we will discuss how you might get clients to write when you are conducting group therapy. Group therapy is a modality that has benefits that individual therapy does not or does not in the same manner. Yalom and Leszcz (2020) proposed 11 primary factors for group therapy, including the instillation of hope, universality, imparting information, altruism, the corrective recapitulation of the primary family group, development of socializing techniques, imitative behavior, interpersonal learning, group cohesiveness, catharsis, and existential factors. For those clients who are involved in group therapy, the writing and/or reading of their letters in a group format may be quite useful. It hits upon many of the primary factors of group therapy where group members know that others are having similar experiences and trying to cope with them similarly. Further, group members receive and become witnesses to someone else's growth process. Therapeutic writing in group therapy helps members to explore their individual experiences and then to express themselves in a social situation.

Letter writing in a group format provides members with an opportunity to be heard in ways that they may not have previously. For example, Signs (2015) worked with individuals experiencing sickle cell disease, where they met in group therapy once a month. These patients had many experiences where people didn't validate them because they did not look like they were in pain while they were dealing with the serious physical consequences of the disease. Letter writing was introduced to help the members cultivate their voices and explain their disease and experiences. The therapist prompted the group members to first write about what they wanted people in their community to know about sickle cell disease. Thus, they were encouraged to educate others and advocate for themselves. Reading their letters aloud in group, before giving them to those they wrote them for, provided space for group members to share their experiences, finding that they had become inspirations for one another. They then were able to talk with one another and share strategies for managing their disease.

Zimmerman and Shepherd (1993) engaged in a similar format where they had group members dealing with bulimia write letters to the externalized problem. In their group process, using a narrative therapy modality, they first had the clients give their own name to bulimia and then draw what bulimia looked like. They then gave a homework assignment where each member was supposed to write a letter to the externalized problem. During the next group session, members read their letters out loud. Group members did not have difficulty writing the letter but experienced reading the letter to be quite emotional. While the therapists didn't give specific directions on what to say to the externalized problem, clients tended to use the letter to express their feelings, request it to leave, or say goodbye to bulimia. A benefit found of naming, drawing, and writing letters to a shared problem was that group members felt more connected and supported by one another. People did not feel they were fighting the problem on their own but rather were fighting their enemies together, which highlighted the primary group factor of universality.

Hagedorn (2011) used therapeutic letters in a group counseling format, particularly with clients dealing with addiction. Similar to what was previously discussed in writing to bulimia, these clients were able to take time to address the substance abuse, which likely had the benefit of circumventing some resistance and ambivalence to change that tends to occur for clients dealing with addiction. Hagedorn called this activity **The Letter to My Substance/Behavior** and it can be used at various points along the treatment process. The client is directed to write a one-to-two-page letter to the substance/behavior they are trying to move on from. They then cover five areas:

1   How I love and/or consider my addiction to be a "friend"
2   How my addiction is sensual (appeals to my senses)
3   How my addiction provides healing or is a balm to my emotional wounds
4   How my addiction controls me and/or promotes my feelings of help-lessness and entrapment
5   How my addiction is hated (i.e., what it has cost me).

(p. 115)

The letters might be written in or outside of the group as homework. The therapist then collects the letters and, outside of the session, reads the letters and takes notes of common emotions and experiences while ensuring to avoid personal information. This is usually done by the therapist highlighting these phrases on each client's letter. At a future group meeting, the letters are given back to their author. Going around the room, each person is asked to read the first highlighted text, followed by the next group member's first highlight, then the next person, until every member has read their first highlighted text. The group members then move on to the second. Hagedorn provided an example of what this might sound like:

> You have controlled my emotions (Participant 1)…fill me when I feel empty (participant 2)…I need to connect (Participant 3)…manipulated the feelings (Participant 1)…always there for me (Participant 2)…you make it possible (Participant 3)…turned me into (Participant 1)…I feel abandoned (Participant 2)…never asked for much (Participant 3)…selfish lover of pleasure (Participant 1)…I can count on you to make me feel whole (Participant 2)…asking for my sanity (Participant 3).

(p. 117)

The activity would then be processed in the group. Participants doing this exercise can have a cathartic experience when they write their own letter and then experience universality knowing that others are going through something similar. Integrating the group members' comments provides a sense of cohesion between group members and helps to instill hope that people can move forward. While there are a lot of benefits of doing an activity like this, Hagedorn (2011) cautioned that therapeutic letter writing, especially in a group context, not be used by the therapist when there has been a plateau or when the therapist is not sure where to go. In that case, the activity would be more for the therapist than the client.

As we've been showing, the writing and reading of letters in the group session can be quite useful. Padfield et al. (2017), in working with clients dealing with eating disorders, provided a writing workshop for group members explaining one format for how they might structure their work. However, clients were told they were free to write whatever they wished. Members and facilitators focused on three levels of communication: personal, interpersonal, and whole group. The prompts the group members received changed each week. For instance, for one week they might be asked to design a park, including the park's amenities and the rules of use. After each member writes their own responses, they read aloud what they wrote. The facilitator—and after a time the group members themselves—explore the symbolism present in the writings, how that relates to how people individually felt, were interpersonally connected, as well as larger group dynamic processes. Padfield et al.'s clients found that this group writing/reading process led to higher levels of emotional expression and processing. They felt freer from constraints and were able to engage in greater methods of self-understanding.

The last example of the use of letters in a group format (although there are countless more) is Keenan et al.'s (2014) use of letter writing as an intervention for treating combat veterans who are experiencing post-traumatic stress disorder (PTSD). Many of their group members experience guilt, shame, and grief around a traumatic event. After an initial phase of psychoeducation, they then work in treatment through a trauma group to help individuals describe, in detail, the trauma and develop a narrative about it. Their hope is that the clients will be able to identify and then work through unresolved grief (as well as guilt and/ or shame). They have one requirement for being a member of the group: that the person agrees to write a letter to someone who was directly harmed or lost in regard to the trauma and that the client then reads the letter aloud in the group. The letter should be written in the second person (written to the individual) and that it focuses on the emotions surrounding the trauma. The letter is written after the person has previously discussed aspects of the trauma in the group. As they explain, "the letter facilitates the reestablishing of connections with those lost or harmed, allowing the writer to grieve or make amends for any transgressions" (p. 550). After writing, and then reading, their letters, the veterans of the group tend to experience a healing transformation, especially in the way they experience the person to whom they wrote the letter. This usually demonstrates a repair to the interpersonal breach that had occurred.

Perhaps on first thought, you might think that having group members individually write letters would not be that useful in a group format. Hopefully, after reading this section, you have a better appreciation that this intervention fits in quite nicely with the primary factors of group therapy. If you do decide to introduce letter writing in your group therapy sessions, it will be important to ensure that you have a group consensus to do so. When you don't, this intervention loses focus (Signs, 2015). Thus, it should be voluntary rather than compulsory.

Writing Letters in a Family Format

Usually, clients write individual letters (as the ones presented in this chapter). In a group format, clients will write at the same time in the same place, but each person writes their own letter. The process of doing so, in the presence of others, and then potentially reading these letters aloud, may have special beneficial properties. However, there is another way that you could engage your client in letter writing—this is when the client is multiple people.

For those therapists who practice family therapy, you can have the family write the letter together. This type of letter is called a **collaborative letter** (Hoffman et al., 2010). Here, you ask the family to write a letter together, usually addressed to the problem. What this does is unite the family against the problem rather than against one another. They have likely been at odds, focusing on one person—the identified patient— trying to get that person to act differently. These communications, whether verbally or in writing, are likely to be littered with many blame statements, denials, and counterattacks. By having the family write a letter to the problem, they can see how the problem has infiltrated their family, impacting each person. This frees up the problem maintaining patterns, providing family members a reframe of the problem situation.

You can have the family write a collaborative letter in a variety of fashions. You might give them a prompt, such as "Write a letter to the problem, Fighting, and how it has disrupted your life. And then in the second part, tell it how you will not let it keep its hold on you all." The family, with either pen and paper or a computer, can be allowed to write the letter however they wish. Watching how they engage one another, you can perhaps gain some insight and understanding into the family's current functioning. You can be even more unstructured and say to the family, "Decide together what you want to say in this letter and how you are going to do so." In this form, family members have little guidance and must figure out between them what and how to accomplish the letter.

Another way of using a collaborative letter is by having it be a bit more structured. You might pick someone to start the letter and then each person takes turns adding one line to the letter. This process ensures that every member will be allowed to contribute to what is being put down on paper. This could be important for full member buy-in, as otherwise, one member is likely to take the lead and dominate this activity. Not that that would be totally bad as it would allow you to see the family's likely pattern at home recapitulated in the therapy room. You would then be able to comment on it and attempt to change it.

Family letters have also been used when one member of the family has been placed in a residential setting. Some residential institutions have family members create **impact letters** (Christenson & Runkel, 2017). Born out of intervention letters for those dealing with substance abuse, impact letters have each family member write the client—usually an adolescent—a letter where they express their thoughts and feelings. They might cover the author's perceptions of the history of the problem, the impact of the problem on the family and various members, their positive feelings, as well as their hopes of what might happen.

Impact letters help adolescents who were recently admitted to residential settings to reflect on their behaviors so that they can become more accountable and responsible for their actions. While they are likely to have a sense of how their actions have impacted others, reading these letters provides a new modality to hearing and appreciating other people's experiences. Further, writing the impact letter increases family members' participation in the treatment where they might be able to express themselves in novel ways.

To ensure that the impact letters are impactful, you will need to work with the family members beforehand to help them not use the letter to blame the adolescent. Rather, the letters should allow the person's vulnerability and open expression to come through. You may need to work with family members on several drafts of their letters. In the end, they should focus on factual behaviors and the primary emotions that resulted from them. You can also encourage the family members to include aspects that the adolescent may not have known because of their preoccupation with themselves. Somewhere in the letter, the family member should include the author's appreciation of the good aspects of the adolescent and their positive behaviors.

The impact letters are usually given to the adolescent during group therapy, as most residential settings include both individual and group sessions. The adolescent is asked to read the letters aloud verbatim without trying to counter or justify themselves. The other group members are then allowed to make comments on what they heard, providing the adolescent with an additional medium in which to contact the ramifications of their past behavior. Depending on the adolescent's reaction to reading the letters, several sessions might be needed for them to take ownership and responsibility for their previous actions. Once they have, you can have them write an impact letter where they describe the behaviors of themselves and family members as well as the primary emotions these events evoked in them. The family members—usually the parents—are given the letter so that they can hear the adolescent's perspective and appreciate their struggles and growth.

Once the adolescent has gone through enough treatment and is close to the action stage in the readiness for change, you can work with them to write an **accountability letter**. The adolescent is asked to describe their past problematic behavior and take full responsibility for their choices. They should also write how they understand that their behaviors negatively impacted other people. The accountability letter is the adolescent's apology to their family. The more accountable they become in the letter, the freer they are as they can get everything out on the table and not have to keep secrets anymore. Their open and honest written communication with their parents allows for a new way of interacting as well as a move away from self-loathing.

Writing Letters to Therapist

In many treatment settings, therapy is a once-a-week endeavor. For some clients, you might meet with them every other week or once a month. In a more restrictive environment (e.g., an inpatient facility), you may have multiple sessions in a week or even daily sessions. Whatever the frequency of meetings, therapy can be an expensive process. Not everyone can afford therapy, particularly from therapists working in private practice. Given this, some clients will ask to spread out sessions solely for financial reasons.

One way to ensure that clients are provided services that fit their financial situation and that provide temporal efficiency for treatment is to have the client write you a letter. This process shifts some of the responsibility for change to clients. Instead of using the therapy session as a place to think about what they want to say, where, if we did a cost analysis, each minute of the therapy session is perhaps $2–4, clients can use their own time to compose their thoughts. They can take as long as they want to construct a letter for you. The question here is that you would want to get paid for your time when you are reading the letter. If you read the letter during the session with the client, there is no issue. The client is already paying you for that time. If you read it outside of the session, you should have arranged with the client how you will charge for the time.

Having clients write the therapist letters was an approach utilized by Terpager to help him have more frequent interactions with his clients, even if it wasn't face-to-face (Rasmussen & Tomm, 1992). This guided letter-writing process provided an opportunity to do long brief therapy, where clients were able to carry out their own therapy. During the intake, the therapist has a 10- to 15-minute telephone conversation with the client to determine whether therapy is appropriate. The client is then given three questions that they are to write a brief letter to answer: (1) What is the main problem? (2) What would you like to change? (3) What has been tried before? The therapist then contacts the client upon receipt of the letter. At that point, the client is asked to write a second and more extensive letter that includes their history, important people in their life that have had positive and negative influences, significant feelings and events in their history, their sense of the meaning of their symptoms, and their goals for therapy. The therapist suggests the letter be around eight to ten pages. A face-to-face appointment is then made with a request that the letter is sent so the therapist has several days to read it before that appointment.

During the session, the therapist interviews the client about the process of writing the letter. Terpager's therapy focuses on clients writing to various people in their lives. These people can be alive, dead, real, or imagined. What is important is that clients should write in an uncensored manner, being spontaneous with their feelings and giving full voice to their experiences. Because some people may censure themselves when writing in fear of what the potential recipient might think, you might have them write the letter with the understanding that they will destroy it afterward (more will be talked, in the next section, about writing a letter that is not to be sent).

The therapist might introduce the letter writing with the metaphor of riding a train to explore a country. The train ride is not the goal but the mode of transportation to get you to different locations. You can get off the train at certain stops and explore, then get back on to the next locale. Riding the train is similar to writing. Writing the letter is not the goal but is the mode to get to various meanings and experiences. If the client gets quite emotional during a certain area while writing, they are encouraged to stop writing and contemplate the memories that are connected to the intense feelings.

The intent behind this process of letter writing is that the client begins to become desensitized to the traumatic life events in their past, allowing them to better deal with the lasting pain. By taking one's time in writing the letter—as it should not be written in one sitting but paused each time intense emotions surface—the client better tolerates and reflects upon their experiences. In the session, these experiences are talked about, redefined, and understood differently.

When doing an intervention like this, it is important to keep in mind that the client doesn't just write. You, as the therapist, would give them specific prompts based on their concerns and goals. For instance, if a client came to therapy expressing guilt from their relationship with their mother, you might assign them to write a letter to their mother about their feelings for her. A second letter could be what they wish they would say to their mother if she was dying. Progressive letters become more emotionally intense as asking the client to emote too quickly could prevent them from opening up and utilizing the letter writing effectively. The client could then be directed to write another letter from the vantage point of the person to whom they wrote the letter to answer the previous letter.

Given that clients are writing at home, it is important that you let them know that the writing prompt is not set in stone. They should know they can change the prompt, omit certain parts, or add other parts based on their sense of what will be most useful. Most prompts will explore multiple aspects of a person's life. As an example, if in the initial personal history letter the client describes a childhood of chaos, a writing prompt may be, "Write about three instances in your life where you felt that it was chaotic and then three instances you felt were stable."

As therapy continues, the writing prompts will likely shift from being suggested by the therapist to being negotiated between therapist and client in the session. Toward the end of therapy, the client will independently decide what the letters will focus on. This movement highlights the growth of personal agency of the client where they have directed the focus of the therapy. One of the benefits of this type of therapy, where the primary method of treatment comes in the form of client-written letters, with periodic face-to-face sessions, is that clients form a strong therapeutic relationship with themselves. The therapist is more of a coach, but the client is truly empowered and can engage in self-healing.

The process just discussed is somewhat structured, lasting over many sessions. This may not be appropriate for all clients and contexts. You can always ask the client to write you a letter as a one-off experience. That is, where you might only write one therapeutic letter for them, you can ask them to write you one. This can be done at any point in the treatment process. In my experience, having the client write you a letter is best used toward the latter stages of therapy because the client will have made progress and the letter can focus on and reinforce their positive movement. You might introduce this idea with the following,

> We have been meeting for several months and you've made a lot of changes that we've talked about here in session. I was thinking it would be useful for you to recognize these changes. This week, can you write me a letter where you discuss your growth in therapy? Perhaps you can talk about the specific ways that you have changed, how you have moved closer to your goals, and where you want to continue moving toward.

Writing Letters Not-To-Be-Sent

In this chapter, we've talked about how clients might write letters to significant individuals in their lives, to their problems, or to the therapist. Most of the letters written to people are written so that they can be given to and read by the other person. The person reading the letter may be able to hear and appreciate the author in ways that they have not previously.

However, there is also the therapeutic benefit of having the client write a letter fully knowing that they will never share this letter with anyone else. Usually, when we are communicating with someone, we think about what we are saying and tend to censor ourselves so that we don't "say the wrong thing" and hurt someone's feelings (sometimes we do the opposite; usually when we are extremely upset and intentionally say something to hurt the other person). By letting the client know, from the outset of writing the letter, that it will never be sent, they have freer rein to explore and express their thoughts and feelings. This section explores the rationale for asking the client to write a letter that will never be sent.

One formalized task that involves writing a letter not to be sent is the **write-read-burn exercise** (de Shazer, 1985). This task is usually given to someone who wants to decrease a behavior or is obsessing about something. The client is asked to choose a comfortable place each day at the same time to do the activity. On odd-numbered days they are to write down all their thoughts, both good and bad, about the concern they are dealing with. Then, on even days, they are to read the previous day's writing and then burn it. The client is directed to try to think about the concern only during the scheduled time (usually they are asked to do this for one hour per day). This activity seems to be effective because it helps concretize people's concerns, reduces their time thinking about it as they are doing so only during the designated time of the day, and allows them to think about other things. Since the problem is no longer forbidden from thinking about, the client realizes they have better things to do, and then, literally, their problems go up in smoke.

Many therapists believe it is important to have experienced the process that clients go through (rather than the content—you don't need to have experienced depression, divorce, or anxiety to work with people who have). By being a client, engaging in growth activities, or writing a therapeutic letter, you gain first-hand knowledge of what it may be like for your client to do the same. Thus, at the end of this chapter, it might be useful for you to engage in writing a letter that can be potentially therapeutic. Here is my suggestion and it will be up to you to decide whether to do so or not. If you take me up on this challenge, then follow this prompt: write a letter to a person whom you feel you are currently having difficulties with. This might be someone with whom there is a severe conflict or someone you have drifted away from. Knowing that you will not give them this letter, express your disappointment in the current state of the relationship. Then, write about what you are hoping for in the relationship. It may be that you want closeness, or you never want to talk to the person again. There is no right way to want the relationship except for your want to be honest. Again, the person is not going to read it, so you can write what you want. When you finish writing the letter, put it away for a week. Once the week ends, read the letter, and then destroy it. You might get creative in how you do so. This might be by burning, shredding, or painting over it. Once you finish, sit with your feelings about doing so. What was it like for you to write the letter? Given the freedom of knowing you were not going to give it to the person you were writing to, how did that change your view of self, other, and situation? How did destroying the letter impact you? What are your thoughts on how your clients might react if you asked them to engage in this activity?

Summary

Therapists are not the only people in therapy to write letters; clients do as well. This chapter covered the usefulness of client-written letters, where clients can gain new perspectives on themselves and their situations. You can get clients to write letters to themselves, you, their partners, or other people in their relational field. They might also write a letter to their problem. This letter can be written from the present or even from the future. Client-written letters can occur in individual, couple, family, or group therapy. While there will be times when you want the client to give the letter to the person that they wrote it to, there are other times when the letter was written so that it would not be sent. The client usually develops a new understanding of self and the situation in the process of thinking about and writing the letter.

References

Anderson, C. M., & MacCurdy, M. M. (2000). *Writing & healing: Toward an informed practice.* National Council of Teachers of English.

Berg, I. K. (1994). *Family based services: A solution-focused approach.* Norton.

Borkin, S. (2014). *The healing power of writing.* Norton.

Christenson, J. D., & Runkel, A. L. (2017). The use of letters to create movement in residential settings with adolescents and their parents. In J. D. Christenson & A. N. Merritts (Eds.), *Family therapy with adolescents in residential treatment* (pp. 13–27). Springer.

de Shazer, S. (1985). *Keys to solution in brief therapy.* Norton.

Dolbin, M. L. (2014). Becoming the author of your life: Writing stories of change. In C. F. Sori & L. L. Hecker (Eds.), *The therapist's notebook for children and adolescents* (pp. 238–241). Routledge.

Ellis, C. (1989). Epistotherapy. *British Medical Journal, 299*(6709), 1230.

Hagedorn, W. B. (2011). Using therapeutic letters to navigate resistance and ambivalence: Experiential implications for group counseling. *Journal of Addictions & Offender Counseling, 31*(2), 108–126.

Jolly, M. (2011). What I never wanted to tell you: Therapeutic letter writing in cultural context. *Journal of Medical Humanities, 32,* 47–59.

Keenan, M. J., Lumley, V. A., & Schneider, R. B. (2014). A group therapy approach to treating combat posttraumatic stress disorder: Interpersonal reconnection through letter writing. *Psychotherapy, 51*(4), 546–554.

Kress, V. E., Hoffman, R., Thomas, A. M. (2008). Letters from the future: The use of therapeutic letter writing in counseling sexual abuse survivors. *Journal of Creativity in Mental Health, 3*(2), 105–118.

Lange, A., van der Wall, C., & Emmelkamp, P. (2000). Time-out and writing in distressed couples: An experimental trial into the effects of a short treatment. *Journal of Family Therapy, 22*, 394–407.

McCarthy, B., & Wald, L. M. (2013). New strategies in assessing, treating, and relapse prevention of extramarital affairs. *Journal of Sex & Marital Therapy, 39*(6), 493–509.

Nau, D. S. (1997). Andy writes to his amputated leg: Utilizing letter writing as an interventive technique in brief family therapy. *Journal of Family Psychotherapy, 8*(1), 1–12.

Padfield, B., Tominey, R., & Matthews, L. (2017). Therapeutic writing groups in specialist inpatient eating disorder treatment. *The Journal for Specialists in Group Work, 42*(4), 316–337.

Pennebaker, J. W., & Beall, S. K. (1986). Confronting a traumatic event: Toward an understanding of inhibition and disease. *Journal of Abnormal Psychology, 95*(3), 274–281.

Pennebaker, J. W., Mayne, T. J., & Francis, M. E. (1997). Linguistic predictors of adaptive bereavement. *Journal of Personality and Social Psychology, 72*(4), 863–871.

Phillips, L., & Rolfe, A. (2016). Words that work? Exploring client writing in therapy. *Counselling and Psychotherapy Research, 16*(3), 193–200.

Rasmussen, P. T., & Tomm, K. (1992). Guided letter writing: A long brief therapy method whereby clients carry out their own treatment. *Journal of Strategic and Systemic Therapies, 11*(4), 1–18.

Roberts, M. (2009). Recursive and connecting dialogues: Spoken and written conversations. *Journal of Systemic Therapies, 28*(4), 12–25.

Rudes, J. (1992). Interactional letters: A reorganization of a couple's communication. *Journal of Marital and Family Therapy, 18*(2), 189–192.

Schlossberger, E. (1998). Letter from the grave. In L. L. Hecker, S. A. Deacon, and Associates (Eds.), *The therapist's notebook: Homework, handouts, and activities for use in psychotherapy.* (pp. 299–301). Haworth.

Signs, T. L. (2015). The art of letter writing in medical family therapy. *Journal of Family Psychotherapy, 26*, 243–246.

Voskanova, C. (2015). A letter does not blush: In-session writing to deal with shame in brief therapy. *Journal of Family Psychotherapy, 26*, 56–61.

Watts, D. (2011). The healing art of writing. In J. Baranow, B. Dolan, & D. Watts (Eds.), *The healing art of writing* (pp. 1–9). University of California Press.

White, M., & Epston, D. (1990). *Narrative means to therapeutic ends.* Norton.

White, V. E., & Murray, M. A. (2002). Passing notes: The use of therapeutic letter writing in counseling adolescents. *Journal of Mental Health Counseling, 24*(2), 166–176.

Yalom, I. D., & Leszcz, M. (2020). *The theory and practice of group psychotherapy* (6th ed.). Basic Books.

Zimmerman, T. S., & Shepherd, S. D. (1993). Externalizing the problem of bulimia: Conversation, drawing and letter writing in group therapy. *Journal of Systemic Therapies, 12*(1), 22–31.

Chapter 8

Client Writing Therapy

Michael D. Reiter

Thus far in this book, we have been discussing how you, the therapist, utilize writing in various ways in your practice. This included you writing progress notes, treatment plans, assessments, and letters to clients. However, client writing is also an extremely valuable aspect of the therapeutic process. Chapter 7 presented how you might get clients to write letters to you, self, or others to help them in their therapeutic progress. This chapter explores four other unique types of client writing—journaling, autobiographies, poetry, and lyrics.

We can call these interventions **Writing Therapy**, which "is defined as a process of investigation about personal thoughts and feelings using the act of writing as an instrument, with the aim of promoting self-healing and personal growth" (Ruini & Mortara, 2022, p. 23). You can use writing therapy as a standalone treatment or as an adjunct to whatever method of therapy you are utilizing. These client writing activities have several therapeutic benefits, including reductions in symptoms and increases in psychological well-being. Further, self-writing provides clients an opportunity to represent themselves in their own words. Litowitz and Gundlach (1987) explained,

> It [writing] serves, along with other semiotic systems (such as gesture, facial and body expression, dress, and speech) as a means of representing who one is, how one feels, what one knows and wants, and so forth, in culturally appropriate ways.
>
> (p. 85)

This allows the client to become more self-reflective and, if they choose to share their writings with you, your own better understanding of who the client is and how they make sense of their experience. This chapter presents several different ways for clients to engage in writing. After reading this chapter, you should be able to begin to implement one or more of these interventions into your therapeutic tool pouch.

DOI: 10.4324/9781003294702-8

Journaling

Journaling has been a common practice for people for hundreds of years. Likely, they would have explained that they "kept a diary." We all are likely to recall watching a television show, probably a family sitcom, where a parent or sibling finds an adolescent's diary and struggles with the morality of opening and reading it. To offset this practice, many manufacturers began making diaries that had a lock and key. The message being sent here is that the person's expressions were so important and so private that no one else should be able to read this written expression.

The words *diary* and *journal* have been used synonymously in the history of psychotherapy practice—as such, we will, for convenience's sake, use the word journaling. In its basic iteration, **journaling** is writing down your thoughts and emotions. This may be describing what happened during the day (or since the last time that you journaled). It may be written in distinguished prose or just random words. There is no set way that people journal. This is one of the benefits of journaling; it is up to the author to write in a way that they find the most beneficial.

We can also journal through many different mediums. Traditionally, journaling has occurred in a diary—a smaller book that has blank paper where people put the date of the entry and write whatever they may. The next page is used for the next entry, etc. Thus, the journal becomes a chronological recording of the individual's experience. However, with today's technology, journaling does not have to occur with pen and paper. You might journal by opening documents on your computer and typing your thoughts or feelings. Or you could use an app on your smartphone and keep your journal there. The location of your journal doesn't matter. What is important is that you engage in expressive writing.

Journaling helps people to organize their thoughts. When we do this our brains do not have to keep on trying to process the experience and we may be able to focus on other things or just relax. In some way, expressing ourselves in a journal is a way that we engage in a cathartic experience. We have gotten it out. While this doesn't make our lives perfect, it is the start of a process. Given the general public's predisposition to have at some point kept a diary, or at least know that it is a somewhat common occurrence, as well as the emotional, physical, and psychological benefits of journaling, it has become a significant tool in many therapists' toolboxes.

Journaling in Therapy

Journaling has been extensively used in psychotherapy as it helps to bridge the work done in therapy with the client's daily life. Borkin (2014) explained that "therapeutic journaling is any type of writing or related expressive process used for the purposes of psychological healing or growth" (p. 5). You might have the client write the journal in session or assign it as homework. You will also have to decide whether you want to ask the client to show you the journal entries or keep them private. To help you with this decision, most therapists have clients write their journals at home and don't ask to see them. However, depending on the type of therapy you are doing and the comfort level of the client with you, this is something that you could negotiate with the client.

Journaling is about expression and potential introspection. Snyder (2018) explained, "Journal writing is one of a group of therapies that provides an opportunity for individuals to reflect on and analyze their lives and the events and people surrounding them, as well as to get in touch with their feelings" (p. 201). By placing thoughts and feelings onto paper (or computer screen), clients can potentially see connections and patterns between themselves and others or patterns in how they tend to handle life events. This awareness and insight might then be useful for them or used in therapy about a possible pathway toward change.

Therapists usually ask clients to journal at least once every day. One of the benefits of doing so is that the writing of the journal then becomes a ritual. Gilligan (1993) believed that one of the oldest forms of therapy is ritual. He defined ritual as "an intense, experiential-symbolic structure that recreates or transforms identity" (p. 239). While most people think that journaling should be done every day, that is not always the case. Journaling should be done as often as it is useful for the client. If writing every day keeps the client perseverating on a distressing topic, then perhaps they should cease writing about it so often. Journaling can be useful if done only one time or several times per week. It will be important for you to check in with your client to find what works for them.

You can suggest to clients to begin journaling for several reasons. First, by taking time outside of the session, the client can get in touch with their thoughts and feelings. For many people, we are so busy engaged in activities during the day that we do not take time to really think about what those activities mean to us. Journaling slows us down and gets us to take both an internal and external perspective on ourselves. Second, you can let clients know that journaling provides a safe space for them to say whatever they want to say without any constraints and restrictions. They do not have to worry about hurting someone else's feelings. They don't even have to worry about hurting their own feelings. Third, you might explain that since the journal is not intended to be read by anyone else, the client doesn't have to think about how to word things, either to not hurt someone's feelings or to ensure that it is grammatically correct. Rather, they should just write. Like free association, once a flow begins, the client will not know what will make it onto the paper. They may be surprised by what comes to the surface.

Journaling has been used mainly with adults regardless of presenting problems. Clients can utilize it whether they are coming to therapy due to feelings of depression, anxiety, relationship problems, or just trying to have a better sense of self. In most cases, client journaling has been beneficial psychologically, emotionally, physically, and interpersonally. However, the use of journaling in the therapeutic context has not yet been utilized to its fullest potential (Alexander et al., 2016).

You can get your client to journal in a variety of contexts, whether it be in a session, on their own at home, or through telehealth. For instance, mothers who were experiencing maternal stress because of poor mother-child relationships were asked via telehealth to keep an online journal (Whitney & Smith, 2015). Those who journaled experienced lower levels of maternal stress and improved mother-child interactions. The researchers believed that the elicitation of emotional disclosure was the active ingredient for the positive changes made by these mothers. The results of this and similar studies give you support in encouraging your clients to write their journals with emotionally laden vocabulary. This may go counter to some people's belief systems that you should not verbalize negative feelings. Knowing some of the science behind your interventions can help you provide clients with the encouragement to engage in journaling—particularly emotion-based writing.

While the use of journaling is primarily utilized with adults and older adolescents, it can also be helpful with young children. Palmer and Bowers (2015) worked with children aged 4–12 where they introduced the child to writing in a journal as part of the therapeutic process. In this way, they first talked with the parent(s) about the journal and the need for confidentiality of what is written in it. The therapist would explain that unless the child offers to disclose what is in the journal, neither the parent nor the therapist should look at it.

When explaining the journal to the child, you can have a variety of art materials, such as crayons, markers, pictures, or other things the child can glue onto the journal. The child can then decorate the journal in session, which is beneficial since it is a symbol that the child is taking ownership of the journal. Creating, decorating, and writing in the journal provides a sense of ownership of the diary. The child is then more likely to have an investment in using it throughout the week.

Throughout therapy, you can ask the child client to write in the journal. This may be drawing a picture, writing a phrase, or writing a paragraph or more where the child is able to express themselves. If the child is too young to be able to write, you might ask for permission to write what the child tells you to. Thus, some portion of the therapy session can be spent with you and the child client making a journal entry. If the client wanted to do it at home, with their permission, you might recruit a parent or older sibling to help them with their entries.

By dating each entry, the journal then becomes a timeline of therapy, providing a personalized guide to demonstrate the client's progress in therapy. Further, based on the child's desire to share it or not, the journal could be shared with parents or other important individuals in their life. Another benefit of using this type of journal with young clients is that it is a tangible object that they take with them at the end of therapy so that they can return to it whenever they feel the need to ensure that they are staying on the positive path that they made during therapy.

While journaling is quite therapeutic for many clients, it may not be useful for everyone. You will need to think about the client you are working with and decide if talking about and introducing journaling will make sense in that situation. Borkin (2014) suggested that individuals with dyslexia and other learning disabilities may have difficulties engaging in journaling. Further, she expressed hesitation in using journaling with those dealing with thought disorders.

Another consideration is the language in which the journal is to be written. For those clients who are multilingual, you can ask them which language they prefer to write in. Since they are likely not to show you the actual journal entry, they should be free to write in their primary language or the language they believe they can express themselves most easily. Again, since no one is reading the journal, it is not a matter of writing well. Rather, it is writing in a language that provides the best medium in which to allow one's inner world to come out.

Up to this point, we have been discussing a more free-form type of journal where the client writes whatever they want to, usually whenever they want to. However, you can also assign them more focused journals. You might ask them to write about a specific event from their past, that current week, or their thoughts about a future event. Another possibility is to have prepared journals. This would be in the form of worksheets. These journal entries could focus on a variety of topics, such as self-esteem, gratitude, or who am I. Figure 8.1 presents a potential self-esteem journal that you could give your client for them to fill out throughout the week. You could then have them come in the next session and share it with you or just have them keep track of it on their own.

An alternative procedure for journaling is having the client create a **dream diary** (Pirjo, 2018). You can request your client to write down their dream immediately upon waking. The longer the client does this, the more material can be utilized in the session so that you and the client can explore them for recurring events, feelings, moods, and themes. In session, you can discuss with the client their reactions to the material in their dreams and connect it to various aspects of their life. The individual entries in the dream diary then become a fuller story providing pieces of a puzzle that help you and the client understand their full gestalt.

Self-Esteem Journal

Monday:
I experienced myself positively when I _____
I liked that I _____
I appreciated _____

Tuesday:
Something I did for someone today is _____
Today, I did well when _____
I feel good about myself when _____

Wednesday:
I enjoyed _____
I overcame _____
Today I helped someone _____

Thursday:
I had a positive experience with _____
I felt good when _____
I was happy when _____

Friday:
Three things I like about myself are   _____
Today, what I did for myself was _____
My favorite personality trait is _____

Saturday:
Something I did for someone today was_____
I felt comfortable when _____
I accomplished _____

Sunday:
I achieved _____
I am good at_____
I deserve _____

Figure 8.1 Sample of a Self-Esteem Journal Template.

Expressive and Positive Writing

Two more specific types of journaling are expressive and positive writing.
Expressive writing interventions get the client to write about negative
emotional experiences. Primarily developed by John Pennebaker, clients
are asked to write about past trauma, focusing on their deepest thoughts
and feelings regarding the trauma. To introduce expressive writing, you
might tell the client:

> What I would like you to do for the next week is to reserve some time
> each day to devote yourself to writing. The writing should focus on
> the most traumatic experience of your life, where you don't censor

yourself or have any inhibitions. Rather, let yourself go and allow your deepest thoughts and feelings to come out on the paper. Some things that you might write about include the impact of other people such as parents, siblings, partners, or others. You might also write about your thoughts about who you were when the trauma happened, who you are now, or who you want to be. Each day write about something different.

This is only one possible explanation of expressive writing among thousands of openings. The key is to get the client writing and expressing themselves.

Expressive writing has been rigorously studied and has led to significant physical and mental health improvements for those who engage in it (Pennebaker et al., 1997; Pennebaker & Beall, 1986). Further, the writing doesn't have to be for a great length of time. With as little as 15 minutes of writing over a three-day period, people who write about important personal experiences find that their mental and physical health improves (Pennebaker & Seagal, 1999). This is the case across ethnic, racial, and cultural groups and regardless of age, social class, or personality type. Those who engage in expressive writing describe it as being quite valuable and meaningful for them in their lives.

Positive writing interventions get the client to write about the positive aspects of their lives, particularly the positive experiences and personal strengths (Suhr et al., 2017). These authors explained, "Through positive writing, a constant reflection of the positive aspects of one's personal characteristics and living situation is induced, and participants could become more aware of and have better access to their personal resources" (p. 1587). Positive writing has also been referred to as a **resource diary**. Examples of some question prompts that you might use with clients who are utilizing a resource diary include:

- What gave you strength today? How did this become apparent to you? Please describe your thoughts and feelings.
- Which aspects of your personality are you content with? What do you like about yourself? What do you think others (friends, family, partner) like about you?
- Assuming you were to make a film about today, what would the viewer see if everything had gone exactly as you wished? What would have happened today? What is the first small step toward the fulfillment of your wishes?

(Toepfer et al., 2016, p. 127)

One of the benefits of positive writing is that it is usually done outside of session. Those individuals who write about positive experiences have more positive moods and fewer health center visits than those who don't write about positive experiences (Burton & King, 2004).

Adolescents using a resource diary as a positive writing intervention decreased depressive symptoms, including worrying, dysphoria, and low self-esteem (Reiter & Wilz, 2016). A resource diary has also been found useful in reducing depression symptoms in adults recently released from psychiatric inpatient facilities (Suhr et al., 2017) or for socially inhibited individuals, even when the writing occurred online (Allen et al., 2020).

One of the interesting findings regarding expressive and positive writing is that they both lead to fewer mental and physical symptoms (Baikie et al., 2011). This is because writing in and of itself may bring some type of structure to individuals, leading them to better handle emotional regulation. However, other researchers have found that positive writing through a resource diary leads to greater perceived social support and better mood than those who kept an expressive writing diary (Toepfer et al., 2016). Regardless, the data is overwhelmingly positive that when clients write they have emotional, psychological, and physical benefits. The question then isn't, "Should I get my clients to engage in expressive or positive writing?" but rather "*How* should I get my clients to engage in expressive or positive writing?" The more that you ground your understanding and interventions into the research literature, the more that you will come to expect that these types of writing interventions will be useful for your client. When you have this type of expectancy, you will help to impart hope and expectancy of change in your client. This is extremely important since hope and expectancy is a common factor of positive change for clients (Lambert, 2001).

Couples Journaling

As just presented, the use of journaling is an extremely useful skill to get the individual to be able to get in touch with their own thoughts and find a way to express them—if even only to themselves. To further the benefit of journaling, you can also use this technique with couples. **Couples journaling** helps couples who are having communication struggles to find a different way of expressing themselves to each other. What has likely happened for conflictual couples is that they have acclimated to each other's communicational strategies. In doing so, they have developed a pattern of non-listening or listening with the intent to discount. They tend to communicate to convince and listen to deny. Asking them to engage in couples journaling is one means of bypassing their dysfunctional interactional strategies.

Couples journaling can be used at any point during couples therapy—whether it be at the beginning, middle, or toward the end after much progress has been made. Usually, the couple is told to journal every day but to do so separately and not talk about what they wrote until the next session. Lemberg (1994) provided the following writing prompts that you can give to the couple to perform the exercise:

- How I feel about my partner today.
- How I think she or he feels about me.
- How I would have liked to have felt about him or her or about the relationship, today.

(p. 64)

One of the benefits of the Couples Journal is to have each member become aware of their fixed beliefs and unwarranted stereotypes. These can then be processed during sessions where the couple might move from more distant positions to a greater sense of connectedness.

Another benefit of couples journaling is that each partner may be more curious and open to how their partner is perceiving them. Many times, members believe that their partner has more negative feelings toward them than that person actually does. Hearing that your partner is having positive thoughts about them tends to bring a sense of surprise into the relationship, opening a space for new beliefs and expectations of what might occur in the relationship.

The Couples Journal is also useful to help shift each person's focus from the problem-saturated past to a future where they are having positive feelings for each other. Instead of hearing from the other person about things the other person is upset about and doesn't want them to do, daily journaling helps shape each person's focus to bring to the forefront those ways of interacting that each want. This helps to promote positive goals and expectations for the relationship.

Zimmerman and Haddock (2016) engaged in a very similar process that they described as **Shared Journaling**, explaining, "The purpose of the Shared Journaling technique is to provide couples with a structured and intentional means of successfully practicing new communication and conflict resolution skills at home" (p. 66). Shared Journaling is usually used with couples who are having difficulty taking the skills that they are learning in the therapy room and applying them when they are at home. While this technique was designed for use with Gottman Method skills, the ideas behind it can be used with just about any theoretical orientation. In therapy, you can focus on any positive communicational skills.

When explaining this technique to the couple, you should summarize all the skills that have been covered up to that point in the therapy process. You might write these skills down for each member so that when they leave the session to do the journaling later as homework, they are able to remember the skills. On their own, each person writes what they want to communicate to their partner. They are then to review their journal and circle and name the various skills that they used when writing the entry. By having everyone point out the skills they used, they are asked to be more conscious of how they are communicating with the other person. Second, they are then self-assessing their communication and whether it is coming across the way they want. Once this is done, the partners give their journal entries to each other. Reading not only what the other person has written but also seeing the person's circled attempts to use the skills they have been going over in therapy provides both parties confirmation that they are each trying to make the relationship better. The partners then write a response, again using the skills they have learned in therapy, and again circling and naming the skills they used in the writing of the journal entry.

At the next therapy session, the couple would bring in the journals and you would go over them together. Reading their attempts at using the skills you would be able to highlight how they utilized the skills well and how they could have done them a bit differently. Having people learn how to communicate more effectively is an extremely important component in therapy, particularly the interactional therapies when working with couples and families. Poor communication is an unfortunate bad habit. People have repetitively used ways of communicating that are ineffective and even harmful. Using a Couples Journal or, even more so, Shared Journaling enables you to work with them to more consciously apply the concepts that you have been engaging with in therapy to their life.

Autobiographies

Thus far in this chapter, we have talked about you getting your clients to write about themselves, but only in a snapshot format. This next section describes a more in-depth self-writing that clients can do that highlights the greater breadth of a client's experience, autobiographies. An **autobiography** is an account of a person's life written by that person. This contrasts with a biography, which is the story of a person written by someone other than that individual. You have likely read a few biographies during your life, probably of a favored celebrity or historical figure such as Abraham Lincoln, John F. Kennedy, or Steve McQueen. Usually, there are more biographies written about people than autobiographies. However, there has been a recent trend of celebrities and important figures writing their autobiographies (most likely right after a significant event that puts them even more into the public spotlight so that they can cash in on this infamy). Given that the individual is writing about themselves, it may seem like autobiographies and diaries are the same thing. However, they are different in that autobiographies focus on the past while diaries focus on the present (Ressler & L'Abate, 2011).

You can use autobiographies with a wide range of clientele and presenting problems. Ressler and L'Abate (2011) explained that autobiographies are easy to administer and are highly versatile. They have been effectively used with those presenting with obesity, dementia, cancer, autism, and addictions, as well as with sex offenders, senior citizens, and a variety of other populations and with those dealing with physical and mental difficulties. Ruini and Mortara (2022) explained some of the benefits of autobiographies, "The first therapeutic effect is the possibility to define a sense of identity through autobiographical narratives by the identification of significant personal changes and by giving meaning to them" (p. 26). Further, because it is the client writing their own story, they develop a greater sense of personal agency.

Another benefit of autobiographies is that they provide a structure for clients to explore their lives. They may be able to recall long-forgotten episodes, as they are trying to explore their life on a more specific event-focused basis. By exploring the course of their life, from early childhood to the current, clients may be able to connect events and see some of the common threads and themes that have been present for them.

To help move people forward, you might have your client also focus on their future history. You can phrase this portion of the writing as

> You have written about how you came to become the person you are now. While the future is not yet written, you can help shape it by having a sense of where you would like it to go. So, take some time and write about what you think the next chapter of your life will be.

Future autobiographical writing provides clients an opportunity to focus on goals and potential strategies to get there.

For many clients, you can have them write, on paper or on a computer, their autobiography in the format that they prefer. Some would like to do so in a more literary format while others may just want to get the facts out. You should be flexible and inquire from the client how they would like to write so that this activity can be most useful to them. Figure 8.2 provides a more structured worksheet that you can use with clients. They can either write their autobiography in session or take the worksheet home and do it as homework.

The use of autobiographies can also be used with couples (Hoang, 2005). Usually, couples enter therapy with frustration about the other person whom they thought was like them and is now quite different. You can introduce this activity to the couple by explaining that while they think they understand what is happening for their partner, there is likely a difference in culture occurring. This is probably why they are not understanding one another. While they may see a lot of similarities between themselves (perhaps based on age, race, or ethnicity), they are

Autobiographical Worksheet

Who you are now is the culmination of where you have been in your life. This worksheet is designed to help you explore your past, so you have a better sense of who you are right now, in the present. Then you will be asked about the future, and where you want your life to go from here.

The Past
Write about the significant events, both good and bad, that occurred in your life. What did going through these events teach you about who you are as a person, what you value, and what you desire?

The Present
Write about who you are now. What are the current challenges in your life? What have been your major accomplishments? What are the skills that you are using to help you succeed in what you are doing?

The Future
Write about whom you want to be. What aspects of self from your past or present do you want to bring out more and which would you prefer to minimize? How do you want people to think about you? What things might you be doing that you and other people hold value to?

Figure 8.2 Sample of an Autobiography Worksheet.

not the same person and did not have the same history. In essence, the couple is engaging in a cross-cultural experience. Because of this, there is likely a lot of guessing about what the other person meant. You can then inform them that at some point in the therapy you will begin autobiography work where you will work with one member first to write about their life while the other person observes—in essence, the partner is the reader of the autobiography.

The client should write from their current age, contrasting how they are now with how they were then, when they lived with their family of origin. The focus can be on how they were in relationships when they were younger and then compare that to how they are in relationships now. The autobiography is designed to help people learn: the client about the possible etiology of how they function and the partner about how they might have misunderstood their partner. Each party may then be more open to framing their relationship and changing the expectations for themselves and others.

It is useful when doing couples autobiography that the clients feel safe, supported, and that you are a neutral party in their complicated dynamics (Hoang, 2005). You may need to block the reader from trying to intervene when their partner is the writer. You might also have them each write portions of their autobiography at home and then bring what they have written to the therapy sessions to be read aloud. At the end of the autobiography work, people should have a better sense of what have been the factors, events, and values that have impacted them throughout their life and that play a significant role in their current functioning. This insight should then lead them to make more conscious choices of how they want to conduct themselves in the present and/or the future.

Poetry in Therapy

So far in this chapter, we have talked about how expressing oneself has positive physical, emotional, and psychological benefits for the individual. Creating a journal, expressive writing, and autobiographies are just a few ways of being able to express oneself in text. Another pathway is through poetry. The use of poetry in therapy can enhance people's ability to reflect on their own experience and express it in ways that they may not have previously done.

Poetry is a medium that allows a variety of possible ways that the author can express themselves. While there are various types of poetry that contain some rules (e.g., a haiku, limerick, or acrostic), it is up to the author to write in a way that brings out their authenticity. Poems can rhyme or not rhyme. They can have five lines or nine. They can be overt or sublime. They can go on for a long time or they can stop on a dime. It is up to the author to decide what type of poetry best enables them to express themselves in the way that they want to.

Therapists have used poetry to help clients achieve personal growth for almost the whole of the field of psychotherapy's existence. While usually not taught in the academic classroom, except if it is a specialty class or program, poetry can be a quite powerful intervention. Many therapists utilize this medium leading to groups of professionals who continue to explore its usage. There is a National Association for Poetry Therapy, which also sponsors a journal focused on this area, *Journal of Poetry Therapy*.

While anyone who can write (or type) can create a journal, poetry has a more specific meaning for people. Those who view themselves as creative and artistic are likely to be better suited for utilizing this medium. Others may have negative viewpoints about writing poetry or about those people who write poetry. Given this, you might be a bit more hesitant in your introduction to the use of poetry in the therapy process. For instance, you can say to a client, "I'm not sure if this is up your alley, but something that others have found useful is to be able to express themselves through poetry. What would be your thoughts about this?"

Like the other forms of writing therapy, poetry can be used with a variety of clientele and presenting problems, even in situations where your client is dealing with intimate partner violence (Masson, 2020). The conjunction of talk and poetry therapy allows the client to explore their decision-making process in leaving the relationship by creating a timeline of the abuse, bringing out feelings using metaphor and imagery, and acknowledging and validating the abuse by putting the experiences into words. By writing in the form of poetry, clients may uncover aspects of self not realized previously. These aspects will likely be contradictory as the person both loves the abuser and hates what they are doing to them. These poems will likely help the person move from victim to survivor.

The use of poetry can also be used with a couple. You might have them sit together, either in session or at home as a homework assignment, and write a poem together. One of the benefits of this is that it gets them connected and doing something *with* the other rather than trying to do something *against* the other person. You could decide to provide the theme of the poem; for instance, with a couple who have been going through the motions with one another, you can ask them to jointly write a poem whose title is "Passion." Alternatively, you can ask them to jointly develop the theme, which will require them to have a conversation about what is important to them.

One use of joint poetry is between the therapist and the client (Kreuter, 2015). Here, you can go back and forth with the client, each adding to what the other person has written, to create a poem that was created by both of you. The client usually starts the poem and therapist and client add lines until the both agree the poem is finished. This technique is usually used when the client tends to have a more negative outlook, using darker imagery. By asynchronously journaling, you can counterbalance the client's tone and mood with a lighter and more positive position. The thought is that having read the more positive imagery and tone by the therapist will help the client begin to shift and add more positive ideas into the poem (and their own understandings of self and life).

This joint poetry process provides an opportunity for both parties to develop trust in one another. Each is sharing their perspective with the other, which helps connect the two. They can take in their own point of view more clearly as they are receiving a counterpoint to their ideas. When the therapist is one of the dyads, they are likely to be adding more positive and optimistic perspectives into the poem, providing light in a potentially dark place for the client.

Not every client will appreciate the use of poetry in therapy. This may be especially the case for male clients who must deal with the hegemonic masculinities that our society instills (Furman & Dill, 2012). Generally, men are socialized to be independent and autonomous where they learn to be utilitarian, solving problems rather than being emotional. The demands of masculinity may sometimes go against the demands of psychotherapy. Masculinity demands men to maintain control, show strength, act invincible, be self-reliant, stoic, omniscient, conflict avoidant, and free of pain. Psychotherapy, on the other hand, demands clients to relinquish control, show weakness, act vulnerable, seek help, express feelings, acknowledge failure, address conflict, and confront pain. The writing of poetry tends to fall in line with the expectations of psychotherapy, where people tap into the expressive and vulnerable aspects of self.

Given the conflict demands placed on men in psychotherapy, you will likely find yourself needing to find ways to avoid shaming men and provide them with a safe space where they can engage in the therapeutic process while feeling supported. A strengths-based perspective is one way to do so where you focus on the client's resources and goals. Further, openly exploring the way in which the man you have in your office understands their masculinity will give you insight into their worldview. This will then allow you to frame the introduction of poetry (or any other written intervention) in a way that will fit for that client.

One option is to help men create poems that highlight the usefulness of their attributes (Furman & Dill, 2012). For instance, you might provide them with a starting point for a poem:

"My resentment is useful to me." The client would then write a poem using this as a first line. Once they are finished writing that poem (and likely reading it out loud during the session), you could then have them write a poem that starts: "My resentment is not useful to me." This provides them an opportunity to explore their multiplicity.

While not all men are the same, not all females or nonbinary individuals are the same. This holds true for people from a variety of cultural groups. When utilizing poetry, or any of the writing techniques presented throughout this book, please think about how you might need to frame and/or adapt that technique to fit for that person from that cultural group.

Lyric Writing

An associated therapeutic practice to having the client write poetry is to ask them to write lyrics (that would coincide with some type of music). This process of songwriting (without having to compose the music) has been widely used, especially with adolescents as they may be more amenable to working in lyric format rather than poetry. While therapists from any orientation can have clients write lyrics to aid them in their growth in therapy, this technique tends to be used by those who are music therapists. Regardless, those who do have clients write lyrics tend to do so to help clients gain insight, clarify their thoughts and feelings, tell their story, develop a sense of self, enhance self-esteem, and provide them an opportunity for decision-making (Baker et al., 2008). By taking content that was internal and perhaps "hidden," the individual is able to make these external, in essence, "purging" them, leading to an experience that is healing (Turner, 2014).

The use of lyrics in therapy has primarily been used with adolescents. One reason lyrics may be more useful than poetry is that adolescents may find poetry to be dull and impractical (Ko, 2014). Lyrics, on the other hand, are associated with music which plays an integral role in most adolescents' lives. Further, music and the associated lyrics are frequently experienced in a group context (i.e., at concerts). Thus, this modality is useful when working with individuals, families, or groups.

When writing lyrics, you might give some structure to the client. One possibility is to have them write from the first-person perspective. That is, they are to write from their own point of view. You might encourage them to utilize "I" as the narrative voice. For instance, a lyrical verse might be:

> I look inside to try to find
> A way to get some piece of mind
> I try I try I try so hard
> To finally let down my guard

You might also have the client write from the point of view of someone whom they are having difficulty with. As an example, a teen who is coming to therapy complaining about an overbearing parent might be asked to write a song from the parent's perspective. This may provide new insights for the adolescent as to why the parent is taking the position they are. This small point-of-view change may then lead to significant changes as the meaning of the parent's behavior changes (perhaps from control to caring).

You will need to decide how central or not you are in the lyric writing process. Depending on the age of the client, their comprehension and variety of vocabulary, as well as their creativity level, you might need to help some clients more and some less when they are developing their lyrics. For older clients who are more motivated and creative, they can have full autonomy in their lyric construction. This may be done inside or outside of session. For clients who may need some assistance—even if it is where to begin—there are various methods for creating lyrics (Baker et al., 2009). These include brainstorming, providing a list of rhyming words, using previously composed poems by the client, having them answer open-ended questions (where the answers can later be modified to be the song lyrics), or having them fill-in-the-blank from a form that you provide them. Having your clients write their own lyrics helps them to describe their own story, which is important to them, while helping them to be creative in ordering and expressing their thoughts and feelings (Urbanek et al., 2021).

Writing lyrics is usually a process and can be enhanced when connected to a specific musical genre. For instance, Levy et al. (2022) used lyric writing with adolescents in relation to hip-hop to help them to support emotional development and regulation. While this intervention was primarily used with Black and Brown youth, it can be used and/or adapted for a variety of clientele. These therapists utilize a four-stage process to help youth write lyrics that enable them to express themselves around a singular personal issue. First, in the engaging process, the students free-write, utilizing rhymes with hip-hop instrumental music as the medium to write over. In the focusing phase, the therapist discusses the lyrics with the client, exploring a personal issue(s) that they want to change. Next, in the evoking process, the student identifies one specific personal issue and writes a 16-bar verse that relates to that issue. Lastly, in the planning phase, the student writes a second verse that describes a plan on how they can address the personal issue.

Lyric writing, as well as the music that goes along with it, can be used with a variety of presenting problems. Many typical topics adolescents struggle with include substance abuse, depression, delinquency, family concerns, grief, communication, and self-identity (Ko, 2014). Each of these can be a lyrical focal element. Exploring and analyzing the lyrics may present openings into the client's experience that may not have been breached otherwise. Lyric discussion tends to be more non-threatening and relaxing than a straightforward focus on the client's difficulties and concerns.

As stated, lyric writing is used with a variety of presenting problems. One significant area that is powerfully explored through lyric writing is grief. Dalton and Krout (2006) worked with adolescents who were dealing with the loss of a loved one. With this population they utilized the **Grief Song-Writing Process** to help the adolescents go through the grief process of understanding, feeling, remembering, integrating, and growing. In a group format, they encouraged the adolescents to create lyrics that focused on each of the five grief process areas. This may be:

Understanding	"I don't know why you're gone."
	"How could this have happened?"
	"Why did you leave this world so young?"
Feeling	"I've never been so down before."
	"I can't escape this gaping hole in my heart."
	"The tears flow like a never-ending river."
Remembering	"When I was ten, we threw the ball."
	"Remember the time you caught me sneaking out."
	"Every July we took a family trip."
Integrating	"When I look in the mirror, I see your face."
	"Even though the pain is there I take a step forward."
	"With the tears streaming down my face I can still laugh."
Growing	"I saw what you did wrong and know that can't be my life."
	"I'm a better man from what I've come through."
	"Things can never be the same again."

In the Grief Song-Writing Process, group members work together to create the theme for their song. They then each write a verse for the song, with the therapist developing the lyrics to the chorus. This intervention is done with a music therapist, someone who can play the guitar or piano and write the music based on the style that the group decides. However, if you are not that musically inclined, you could have several instrumental tracks available to you and put the lyrics to a prerecorded song. Each group member sings their lyrics, and all members sing the chorus. The song is then recorded, and a copy is distributed to the group members for them to listen to outside of session. While this specific intervention was developed to help group members grieve a loved one in healthy and adaptive means, it can be adapted for a variety of presenting problems, including parents' divorce, the ending of a relationship, or when dealing with substance abuse.

Having your client create their own lyrics, whether individually or in groups, has many potential therapeutic benefits. In a group format, song-writing is a fun activity that tends to build a strong therapeutic rapport. The group members are likely to be able to connect to the music, the therapist, and each other. However, there are some potential contraindications to its use (Baker, 2015). If you are using existing lyrics and then altering them, the clients may not have familiarity with the songs that you choose. Second, they may not want to alter the lyrics of songs that they really like. In group therapy, there may be disagreement among members about which song to utilize and what lyrics they may put to them. Also, when using a client's preferred song, this type of activity may change their relationship with the song. In the next paragraphs, we present a technique that is based upon the notion that the client's relationship to the song changes from what occurs in therapy; yet that change should be for the benefit of the client.

Besides having the client create their own lyrics, you can use preexisting songs to help move clients closer to their goals. Songwriters tend to write lyrics that include metaphor and simile, leaving ambiguity to the meaning of the lyrics. This provides an opportunity for the client to place their own meanings onto the lyrics so that they are more pertinent to their own situation. Reiter (2019) had clients choose a theme song that was then utilized to help enhance their resources. In this technique, you talk with the client about how boxers, wrestlers, and other sports figures have a walk-out song, which might be considered a theme song. Then you ask them what would be a song that could be their theme song, a song that is probably more based on the lyrical rather than musical essence.

Without having the client think too long about it, the client chooses a song and, in session, you and the client listen together to the song. **The Theme Song for Change** technique usually works best if you have two devices, one to play the song and the other to read the lyrics. You might have a pad and writing implement with you as you listen so that you can write down the keywords and phrases that stood out for you. The client can do the same. These phrases would be those that relate to the client and hint, suggest, and exemplify potential client resources. These lyrical themes highlight the client's values and practices that are related to their identity. Most likely the client has not been honoring these ways of thinking and being.

After listening to the song, you ask the client what words and phrases spoke most to them. The craft here is to relate the phrase to their presenting concern and how they are trying to handle the situation. You might ask them about previous times in their life when they did engage in life from the perspective of that resource. Once you explore the various phrases the client paid attention to you can add the ones that you heard that the client didn't yet mention into the therapeutic conversation. At the end of the conversation, a natural exercise or homework assignment is to have the client listen to the theme song every morning upon waking.

As an example of the Theme Song for Change, you are working with a 30-year-old woman from Philadelphia who is struggling with "feeling down." There are days that she doesn't get out of the house and barely gets out of her bed. Six months ago, she went through the breakup of a two-year relationship. She's still unclear how come her ex-boyfriend broke up with her. You introduce the idea of the Theme Song, and she mentions an obscure local band called Shadow Merchant and one of their songs, *Invisible Energy*. While listening to the song and reviewing the lyrics, you pay particular attention to the following:

Speak not of enemies
Speak not of friends
Carry it inside Up to the end
Bend but do not break
Stretch but do not snap
See through the obstacles Fill in the gap
Invisible Energy
Carried along, Passing through walls

When you talk with her about the song, she first mentions the words, "Invisible Energy." You ask her about her own invisible energy, and she explains that she knows inside of her is a will and a drive but that she can't see it right now. This opens space for you to discuss how she can be more open to the invisible energy inside of her. You then talk with her about how she has bent and stretched but not broke or snapped. The conversation then veers toward how she has coped with her disappointment at the end of her relationship. You then connect this coping to her resources, which you talk about in terms of being invisible energy. At the end of the session, she and you have identified four different resiliencies that she wasn't thinking about previously—resiliencies that are her invisible energy. You then explore how she can "see through the obstacles" (the concerns that brought her to therapy) so that she can "fill in the gap" with her coping strategies and now-identified resiliencies.

Summary

Having clients write about themselves in a variety of ways can help them to connect to known and unknown aspects of self. One of the primary ways that people, inside and outside of the therapy context, have engaged in self-writing is through journaling. Journaling can be a daily regimented activity or engaged in periodically. Writing in an expressive way, usually using positive attributes, is quite beneficial for people psychologically and physically. This type of writing, just a few minutes several times a week, has a significant impact. Adding a temporal aspect to self-writing, therapists can have clients write in an autobiographical fashion. Highlighting the person's past, particularly strengths and resources that have been useful for them in the past, can be utilized to discuss how they can implement these in the present and/or future. Another writing therapy technique is poetry where people can express feelings and ideas in a freer form. For other clients, chiefly adolescents, therapists can have them write lyrics to songs where they are able to express themselves in ways they may not have been able to articulate previously. These self-written lyrics, or using lyrics from a preferred song, can highlight the client's underutilized resources that can aid them in overcoming their current difficulties.

References

Alexander, J., McAllister, M., & Brien, D. L. (2016). Exploring the diary as a recovery-oriented therapeutic tool. *International Journal of Mental Health Nursing, 25*, 19–26.

Allen, K. L., O'Hara, C. B., Bartholdy, S., Renwick, B., Keyes, A., Lose, A., Kenyon, M., DeJong, H., Allen, S. F., Wetherell, M. A., & Smith, M. A. (2020). Online writing about positive life experiences reduces depression and perceived stress reactivity in socially inhibited individuals. *Psychiatry Research, 284*, 1–9.

Broadbent, H., Loomes, R., McClelland, J., Serpell, L., Richards, L., Johnson-Sabine, E., Boughton, N., Whitehead, L., Treasure, J., Wade, T., & Schmidt, U. (2016). Written case formulations in the treatment of anorexia nervosa: Evidence for therapeutic benefits. *International Journal of Eating Disorders, 49*(9), 874–882.

Baikie, K. A., Geerligs, L., & Wilhelm, K. A. (2011). Expressive writing and positive writing for participants with mood disorders: An online randomized controlled trial. *Journal of Affective Disorders, 136*(3), 310–319.

Baker, F. A. (2015). *Therapeutic songwriting: Developments in theory, methods, and practice*. Palgrave.

Baker, F., Wigram, T., Stott, D., & McFerran, K. (2009). Therapeutic songwriting in music therapy, Part II: Comparing the literature with practice across diverse clinical populations. *Nordic Journal of Music Therapy, 18*(1), 32–56.

Baker, F., Wigram, T., Stott, D., & McFerran, K. (2008). Therapeutic songwriting in music Therapy, part I: Who are the therapist, who are the clients, and why is songwriting used?. *Nordic Journal of Music Therapy, 17*(2), 105–123.

Borkin, S. (2014). *The healing power of writing*. Norton.

Burton, C. M., & King, L. A. (2004). The health benefits of writing about intensely positive experiences. *Journal of Research in Personality, 38*, 150–163.

Dalton, T. A., & Krout, R. E. (2006). The grief song-writing process with bereaved adolescents: An integrated grief model and music therapy protocol. *Music Therapy Perspectives, 24*, 93–107.

Furman, R., & Dill, L. (2012). Poetry therapy, men and masculinities. *The Arts in Psychotherapy, 39*(2), 102–106.

Gilligan, S. (1993). Therapeutic rituals: Passages into new identities. In S. Gilligan & R. Price (Eds.), *Therapeutic conversations* (pp. 237–257). Norton.

Hoang, L. (2005). "I thought we came for therapy!": Autobiography sessions in couple work. *Australian and New Zealand Journal of Family Therapy, 26*(2), 65–72.

Ko, D. (2014). Lyric analysis of popular and original music with adolescents. *Journal of Poetry Therapy, 27*(4), 183–192.

Kreuter, E. A. (2015). Asynchronous journaling as a therapeutic devise: Attenuation of negative imagery. *Journal of Poetry Therapy, 28*(1), 11–19.

Lambert, M. J. (2001). Research summary of the therapeutic relationship and psychotherapy outcome. *Psychotherapy: Theory, Research & Practice, 38*(4), 357–361.

Lemberg, R. (1994). Couples journaling technique: A brief report. *The Family Journal: Counseling and Therapy for Couples and Families, 2*(1), 64–65.

Levy, I. P., Emdin, C., & Adjapong, E. (2022). Lyric writing as an emotion processing intervention for school counselors: Hip-Hop spoken word therapy and motivational interviewing. *Journal of Poetry Therapy, 35*(2), 114–130.

Litowitz, B. E., & Gundlach, R. A. (1987). When adolescents write: Semiotic and social dimensions of adolescents' personal writing. *Adolescent Psychiatry, 14*, 82–111.

Masson, C. E. (2020). Writing and healing: Poetry as a tool in leaving and recovering from abusive relationships. *Journal of Poetry Therapy, 33*(1), 1–7.

Palmer, E. N., & Bowers, D. (2015). New twist on a classic tool: Using a journal as a technique for organizing therapy with young children. *Journal of Family Psychotherapy, 26*, 15–18.

Pennebaker, J. W., & Beall, S. K. (1986). Confronting a traumatic event: Toward an understanding of inhibition and disease. *Journal of Abnormal Psychology, 95*(3), 274–281.

Pennebaker, J. W., Mayne, T. J., & Francis, M. E. (1997). Linguistic predictors of adaptive bereavement. *Journal of Personality and Social Psychology, 72*(4), 863–871.

Pennebaker, J. W., & Seagal, J. D. (1999). Forming a story: The health benefits of narrative. *Journal of Clinical Psychology, 55*, 1243–1254.

Pirjo, S. (2018). Messengers in the shadow: A case study in creative writing and dreams. *Journal of Poetry Therapy, 31*(1), 56–67.

Reiter, C., & Wilz, G. (2016). Resource diary: A positive writing intervention for promoting well-being and preventing depression in adolescence. *The Journal of Positive Psychology, 11*(1), 99–108.

Reiter, M. D. (2019). Theme song for change: Utilizing music to enhance client resources. *Journal of Family Psychotherapy, 30*(1), 40–59.

Ressler, L., & L'Abate, L. (2011). Autobiographies. In L. L'Abate & L. G. Sweeney (Eds.), *Research on writing approaches in mental health* (pp. 39–53). Emerald Group Publishing.

Ruini, C., & Mortara, C. C. (2022). Writing technique across psychotherapies—from traditional expressive writing to new positive psychology interventions: A narrative review. *Journal of Contemporary Psychotherapy, 52*, 23–34.

Snyder, M. (2018). Journaling. In R. Lindquist, M. F. Tracy, & M. Snyder (Eds.), *Complementary and alternative therapies in nursing* (pp. 201–210). Springer.

Suhr, M., Risch, A. K., & Wilz, G. (2017). Maintaining mental health through positive writing: Effects of a resource diary on depression and emotion regulation. *Journal of Clinical Psychology, 73*(12), 1586–1598.

Toepfer, N. F., Altmann, U., Risch, A. K., & Wilz, G. (2016). Examining explanatory mechanisms of positive and expressive writing: Towards a resource-oriented perspective. *The Journal of Positive Psychology, 11*(2), 124–134.

Turner, M. (2014). The therapeutic effect of lyric writing on the writer: A narrative perspective. *Journal of Poetry Therapy, 27*(3), 143–154.

Urbanek, A., Kamiński, A., & Chatzipentidis, K. (2021). *Journal of Poetry Therapy, 34*(2), 118–130.

Whitney, R. V., & Smith, G. (2015). Emotional disclosure through journal writing: Telehealth intervention for maternal stress and mother-child relationships. *Journal of Autism and Developmental Disorders, 45*, 3735–3745.

Zimmerman, T. S., & Shephard, S. D. (1993). Externalizing the problem of bulimia: Conversation, drawing and letter writing in group therapy. *Journal of Systemic Therapies, 12*(1), 22–31.

Chapter 9

Documents and Counter-Documents

Michael D. Reiter and Jessica Popham

Many people who find themselves in a therapist's office have had difficulties in various contexts such as school, medical, and legal. Each time they experienced a problem, there likely was written documentation of that situation. These documents then add up, portraying a picture of the person that is less than positive. For instance, a teen who gets in trouble at school may accrue documented school suspensions and expulsions, as well as court transcripts and judge's rulings, all highlighting problematic behaviors the teen engaged in as well as the consequences of them. If you didn't know the person and only encountered them via these documents, a negative picture of the person would develop.

As a therapist, you have the opportunity of incorporating different types of documents into the client's life. These therapeutic documents, awards, and certificates focus on those behaviors the client has engaged in that lead them on a positive pathway in their life. They are usually a celebration of achievement. Because they go against the dominant narrative of who the person is—a narrative that is proscriptive, limiting, and pathologizing—they are called **counter-documents** (White & Epston, 1990).

Therapeutic documents shift peoples' identities from being problematic and limited to resourceful and expansive. Chen et al. (1998) explained, "Specific languaging principles are designed to ensure that the document liberates rather than restricts, opens up rather than closes down, and constructs rather than subjugates clients' experiences of themselves" (p. 406). The document that you give the client should lead to them experiencing themselves in a much greater resourceful position than they previously did.

Typical documents about people, such as assessments and evaluations, are written by others from an expert knowledge position. What we will talk about in this chapter are those documents that provide a different view of people. Counter-documents privilege the voice and expertise of the client. They shift information from another person's expert knowledge to the client's local knowledge—the ways that they know themselves better than anyone else can.

DOI: 10.4324/9781003294702-9

Many therapeutic documents are constructed and given out by narrative therapists. In this vein, Fox (2003) explained that "one of the key purposes of written documents is to record knowledges and preferred stories in permanent form" (p. 26). However, therapeutic or counter-documents can be provided by any type of therapist regardless of theoretical orientation. In this chapter, we provide you with a variety of counter-documents that may be useful for you in your continual pursuit of helping to enrich people's lives.

Documents

Documents are statements of knowledge. These can be written solely by the therapist, or you can co-construct them with the client. They tend to highlight the therapeutic talk, focusing especially on the ways that clients have taken personal agency against the situation and the problems they have been dealing with. Fox (2003) described that documents serve the purposes of recording particular knowledges, spreading news of preferred stories, and highlighting the rite of passage at therapeutic termination.

The **document of knowledge** is usually used when clients have either forgotten or lose sight of certain knowledges of self that could be useful for them in times of distress. In essence, documents of knowledge help people to remember aspects of self that might come more to the forefront of their experiencing. Often, when people are distressed they become overwhelmed. They may think negative thoughts or engage in unhelpful behaviors. They forget, or lose sight of, their solutions, especially if the solutions or skills are newly acquired. For example, take into consideration a person who experienced child abuse and now, as an adult, struggles with believing he deserves love. When he explores a new relationship he often becomes overwhelmed with these negative beliefs and behaves in ways that push people away. Even though he can acknowledge that he deserves love and connection, it becomes difficult to remember when in distress. Figure 9.1 presents an example of a document of knowledge for the example mentioned above.

When creating a document of knowledge, it is helpful to use the client's language. The language does not always have to be positive or uplifting but rather more matter of fact. It can acknowledge past struggles or pain but it does not spiral into a negative picture of the client. It can also be beneficial to have other people related to the client sign the document to give it authenticity (Fox, 2003). This can help the client further recognize and solidify their sense of self. For example, a friend, spouse, parent, child, or colleague can sign the document affirming their belief in these positive aspects of the client's identity. The more people among whom this resourceful understanding circulates, the greater the chance that it can take hold.

Documents of knowledge are related to a person's identity as well as to their skills (Fox, 2003). If a client struggles to remember their newly acquired skills, a document can be created that states what they know will help in relation to the problem. These documents can be written or printed on a small card or piece of paper so the client can easily access them and read them in times of need or distress. Perhaps even taking a picture of it on their phone or writing it in a notes application on their phone would provide even easier access. Figure 9.2 presents an example of a document of knowledge focused on skills that help a client experiencing anxiety.

Documents of circulation are intended to be given to people in the client's relational field where they can encounter the client's preferred story. These documents are usually given to family members, friends, and perhaps legal and helping professionals. What has likely occurred is that a

---

DOCUMENT OF KNOWLEDGE

This document certifies the following knowledges about Phlandrous:
1. Phlandrous has experienced the pain of child abuse.
2. He was not to blame for this abuse.
3. Phlandrous was able to keep his focus in school and be successful and graduate.
4. He is a loving person who wants connections with others.
5. Phlandrous is a person who deserves to be loved.

Certified this 26th day of October 2023

Signed: *Mike White, Psy. D.* & *Phlandrous F.*

Figure 9.1 Document of Knowledge. (Adapted from Fox, 2003.)

DOCUMENT OF KNOWLEDGE
This document certifies the following knowledges that Jane has acquired about anxiety:

1. The anxiety tries to trick you
    - Don't believe it
    - Think of alternative thoughts
2. Breathe
    - Take a deep breath before making any decisions
    - Focusing on your breath will help calm your mind and body down
3. It is okay to ask for help
    - Talking to a friend will help you feel less alone
    - Getting someone's opinion helps to quiet the anxious thoughts
4. This too shall pass
    - The anxiety is temporary and will go away with time
    - You can and will feel better

Certified this 19th day of May 2025

Signed: *Mike White, Psy. D.* & *Jane D.*

Figure 9.2 Document of Knowledge for Skills. (Adapted from Fox, 2003.)

To: Those who know Elizabeth
>   You may or may not know that I spent a few weeks in juvie. I had made a few mistakes. During my time in juvie, I was able to think about where my life was heading and, more importantly, who I was. I didn't like what I was doing and whom people thought I was.
>   Since I've been out, I have made active efforts to set things right. I have enrolled in a GED program, I am doing community service, and I have been drug-free now for seven weeks. The mantra I have been telling myself is: Keep growing.
>   I look forward to re-engaging with you. When you see me, I would appreciate you letting me know how you have seen me grow.
> Thanks,
> *Elizabeth*

Figure 9.3 Sample of a Document of Circulation. (Adapted from Fox, 2003.)

problematic story has been following the individual around. This may be that they are a troublemaker or do not care about other people. Therapy tends to help people shift from a limiting identity to a resourceful identity (Reiter et al., 2020). Documents of circulation are given to people to aid in connection around moving forward and thickening the preferred story. They can also serve as a reminder to both the client and others who view or receive the document as to what needs to be done to continue to embrace the resourceful identity. Figure 9.3 presents an example of a Document of Circulation.

Documents of rite of passage are used at the end of therapy to mark the ending of therapy to something else. These can take many different forms such as awards and certificates.

Awards

Awards highlight the client's achievements. An award could be a paper document, medal, trophy, or item that recognizes the client's success. Presenting an award to a client can help them feel like the hard work they put forth in therapy is valued. It is a sign of approval and gratitude for the work they did and the goals they accomplished. The presentation of the award shows the client that good work gets recognized and rewarded. It also goes beyond verbal recognition, acting as a symbol and representation of the client's hard work.

This can be very important for clients who feel like they are often overlooked or underappreciated. More importantly, it can help clients who struggle with recognizing their own achievements. Clients often come to therapy with a negative outlook on their life and themselves. It can be difficult to see the positive or the small changes they have made. Awards can punctuate those small changes that the client may not initially give credit to. Figure 9.4 shows an example of an award that can be given for small changes and achievements.

Awards can also serve as a rite of passage and a reminder that one small change or goal has been accomplished and now it is time to focus on the next stage or rite of passage. For example, a client could be presented an award for implementing healthy boundaries, as in Figure 9.4. In this case, the client could have chosen to end a relationship that was detrimental to their own self-love and individual growth. This award could signify to the client that one goal has been achieved and now it is time to focus on the next goal. Perhaps, the goal would be engaging in self-care activities to allow the client to continue putting themselves first.

The rite of passage could also be for the end of therapy to something else, as mentioned earlier. Instead of viewing the end of therapy as a loss, it can be celebrated as a passage onto the next stage in their life. The award can be presented to acknowledge the client's overall achievements in therapy. It highlights and celebrates the moment which can counter any fears or sadness with terminating therapy. Figure 9.5 presents an award that can be presented at termination.

Whether the client received the award throughout the therapeutic process or at the end of therapy, the client can take the award home and share it with others to show them their accomplishments. It can serve as a source of pride. Rather than just telling others of their accomplishments

THIS AWARD IS PRESENTED TO

Shawn Smith

for

Implementing healthy boundaries

_____   _____
Signed   Date

Figure 9.4 Award for Small Achievements.

THIS AWARD IS PRESENTED TO

Michelle Gonzalez

for

Successfully completing Mental Health Therapy

_____   _____
Signed   Date

Figure 9.5 Award for a Rite of Passage.

they have an official document or object to legitimize their hard work. If the award is given to the client in the middle of therapy, it can help the client to continue accomplishing more goals. It can push the client to continue on a path of success in multiple areas of their life. Once therapy ends, the client can look at the award and reflect back on the skills they learned and the progress they made in therapy. This could help motivate a client to continue putting in the hard work even though they are not in therapy any longer.

Many Alcoholic Anonymous (AA) groups give a similar award to those who maintain sobriety for a certain amount of time. AA members will receive a chip, token, or coin for their first day, first month, first year, and multiple years of being sober. It serves as a reminder of their commitment to recovery and their progress with sobriety. Awards provided in therapy can serve a similar purpose.

Certificates

Certificates are certified statements that note the training experience a person has. They typically are written declarations depicting the qualifications the person has acquired through the training. Oftentimes, certificates of completion are given once someone has completed training and acquired new knowledge. Jobs may require specific trainings to be completed on a yearly basis to maintain employment. The employee must complete the training and present the certificate of completion, indicating they completed the training and now have the proper qualifications for the job. Think back to your school and work careers. You likely received many certificates. What were they? What did they mean to you? What did the receipt of the certificate tell you about your abilities? Knowledge? Some were likely not meaningful to you (perhaps there was one you got for completing a work training that you really didn't care about). However, others were probably extremely meaningful. These were likely from activities that you put a lot of investment into. The therapeutic certificates we will be talking about will likely fall into this latter category as clients are usually highly invested in themselves and their own growth. Certificates that promote clients' positive growth are likely to hold special significance for them.

Oftentimes therapists do not know when clients will terminate therapy. Sometimes clients don't inform the therapist they will not be returning. Other times, clients don't know they are ready to terminate therapy until it is discussed in that session. Ideally, the therapist will discuss termination with the client prior to the actual termination day. In this case, the therapist has time to prepare a certificate for the client. The therapist can present the client with a certificate of completion, marking the end of the therapeutic process. In the event the therapist does not know the client

CERTIFICATE OF COMPLETION

This certificate is presented to

_____

for completing

_____

_____   _____
Signed   Date

Figure 9.6 Certificate of Completion.

is going to terminate therapy, they can have standard certificates printed where they can fill in the client's name and area of completion. Figure 9.6 presents an example of a blank certificate of completion.

In the above example, the therapist can acknowledge the client for completing mental health therapy or a similar distinction. The therapist could also pull from the client's experience and use the client's language as to what the client believes they have completed, such as completing "another chapter in my book of life" or completing "coping skills training." While certificates of completion are traditionally given at the end of therapy, they can also be presented throughout therapy as clients complete small goals. For example, a client may be focused on improving their coping skills. Each time a client learns and implements a new coping skill, a certificate of completion can be presented such as completing deep breathing skills.

Other types of certificates include certificates of achievement, participation, recognition, compliance, appreciation, excellence, and authenticity. Certificates of achievement would certify specific skills or behaviors the client has attained in or throughout therapy; for example, achieving time management skills. Certificates of participation would note the client's level of participation and engagement in and outside of therapy. A client can be acknowledged for attending eight consistent weeks of therapy or participating in weekly group therapy. They can also be used to recognize certain abilities or accomplishments such as the ability to care for others or the accomplishment of being the most valuable family team player. Court-mandated clients may especially appreciate certificates of compliance that recognize their engagement with services. The certificate can identify the client complied with all court orders and might even detail each order. Showing appreciation or acknowledging a level of excellence through a certificate can encourage the client to continue on a positive path. For instance, a certificate can highlight appreciation for the client's hard work and dedication to their self-improvement. Certificates of authenticity validate the client's resourceful identity and skills. The title of the certificate alone acknowledges the work as genuine and authentic.

In therapy, certificates can be used to show that a client has completed training in a certain life skill and now has the proper qualifications to manage their presenting problem. For example, a client attending therapy for anxiety could be presented a certificate for completing anxiety reduction skills training. It serves as a reminder to the client that they have the skills needed to manage their problem.

Certificates serve as a rite of passage, as mentioned earlier, marking an important stage in the person's life or therapy process. It also serves as a reminder for clients to look back on the things they learned and accomplished. Oftentimes, clients return to therapy because they stop using or forget to use the skills they learned throughout therapy. Certificates are a wonderful way for clients to visualize, keep, and remember the skills they learned in a tangible way. Perhaps presenting the certificate in a folder or with lamination can help the client to keep the document from getting lost or damaged.

Cards

In a non-therapeutic situation, **greeting cards** have been a mainstay of connection, support, and communication for people. If you go to any supermarket or retail pharmacy, you will find a section in the store devoted to greeting cards. Sometimes, these sections are a full aisle. You can buy a card for someone's birthday, engagement, marriage, anniversary, Christmas, Hanukah, graduation, or to express your condolences if there has been a death or loss in the person's life.

Greeting cards are an integral part of our lives, providing a quick means of expressing ourselves to someone else. Further, these cards are usually put up on a mantel or kept by the person so that they have frequent interaction with them, where the card's message or the person's show of due concern is repeated. If you take a second and think back to the last time you received a card from someone, what were your reactions? How did that feel? What meaning did you make about yourself? The person who sent it? Your relationship with that person?

Therapists can also use greeting cards with clients to help commemorate people's movement and growth in the therapeutic process. Hahs (2008) described how he used cards as therapeutic documents, particularly through a narrative therapy orientation. Rather than going to the store and buying a premade card, Hahs works with his clients and drafts what the client would like to be included in the card. Some of the questions you might ask your client to determine what will be included in the card are as follows:

- What achievements could you tell about the problems in your card?
- Would it be useful to highlight what you have done or what has enabled you to challenge the problems?

- Could your card celebrate aspects of your life that have improved since your commitment to overcome the problems?
- What is your main aim in making this card?
- What type of card would you like to send to the problem (i.e. farewell, celebration, or …)?
- Would you like the card to be a private document or more public?

(Hahs, 2008, p. 31)

The client might also be recruited to do the artwork on the card if they are so inclined. Here we present several of these types of cards.

A **"bon voyage" card** can be written for clients who are dealing with some type of problem that they don't want in their life anymore. These problems might be worry, depression, fear, or the like. The card is usually developed once significant steps have been taken by the client to separate themselves from the problem. For instance, a client who entered therapy because of issues with fear of heights might have begun to overcome this fear and was engaging in more situations where they were placing themselves in higher locations (such as doing a ropes course, ziplining, or even hang gliding). Depending on the age and artistic inclination of the client, they might draw the cover of the card, perhaps with a depiction of themselves on the top of some high edifice, such as the Eiffel Tower. Figure 9.7 shows what the therapist might write inside the card:

Clients may also be given an **Anniversary Card**. Usually, anniversary cards are given to married individuals upon the yearly anniversary of their marriage. However, other yearly occasions are noted by people, such as an anniversary of having overcome cancer or recognizing time being sober.

Often, clients come to therapy due to negative circumstances. These circumstances could involve the death of a loved one, the end of a relationship, or a traumatic event. These events stand out and are usually attached to the date the event occurred. Every monthly or yearly anniversary can bring up negative feelings, reactions, and thoughts. In therapy, Anniversary Cards can be given to clients when they have made significant changes regarding their interaction with the problem. For example,

Bon Voyage Fear of Heights
I want to say goodbye
To you and your try
To keep me on the ground
To keep me tied and bound
You are free to go
On a trip far and away
So that I can continue
To rise up up and away

Figure 9.7 Bon Voyage Card.

an anniversary card can be presented to a client who was grieving the end of her relationship with her partner but has now focused on the relationship with herself for a month. The card can use language the client has used to describe their progress and strengths. Figure 9.8 depicts an example of an anniversary card.

Using **Greeting Cards** may also be especially useful in working with children, as talk therapy may be overwhelming for them (Deacon, 1998). Rather than have a whole session where they are asked questions and might feel forced to give answers, having them write Greeting Cards may allow them to express themselves, especially how they feel, in a way that will feel safer and more comfortable. Therapy then becomes less intimidating for the youth. Rather, the use of art and writing provides a possibility of a game-like experience, which allows the child to have more fun in therapy while also having a therapeutic encounter.

To use Greeting Cards with children, you may introduce this process by talking with the child client about when people tend to get greeting cards and what it is like for them to receive one. With the client, you can come up with the variety of occasions on which people may receive a card such as a birthday, graduation, or a holiday. You can also talk about ideas and phrases that you might use in a card, such as "I'm sorry," "Thank you," and "I miss you." In session, you can create a variety of these Greeting Cards. A Greeting Card can be deliberately created for various people in the client's life. During the creation of the card, you can talk with the client about whom they are making the card for, their thoughts around that person, and what that relationship means to them. Depending on the situation and the client, you may encourage them to give the various cards to the people they were created for. This will provide them an opportunity to express themselves in a different way to important people in their life. If the child or client doesn't want to share the card with the intended person, the process can still be beneficial since the person was able to express and release their thoughts and feelings onto the greeting card.

Coping cards are cards that identify and define a coping skill the client has learned. The cards can be created by the therapist and presented to the client or the client can create them in session with the therapist's guidance. Any type of paper or card can be used. Typically index or

Happy Anniversary
One month ago today you chose you
You are deserving of a happy life
You are strong, caring, and capable
Keep on focusing on you

Figure 9.8 Anniversary Card.

flashcards are used. Similar to when students create flashcards to study the information they learn in class, clients can create flashcards (coping cards) to study, or remember, the skills they have learned in therapy. Freedom can be given to the client in how they design their card. Some clients may want to write the name of the skill on one side of the card and write a short definition or explanation of the skill on the back of the card. Some clients may prefer to write the name and definition on the front side of the card. Pictures can be drawn to either further illustrate the skill or can be used to make the card appealing to look at. Stickers can be used in the same fashion.

The coping cards can be hole punched and put on a key ring so they remain together and are easier to flip through. Since they are most likely on index cards, they are easy to transport and keep on hand. They serve as a quick reference and reminder when a client needs to cope with a situation. See Figure 9.9 for an example of a coping card.

Affirmation cards are created in a similar way to coping cards. They can be written on index/flash cards and can incorporate pictures, stickers, or doodles. They are small cards that can easily be referred to and read when a client needs a "pick me up." Affirmations are short statements that emphasize, encourage, and support our positive thoughts and identities. Affirmations are typically I-statements, declarations we make about ourselves. They serve as a counter-document to the negative views and limited identities we have of ourselves. For example, a client may come into therapy thinking they are a failure and not worthy of love since their last partner cheated on them and ended the relationship. The client might connect with affirmations such as "I am worthy of love," "I am capable," "I am strong," and "I will succeed." While some clients might like making cards for their affirmations, others may prefer to write them on sticky notes. This allows the client to stick the affirmation note on a

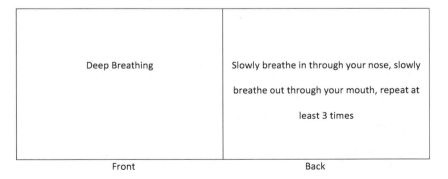

Figure 9.9 Coping Card.

place that is visible or easy to see. Some people like to place affirmations on their mirror so they can look at themselves while saying the affirmation. Others may write the affirmation directly on the mirror with a dry-erase marker. This seems to help the message truly sink in since the person is looking at themselves while saying the affirmation. For the purpose of therapy, it would be beneficial to have the client write down their affirmations on paper. Then, if they decide to put them on a sticky note or write them directly on a mirror they have the paper as a reference. This helps the client remember the affirmations instead of having to keep them in their working memory.

Lists

Documents that are given to clients do not need to be very in-depth or complex. They can be quite straightforward. One of these document opportunities is lists. Lists are especially useful when working with children and youths (Cooper, 2018; Freedman & Combs, 2002).

The **lists** that you write and provide for the client to take home are likely to highlight the client's personal agency. That is, the list contains actions—thoughts, beliefs, or past, current, and future behaviors—that the client can engage in that will be useful for them to challenge the problem. Many times, the lists that therapists use with clients focus on their accomplishments. Freedman and Combs (2002) explained,

> A list of accomplishments can bring forth vivid and meaningful experience of those accomplishments. In making a list with a child, the therapist helps to identify and name things that are worth listing. The process of writing these things down and reading them back makes them more 'real' and more memorable.
>
> (p. 168)

See Figure 9.10 for an example of a list of accomplishments.

List of Accomplishments

1. I have identified my problematic behavior.
2. I have taken responsibilities for my past actions.
3. I have learned new ways of responding to my feelings of anger.
4. I have learned to pause, take a deep breath, and think of my choices before acting.
5. I have learned new communication skills to help with conflict resolution.
6. I have practiced new coping skills to manage my emotions in a productive way.

Minoru Manabe   June 28, 2023
Signed   Date

Figure 9.10 List of Accomplishments.

You might also provide the client with two lists, side by side where one list is the client's positive actions and the second list describes the negative impact of the problem. In this manner, that paper can provide a juxtaposition for the client to see both the challenges they are dealing with and past, current, or future actions that can help them to combat the problem. Figure 9.11 shows an example of a side-by-side list.

While the list that you give the client to take home highlights the positive actions they have previously taken, you might also leave space on the list for the client to add to it when they discover a new thought, feeling, or behavior that they find useful in the goal pursuit as shown in Figure 9.11 (Cooper, 2018).

You can develop lists within the actual therapy session, or you can have clients generate lists outside of session as homework assignments. You may allow them to create the list as they wish or you may provide them with a template with a few examples as a guideline to follow. With a family that was having many conflictual interactions, we asked them to, each day, each write on a piece of paper one thing that they were grateful for about the other family members. They were to then put that in a gratitude jar at the end of the day and then read it the next day. The family decorated a box that they called their Gratitude Box, which they kept in the kitchen.

Dankoski (1998) utilized a similar usage of **Gratitude Lists**. This is used for partners in a couple when one or both feel that they are being taken advantage of. The Gratitude List writing assignment homework attempts to interrupt the pattern of blame and resentment that couples may have. Each party is told to take several days to write a list of what they are grateful for and appreciate about their partner. At some point, perhaps in session or maybe at a special location (i.e., a place that is meaningful to them, such as a favorite hangout or restaurant), the partners

Positive actions I can take	Negative impact of problem behavior (Anger)
Take deep breaths, do muscle relaxation	Brings on physical stress (headache, tension, stomach aches)
Take a moment to breathe and pause before responding	Creates heated arguments
Use communication skills to take responsibility and calmly express my thoughts and feelings	Makes me walk away from people and cut them out of my life
Practice gratitude and mindfulness to be in the moment and be open to various options	Prevents me from gaining opportunities in work and personal life

Figure 9.11 Side-by-Side List.

exchange their Gratitude Lists and read them. Dankoski explained that this writing technique may not be indicated for couples just beginning therapy or about to divorce. Figure 9.12 presents a Gratitude Lists Take Home Sheet.

Gratitude Lists can be beneficial for couples but can also be valuable to individual clients. Often, clients struggle with self-esteem and confidence and may experience self-defeating thoughts related to themselves or others. Creating a gratitude list for oneself or others can help shift the pattern of blame and negative self-talk to a more positive, resourceful identity. Generally, negative self-talk has a heavier and greater impact than positive. It is important to remind ourselves of the positive things that occur in spite of any negative events happening to help balance out our identity and views of the world.

Another type of list assignment is based on solution-focused therapy, especially when you want the client to focus on the exceptions to their problems—those times when the problem could have happened but did not (or occurred but to a lesser extent). You can ask the client to pay attention, from now until the next time that they come in, to what is occurring when the problem is not present or as severe. Another way of wording this is for them to notice what is happening this week that they want to continue to have happen or have happen more of. This technique is known as the First Session Formula Task (de Shazer, 1985). If you just ask the client to pay attention, there may be so many of these occurrences

---

Gratitude Lists Take Home Sheet

This sheet is designed to provide you with prompts to help promote your recognition of what you are grateful for in your life. Try to keep this sheet readily available to you as you should fill it out several times over the course of the week. Please fill in the blanks of the various statements. You can do this in any order that makes sense to you. When filling this sheet out, think about those large things you are grateful for about your partner as well as the small things.

I really appreciate when you _____.

One of my favorite things about you is _____.

In our relationship, I take pride in our ability to _____.

The first thing I tend to notice about you in the morning that I really like is _____.

I am happy in our relationship when we _____.

You are special to me because _____.

You are unique in that you _____.

Figure 9.12 Sample gratitude list sheet. (Adapted from Dankoski, 1998.)

that they forget some of them during the week. By getting the client to write these times down in a list, you get them to mark and hold each of these positive situations. Hopefully, by the time you meet with the client again, their list will be extremely long. During the next session, you can go over this list, primarily focusing on what the client has done to make these happen. Then the two of you can figure out what the client can do so that they do more of what has worked for them.

Worksheets and Workbooks

The documents and counter-documents we have been talking about in this chapter are usually presented to the client in the session. They are intended to be taken home so that the client can frequently look at them or show them to other people as they are a means of reinforcing a new and more desired client identity. In this section, we talk about a type of document that is usually given to the client for them to fill out at home— worksheets and workbooks.

A **worksheet** is a written activity that is given to a client for them to fill out. Worksheets often use prompts to help clients identify their thoughts, feelings, and behaviors. Depending on the length of the worksheet, the time you have available in session, and the purpose of the activity, you may have the client fill it out in session or out of session as homework. This may be a one-off occurrence, or you can have the client fill out multiple worksheets. Many authors have compiled a progressive order of worksheets into books. There are also websites that offer free worksheets for therapists to download and use with clients. Worksheets can be found based on presenting problem (e.g., anger, anxiety) or model (e.g., CBT, DBT).

Worksheets help put concepts, skills, or ideas that have been talked about in therapy onto paper. Writing things down help makes things more concrete. It also helps the client remember certain things with more ease. Instead of having to keep their skills or process their thoughts in their mind, they can put them down on paper which sometimes helps people to develop new insights, learn more effectively, or process differently. The client can also take the worksheet home with them to fill out in between sessions, extending the therapeutic work beyond just the session. Taking the worksheet home also allows the client to reflect on the work done in a session or throughout therapy.

Workbooks "contain systematically written instructions (exercises, prescriptions, questions, tasks) for a specific topic in prepackaged forms, sheets, or handouts to be completed by respondents either in writing or through talk and nonverbal communication" (L'Abate, 2004, p. 3). They can be used on their own or as an adjunct to therapy. Depending on the severity of the presenting problem, clients may be given, mailed, or suggested to purchase the therapeutic workbook and then given a schedule for moving through the book.

There are multiple pathways through which workbooks are effective (Pennebaker, 2004). They help to translate experiences into words. That is, when people write something out, they are better able to understand the phenomenon in that they thought about the issue and how they wanted to put that into words. By utilizing a workbook, people engage in story creation where their experience becomes organized into a greater narrative. Depending on the type of workbook, people are usually able to engage their thought processes and patterns differently. The frequent and consistent use of a workbook helps to train people in thinking differently. When doing this, people can engage in emotional venting where they acknowledge their emotions and find that they gain some type of emotional relief. Putting their emotions and thoughts on paper in the workbook tends to lead people to have a different perspective on them. They may gain a greater sense of control because their situation feels less overwhelming. By writing in a workbook, people tend to perseverate less on the issues they are writing about. This will then free their working memory, allowing them more space to focus on other aspects of their lives such as being with others. Lastly, since workbooks are to be "worked" frequently, they serve as a reminder about change. Having to engage the workbook on a set schedule (say every day or every other day), people keep the idea of change in the foreground of their thinking as they actively make changes in how they think and behave.

Workbooks are useful for a variety of clientele, in a variety of contexts, and by a variety of professional helpers using a variety of treatment modalities (L'Abate, 2004). Clients dealing with depression, communication issues, eating disorders, couples' problems, substance abuse, trauma and abuse, dementia, and a cornucopia of other presenting problems find the use of workbooks to help them deal with their current issues. You might use workbooks if you work in an agency, institution, or private practice. You might also use them whether you are a clinical psychologist, mental health counselor, marriage and family therapist, or any other helping professional. And you might use workbooks if you operate from a cognitive-behavioral, humanistic, psychodynamic, or most any other theoretical model.

The use of workbooks may have some advantages over standard talk therapy as well as manuals and self-help books. These advantages include specificity, explicitness, interactivity, versatility, cost-effectiveness, and verifiability (L'Abate, 2004). Workbooks are specific in that they deal only with the specific topic that they are dealing with. A depression workbook focuses on aspects of depression rather than substance abuse or communication. Explicitness in workbooks occurs because the questions and tasks presented are quite clear in what they are demanding of the client. A well-written workbook reduces potential confusion. Interactivity happens as the client actively engages the material. Further, workbooks are versatile. They can be used on their own or in conjunction with other types of methods (e.g., talk therapy, app usage, online therapy). Workbooks are also cost-effective. Whereas a face-to-face private practice session may cost $100, $200, or even $300 per session, brand-new workbooks probably average around $20. This makes therapeutic change more accessible for a wider array of clients. Further, given some clients' hesitancy to going to a therapist, for either shame, finances, or transportation issues, workbooks can be delivered to one's house, avoiding these potential blocks to accessing therapy. Lastly, workbooks are verifiable in that, since they are in written format, they can be reproduced.

While there are many advantages to workbooks, there are also some disadvantages. If you did not write the workbook, you must check it to ensure that whoever authored it did a good job. A poorly written workbook that is poorly developed may not be useful for the client. Further, the onus of engagement is on the client rather than therapist. It is up to the client to keep motivated and work on the workbook on their schedule. They also may have questions or misunderstandings that cannot be immediately remedied by your clarifications. In order to remedy these disadvantages, the therapist can check in each session on the client's progress with the workbook. If something was not completed, the therapist can explore what prevented the client from using the workbook. For example, if the client did not understand something, the therapist can clarify it in the session and the client can complete it in the following week. While these are potential disadvantages, the benefits of using workbooks far outweigh them.

There are hundreds of different therapeutic workbooks—far too many for us to talk about here. It will be up to you to explore some of them, particularly those that address issues you have more expertise in. Then you will have to determine whether and which workbook may be useful for which client. Not all clients will want to engage with a workbook. Perhaps the best thing to do is to offer it as a possibility to the client and see what their response is to the suggestion. If you believe the workbook will be quite useful, you can recommend the client to use it. However, clients always have autonomy in what type of treatment they want.

Genograms

The documents that have been presented so far in this chapter have mainly been written and created for the purpose of the client. The final document we will talk about is primarily written and kept by the therapist; however, you could always give a copy to the client. That document is a genogram.

Genograms are a multi-generational diagram of the family similar to a family tree. They are used to give therapists a wider understanding of a client's historical and familial context. Genograms usually cover three generations; thus, your client's genogram would include them, their parents and siblings, and their grandparents. Also included would be their children (if they have any), and, depending on how in-depth you wanted the genogram, it could include aunts, uncles, cousins, and potentially great-grandparents.

Genograms allow therapists to visually see who is in the family but, more importantly, to understand family patterns that have occurred over generations. McGoldrick et al. (1999) explained, "For a clinical record, the genogram provides an efficient summary, allowing a clinician unfamiliar with a case to grasp quickly a large amount of information about a family and to have a view of potential problems" (p. 1). In essence, the genogram is a snapshot of the history of a client's family.

When introducing the production of a genogram to a client, you might begin by explaining its purpose with something such as, "It is usually helpful for me to get a full understanding of what is going on for you. To do so, I would like to create a family tree." Genograms require the therapist to note a lot of information so the therapist will want to inform the client they will be taking notes and drawing the diagram during the session.

While you can use whatever symbols you would like to create genograms in your sessions, there are some standard symbols, with males being represented by squares and females by circles. Transfemales are usually notated with a square within a circle while transmales are represented by a circle within a square. Some of the common information that therapists put on genograms include people's name, sex, sexual orientation, age, and whether they are deceased (and if so, what age they were when they died and perhaps what the cause of death was).

Usually, therapists begin the construction of the genogram with the client in the room. If working with a family, probably starting with the couple, then documenting their children, and then going back to the couple's parents, siblings, and grandparents would make sense. One of the things that genograms are primarily used for is to explore the relationships between people. Besides whether two people are married, separated, or divorced, genograms tend to depict how close or distant people are and whether they get along well or have a conflictual relationship (Kerr & Bowen, 1988). This is depicted by drawing different kinds of lines between each family member. Standard relational lines include a single straight line to depict a good relationship, double straight lines to depict a close relationship, triple straight lines to depict a fused relationship, a dashed line to depict a distant relationship, a zig-zag line to depict a hostile relationship, and a straight line with a break in the middle to depict a cut-off relationship. There are additional relational lines but these tend to be the most common ones. See Figure 9.13 for an example of a genogram.

Once a client starts to describe relationships among family members in the genogram, the therapist will connect these family members on the genograms with the different types of relationship lines mentioned above. These lines will start to form triangles among family members. These triangles represent a way the system tries to maintain stability amongst chronic anxiety (Kerr & Bowen, 1988). It can reveal who is in conflict with one another, whom people turn to when they are in conflict with someone else, and how anxiety and stress are managed overall. Patterns will be revealed. The client might gain insight into how everyone in their family cuts people off when they do not get along. This realization may allow the client to change that response for themselves, therefore, creating a new pattern in the family system.

Standard practice is to have the male of the couple on the left with the female on the right. However, in same-sex relationships which side they are on does not matter. While most people tend to organize the location of a couple based on gender, others do it based on age where the older person in the couple is drawn on the left and the younger partner on the right. For children, they are drawn chronologically, going from left to right, from oldest to youngest. This helps to depict sibling position, as Kerr and Bowen (1988) believed birth order played an important role in people's roles and functions in the family system. Older siblings tend to

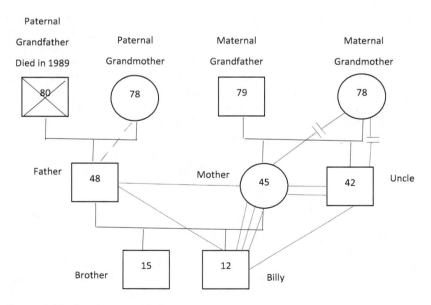

Figure 9.13 Genogram of Billy.

be more responsible, controlling, reliable, and motivated. Middle siblings tend to feel left out, be more social, adapt easier, and are seen as the go-between person. Last-born children are viewed as uncomplicated, attention-seeking, outgoing, and manipulative. While a person's actual position refers to the person's actual order and the role they were born into, functional position refers to a person's actual function as that sibling position role. For example, a person can be the firstborn but function more as a last-born child acting in ways that are attention-seeking or manipulative.

While it is important to include racial, cultural, ethnic, and social class factors on a client's genogram, as these play a significant role in the individual and family's functioning, most genograms highlight family patterns in general. Before working with clients, you might consider developing your own genogram, specifically a cultural genogram, as its development will help you understand your cultural identity so that you can gain cultural awareness and sensitivity (Hardy & Laszloffy, 1995). The cultural genogram adds an additional layer to a genogram, including exploring the person's culture of origin—the major group(s) the person is descended from. Additional symbols are used that help to elucidate the pride and shame issues the individual has encountered from their cultural affiliations. These symbols are presented in the cultural framework chart; for instance, a symbol related to interracial marriage involves color coding (e.g., someone might use red when depicting anything from their Jewish heritage and blue for their Irish ancestry). The symbols or colors help to show patterns in the family system related to culture. This can also lead to a deeper exploration of identity involving all the factors mentioned above.

We often think we know our families very well but once we see these depictions on paper we open up a new way of viewing our family system and the patterns we engage in. Knowing our own history, patterns, and beliefs can help us manage those in the therapy room with our clients that come with similar or different backgrounds and histories from us. It is also important to note that a genogram is an ever-changing document. As new family members are born, family members pass away, and relationships change, the genogram will change. What we understood about our family at one moment in time may be very different from the family dynamic at a later point in time.

While genograms are mainly created to help the therapist better understand the client and their family system and patterns, genograms can be shared with the client as well. Sharing this document with our clients can serve as a reminder as to where they come from, who they belong to or are connected to, and their previous ways of responding and interacting. When a client goes to engage with a family member, they can reflect on the genogram and choose to engage in a different way to hopefully create new patterns of interaction that will help strengthen the family system. If they understand how the genogram is created, they can also continue to develop their genogram once therapy has ended. This allows the client to use the genogram as a tool to continue to understand their family over time or as things change, and to continue the progress they have made from therapy.

Final Considerations

The use of any of these documents can be quite beneficial, depending on the situation, the client, and the context. Each client is unique and holds autonomy for their therapeutic process. A document we use with one client may not be effective with another client. Having this vast array of counter-documents at our disposal allows us to assess each client's needs and utilize the document/s we deem most helpful.

Before you give the client any of these types of documents to take home, ask the client if they would like to take it with them (Cooper, 2018). This could be important for some clients who may not be able to keep the document private. If they happened to be in an unsafe environment, taking home the document could put the client in jeopardy. However, luckily, most clients can safely take any documents that you create home with them. Also, now with smartphones, clients can take a picture of the document with hopes of greater privacy. Further, almost all clients, at least in our experience, are extremely grateful and appreciative to not only receive the document but also be able to take it with them.

If clients decide to take the document home with them, it is beneficial to make a copy of the document to place in the client's file. This follows good documentation protocol but also allows you to provide copies to the client in case they lose the original document they took home. In addition, it lets the therapist review the information from the document in preparation for future sessions or to recap any progress made.

When giving clients documents, to further help ensure privacy, it is best to keep any information that may identify you as the therapist or place of therapy to a minimum. For example, ensuring the document is not printed on a letterhead that clearly identifies a mental health facility may help a client who does not want anyone to know they are in therapy or where they go to therapy feel more comfortable with taking the document home with them. How a therapist signs a document may further aid in the client's comfortability. Sometimes it may be appropriate to sign a document as "Your therapist" and other times it may be appropriate to only sign your name. This will depend case by case on your best clinical judgment. If the client mentions they do not want to take the document home due to the labels, headings, or signatures, you can offer to change or omit the information so the client feels more comfortable.

Taking home the document has many potential benefits. Many of these benefits have been discussed earlier throughout this chapter. During session, you might consult the client for them to think about the meaning of the document for them and how they might get the most out of it. Cooper (2018) provided some questions that you might ask clients to make the most out of these documents:

- How many copies would you like to take with you?
- Where would it be useful to keep this document?
- When would be a useful time to read/review your document so that it has the most influence?
- What difference will it make to have this with you when you leave?
- What might it make possible for you as you are continually reminded of this information?
- What will this remind you about who you are becoming that the problem would want to blind you from?

(p. 266)

Hopefully, these guidelines and suggestions will help you and your client utilize documents to their utmost possibilities.

Summary

This chapter highlighted many different types of documents and counter-documents that can be used with clients such as awards, certificates, cards, lists, worksheets, workbooks, and genograms. Each of these can be used by any clinician regardless of their theoretical orientation and model. They can be in-depth and complex or very simple and straightforward.

As discussed, there are many benefits to using documents and counter-documents in the therapeutic process. They can help the client highlight achievements and successes, remember skills learned, celebrate big and small accomplishments, shift patterns of negativity, and reinforce new and more desired identities. Using these documents allows the client to develop a more resourceful identity instead of the limited identity they may have formed from documents acquired from life experiences that paint a negative picture of them.

The different types of documents tend to emphasize the client's voice and often the creation of a document can be a collaborative process between the therapist and the client. Documents and counter-documents can be created by the therapist, in session with the client, or at home by the client. Providing a document to a client extends the therapeutic session beyond the office. It allows the client to look back on things learned and accomplished and can help the client continue to develop a different perspective, a better understanding of themselves or the problem, and a deeper exploration of identity. Overall, the goal is to help reinforce the client's new and more desired identities.

References

Chen, M., Noosbond, J. P., & Bruce, M. A. (1998). Therapeutic document in group counseling: An active change agent. *Journal of Counseling & Development, 76*(4), 36–43.

Cooper, S. (2018). Co-crafting take-home documents at the walk-in. In M. F. Hoyt, M. Bobele. A. Slive, J. Young, & M. Talmon (Eds.), *Single-session therapy by walk-in or appointment* (pp. 260–269). Routledge.

Dankoski, M. E. (1998). Gratitude lists. In L. L. Hecker, S. A. Deacon, and Associates (Eds.), *The therapist's notebook: Homework, handouts, and activities for use in psychotherapy* (pp. 147–149). Haworth.

Deacon, S. A. (1998). Greeting card messages: Reading between the lines. In L. L. Hecker, S. A. Deacon, and Associates (Eds.), *The therapist's notebook: Homework, handouts, and activities for use in psychotherapy* (pp. 333–334). Haworth.

de Shazer, S. (1985). *Keys to solution in brief therapy.* Norton.

Fox, H. (2003). Using therapeutic documents: A review. *The International Journal of Narrative Therapy and Community Work, 4*, 26–36.

Freedman, J., & Combs, G. (1996). *Narrative therapy: The social construction of preferred realities.* Norton.

Hahs, A. (2008). Cards as therapeutic documents. *The International Journal of Narrative Therapy and Community Work, 1*, 30–33.

Hardy, K. V., & Laszloffy, T. A. (1995). The cultural genogram: Key to training culturally competent family therapists. *Journal of Marital and Family Therapy, 21*(3), 227–237.

Kerr, M. E., & Bowen, M. (1988). *Family evaluation: An approach based on Bowen theory.* W. W. Norton & Co.

L'Abate, L. (2004). The role of workbooks in the delivery of mental health services in prevention, psychotherapy, and rehabilitation. In L. L'Abate (Ed.), *Using workbooks in mental health* (pp. 1–64). Hawthorn Reference Press.

McGoldrick, M., Gerson, R., & Shellenberger, S. (1999). *Genograms: Assessment and intervention* (2nd ed.). Norton.

Pennebaker, J. W. (2004). Foreword. In L. L'Abate (Ed.), *Using workbooks in mental health* (pp. xix–xxii). Hawthorn Reference Press.

Reiter, M. D., Jung, W. F., Popham, J., Fitzgerald, C., Garcia, E., de Perez, M. G., Lockhart, T., & Villanueva, N. (2020). Training through naming: A process of psychotherapist skill developing utilizing recursive frame analysis. *The Qualitative Report, 25*(8), 2085–2099.

White, M., & Epston, D. (1990). *Narrative means to therapeutic ends.* Norton.

Chapter 10

Writing in Psychotherapy via Technology

Michael D. Reiter and Natalie Rothman

Therapists have been utilizing technology in their psychotherapy practice since technology has been available. In the 21st century, the current technology is quite different than when psychotherapy began over 100 years ago. Computers, smartphones, virtual reality, and videoconferencing are means of communicating that were probably not imaginable when Freud was sitting in his office looking at the client on his couch. Fifty years ago, psychotherapists incorporated state-of-the-art technology such as reel-to-reel recordings. For most of the history of our field, the technology we could use was more auditory. For instance, with the technology of the telephone, therapists began to provide contact and therapeutic services over the phone. When the internet became popularized in the 1980s, creative therapists began to use computers as a part of their practice.

In this chapter, we talk about how therapists utilize technology—specifically those technologies in which the written word is used. In 2020, with the beginning of the COVID pandemic, most therapists shifted from seeing clients face-to-face to alternative means so that they could continue providing services. Many therapists utilized video conferencing platforms, where therapist and client could see and hear each other, but were situated in separate locations. We will not be talking about this type of use of technology as it is auditory and visual. Rather, we will explore how therapists utilize their phones and computers to contact clients. This includes the use of text messages, emails, and online chats.

The use of technology is extremely beneficial for many people. We have become reliant on the connection that technology provides us. Today, most people across the globe have a smartphone. We have moved from primarily talking face-to-face with one another—or at least on the phone—to texting one another or posting statements and updates on social media. Technology allows people in very disparate locations to be connected at the touch of a button (or a few buttons on the keyboard). You can be in North America and almost instantaneously communicate with someone in Asia. Additionally, the US federal government has indicated the beneficial nature of smartphone technology which is displayed

DOI: 10.4324/9781003294702-10

through the LifeLine Program (USAC Lifeline Support, 2022), a federal program designed to provide phone and internet services at affordable costs for those who meet the income poverty guidelines. Essentially, this form of technological connection can be quite economical. Besides the price of the smartphone or computer (and the internet package), you can communicate with others through technology as much as you want for very little money.

Technology also helps to provide access to information. Think about the last time you didn't know the answer to something. What was your first thought? It might have been, "I need to Google that." You typed in a query and received a plethora of websites that you could peruse to gain the answer. As easy as it is to get an answer to your inquiry, it is important to keep in mind that not all answers found through a Google Search come from credible sources.

While most people across the globe are intimately connected to technology, traditionally therapy has been technology limited. For most of our profession, therapist and client have met face-to-face in the same room and talked with one another. Engaging with clients outside of this standardized method of service delivery was more of an anomaly than a universal form of therapy. Yet, within the last 20 years, technology has been increasing in its usage in psychotherapy. For example, therapeutic services are now available through videoconferencing, emails, text messages, websites, chat functions, and computer-assisted interventions. The various technologies have opened pathways for telehealth communications, which have led to the discovery of several benefits for the mental health field, such as removing structural and psychological barriers for clients and therapists. Technology has enhanced therapy services as the mental health field transitions to be more flexible and, most importantly, convenient for all populations.

One of the first benefits of this transition is that the more contact is made electronically, the less the client must travel to the clinic. This can be extremely useful to clients who may not have the time to go to therapy because of having to work and/or take care of family. Further, it is useful for those clients who are infirm and cannot easily leave the house or live in an area where mental health services are not easily attainable.

The use of technology as a significant modality of therapy helps to increase equity as those who may not have been able to gain services are more able to. Instead of maybe needing to take a train, bus, taxi, rideshare, or walk, clients can engage in services from the comfort of their own homes. However, not all clients have access to the internet or smartphones. When using technology with clients it is important to find out from them what type of access they have so that if you do use technology, you can do so in a way that fits with their abilities and usage.

Besides these benefits for clients, they also hold for therapists. Today, if you want, you can engage in the therapy process from a work office, a home office, the beach, while you travel, or anywhere you have access to the internet. Depending on where you live, the incorporation of technology in your therapy practice also reduces your commute time. If you work from your home, you will have an extra hour or two to do what you want: exercise, sleep, eat, watch TV, or maybe even work with an additional client whom you didn't have time for previously.

Second, exchanges made electronically may decrease the possibility of the stigma of therapy. The client will not have to come to the therapist's office and potentially be seen by others walking into or out of the office or sitting in the waiting room. Or conversely, if home-based therapy were occurring, no therapist is showing up at the client's house. Rather, from the safety of their own home, a more private conversation happens between the client and the therapist. For many people who still have some internal stigma or perceive social stigma against counseling, having interactions with therapists through technology may break a few of these barriers.

A third benefit of the use of technology in psychotherapy is that treatment can occur at a different time frame than traditional psychotherapy. Sessions may be of a shorter duration than the standard one hour (or 45 minutes that is allowed by managed care) but may occur more frequently (Fairburn & Patel, 2017). This results in the overall treatment length being shorter when digital technology is utilized. The one-hour once-a-week therapy that has become the norm is an arbitrary designation. One hour works well in appointment calendars. However, it may not be an appropriate time frame for all clients. For instance, it may be way too long for young children. However, it is likely too short for the group format. One hour is also not enough time when doing an in-depth and immersive experience such as marathon sessions (Reiter, 2010). Based on the technology being used, clients may be able to engage in therapeutic interventions/sessions/lessons whenever they want. If they can't sleep at 3 in the morning, they can go online or access an application on their smartphone and engage in treatment.

Lastly, technology in psychotherapy provides a range of possible delivery systems (Fairburn & Patel, 2017) instead of the common face-to-face format that almost all of us were trained in and that most of society visualizes when they think of what psychotherapy looks like. With technology, clients can engage in treatment autonomously, where they engage the content of a problem (either via a website or an app) on their own without any support or contact from a therapist. They can also utilize an online therapy program that does have human support available but not by a trained psychotherapist. Clients can engage in blended treatment where they use technological interventions under the supervision of a clinician.

Finally, they can receive therapy from a therapist who incorporates technological interventions. These options provide the client the ability to contact and utilize psychotherapy interventions in ways that best fit their current circumstances and finances (as autonomous treatment will be the most cost-effective).

Online Therapy

Online therapy, also known as **cybercounseling** and, more recently, **tele-mental health**, has been a part of our field for over 30 years. Instead of the therapist and client meeting in person, interaction happens through a computer-based medium. As technology expands, online therapy has been able to take a wider range of forms, such as emails, chats, text messages, and computer-assisted interventions. The recent rise in popularity of these services can be attributed to the COVID-19 pandemic. There was a large-scale need for mental health services at a time when individuals were unable to physically be in a room together for fear of their lives.

Online therapy provides a unique and innovative atmosphere when working with clients. Suler (2005), in an article titled *The Online Disinhibition Effect*, suggests that in online interactions people seem to be more uninhibited compared to face-to-face interactions. This phenomenon is attributed to the following seven factors:

1   Dissociative Anonymity
2   Invisibility
3   Asynchronicity
4   Solipsistic Introjection
5   Dissociative Imagination
6   Attenuated Status and Authority
7   Individual Differences

Dissociative anonymity refers to the concept of online identity as being discrete. Usernames, emails, and social media handles are all personally created and customizable. Therefore, anonymity is easily obtainable as these identifiers do not reveal your true self. When people feel distant from their online persona, they are more inclined to self-disclose or act out.

Invisibility connects with the concept of not physically being able to see the person on the other end of the communication. When people do not have to view the physical attributes and body language of others, they feel less inhibited. This is an innate characteristic of online therapies.

Asynchronicity occurs when two people communicate at different times. Here, you will send a message to the client who later reads it and then responds. You will then later read their response to you. The idea here is being able to send an emotionally charged communication while creating space for the sender and processing time for the receiver. Emails and text messages are forms of asynchronous communication.

We also have a way of utilizing technology in real-time interactions. This is known as **synchronous communication** which occurs when both people on either end of the interaction are doing so simultaneously. That is, you are in your office on a device talking and/or writing to the client who is on their device at the same time. Videoconferencing and telephone conversations are done synchronously.

It is important to note that individual differences play a significant role in how Suler's Online Disinhibition Effect impacts them. Throughout this chapter, you will encounter this as it applies to emails, chats, text messages, and computer-based interventions. As you read along in the following sections focus on various uses of online therapy and pay attention to how these factors are being displayed.

Emails

The first form of **email** was introduced in the 1960s via the Massachusetts Institute of Technology; however, messages could only be sent to people using the same computer. In 1971, Ray Tomlinson invented networked email, where people could send messages to one another on different computers. Since then, emails have become a primary mode of interpersonal communication. More than 4 billion people around the world—over 50% of the world's population—use email for personal and professional reasons.

The most common form of technology that psychotherapists engage in is email. Therapists use email for a variety of purposes. They might contact other professionals or refer sources to promote themselves, provide updates on clients, or request information. They also use emails to contact clients. The brunt of this section will focus primarily on your potential use of email with clients.

First, you might email clients regarding appointments. While one means of responding to clients or providing an appointment reminder is through the telephone, you might also use emails. Emails can be useful because you can send them at any time and not have to worry about inconveniencing the client (i.e., calling early in the morning, while the client is working, or late at night). Further, if the client did not answer the phone, sometimes their message box is full, and you won't be able to leave a message. There is not that same worry with emails. However, the concern is that you have the correct email address for the client. We highly recommend that if you plan on contacting clients via email you confirm with them the email address to which they want you to send messages. You should also have a conversation with them about online content safety and confidentiality.

The second use of emails with clients is for actual therapeutic purposes. We can do therapy fully via email; however, this is rare. Face-to-face meetings are still the dominant modality. For those therapists who use email only in therapy, there are some potential advantages (Murphy & Mitchell, 1998). One of those advantages is meeting the client where they are at. Meaning, sometimes people can better communicate their feelings when thinking about the words they are choosing to use when writing an email, rather than expressing themselves directly to another person. Email therapy also slows down the process of responding as clients are developing a written articulation of their experiences. In turn, this also shifts the processing of the information being discussed. Since everything discussed between the client and the therapist occurs via writing in emails, the whole therapeutic process is documented. Thus, there is a permanent record of what transpired.

This also helps supervisors who can read and see what was actually said in therapy rather than having the therapist summarize what they think happened. An additional supervisory benefit is that therapists can write a potential email to a client and go over it with their supervisor (or colleague) before sending it. This slowing down of responses where you don't have the client sitting across from you waiting for a response allows you to calm down, think about what you want to say, and then take time to compose the email, using the most appropriate and descriptive language to convey the message to your client. The benefit for clients here is that they can more easily point out aspects of what the therapist said that they either agree or disagree with, which puts them in a more honored position.

You will be using emails in your practice, so let's discuss some common considerations to keep in mind. Whether you are just emailing the client for a one-time message or are engaging in email therapy, this medium has a few issues that you should consider (Gutheil & Simon, 2005). Emails lack nonverbal cues. In face-to-face therapy, we use paralanguage whenever we communicate with someone. This includes our voice tone, volume, and quality, as well as our facial expressions and body gestures. All of these are missing in emails. This leads to a potential coldness when conversing via text-based methods. Because we are not able to send our nonverbal cues (we will talk about emoticons later) and are not able to receive the client's nonverbal cues, there is a serious potential for misunderstanding. Usually, when talking with someone, we can gauge, in the moment, how the other person is reacting to us. This allows us to adapt either the mode in which we are conveying information or the content of that information. The same does not happen when communicating through email. Thus, there is a lack of control as the client is reading your email at a time and place that you don't know and which they may not be in a good mental or emotional space to receive. For example, a client may be checking their email at a time when they may not be receptive to the contents of the message or when they are in line at Starbucks. It is these types of situations that make email therapy a bit more difficult to navigate regarding the therapeutic relationship with the client.

When utilizing email as the primary modality of therapy, there are different aspects of developing the therapeutic relationship than there are in face-to-face meetings. Traditionally, therapists join with clients through their demeanor as well as what they talk about. The time you take to walk with the client from the waiting room to your office is usually spent in small talk. However, that talk is also the beginning of your connection with your client. Your aura, presence, and visual and auditory engagement are signals to the client that you are beginning to make an investment in them and the therapeutic relationship. Therapy via email is quite useful for providing information; however, it is quite difficult to develop a therapeutic space (Murphy et al., 2008).

In the online environment, particularly when making contact via email, the initial connection becomes much more difficult. We don't have the variety of tools that we have in face-to-face interactions. The normal repertoire of nonverbal communicational tools is not available for us, such as our smile, a warm voice, and engaging eye contact. Via email, we have just the letters on the page.

When we think about whom we might use email therapy with, we can think about various populations that might be difficult to navigate when joining face-to-face. One such population is adolescents. Adolescents tend to utilize the internet at higher rates than any other age group. This can be attributed to the noted perceived anonymity of communicating online (Suler, 2005). Not speaking directly to an individual may contribute to an overall level of comfortability for adolescents as the assumed judgment is removed. The previously stated limitation of the absence of body language in text-based therapies is the identified strength when working with the adolescent population via text-based therapies. With the removal of nonverbal cues, adolescents may feel less inhibited because the preconceived assumed judgment from the therapist is removed. Disinhibition provides adolescents with a sense of control regarding the information they may share, which may also be impacted by the rate at which a response is expected.

Like therapeutic letters, using emails in therapy allows both therapist and client to take time in thinking about what they want to say and then compose their thoughts in a manner that describes their experience. Further, once their own or the other person's thoughts are put into an email, both parties can go back and reread what was written. This provides another opportunity to expand the scope of therapy so that it can happen more than just one specific time. This is like studying for an exam. Most people do much better in retaining and understanding the material (and thus better on an exam) when they frequently engage with the information rather than trying to do one cram session.

Typically, therapy has been a localized event that only takes place in the therapy room. While the number of sessions per week, and the duration of each session, depends on the context, most therapy happens in a prescribed time. For most outpatient therapy, this is usually one time per week for one hour. Inpatient therapy tends to happen every day (with perhaps the exclusion of a day or two on the weekend), with multiple sessions per day where the residential client has many hours of therapy per day. For the typical client, one hour per week may not be enough. One thing you can think about is what happens for the client for the remaining 167 hours of that week. The more that you can have them focus on the treatment goals of therapy, the more likely they will engage in the skills and behaviors that therapy is targeting. Utilizing semi-frequent emails is one way to help enhance the amount of contact the client is encountering the therapeutic ideas.

When in front of your client, you can adjust your therapy based on the client's immediate reactions and feedback. If you see that they are extremely emotional, you may not push and challenge them as much. If you see that they are not engaged, you might raise the intensity. However, you do not have these same cues when you are working through emails. You might talk with your client early in the therapy about suggestions for when they might read and/or write the emails that you send back and forth. The structure of email therapy should be established in the initial email communications when developing the therapeutic relationship with the client. Implementing a clear structure from the beginning of services will establish the foundation of how future emails are interpreted. One way of trying to ensure that your email is read in a way that becomes meaningful to the client is to think about your sentence construction and pacing (Murphy et al., 2008). You do not need to write in full sentences which are constructed into paragraphs. Just like reading this chapter—sentence after sentence, paragraph after paragraph—might at some point become monotonous (we are hoping not!), the same could happen when you write your client an email.

Think about the different ways that you can write the following sentence in an email that will draw the reader's focus:

What do you really want to do?

This could be written like it is above, which is fine dependent on the context of where it is in the email, how many other sentences are around it, etc. You could also write it like:

What.
Do You.
Really.
Want.
To Do?

If you were talking, you would be able to use vocalics such as volume and pitch. When writing, you can emphasize certain words based on capitalization, bold, italics, and underlining. Here is that same sentence using each of these opportunities:

What do YOU really want to Do?
WHAT do you really want to do?
What do you REALLY want to do?
What do you really want to **do**?
What *do you* really want *to do*?
What do you really want to do?

Or you can combine all these various modalities to get the client to read your message in the way that you intended.

WHAT do **you** really want to **DO**?

We have provided several of the advantageous aspects of exchanging emails with clients. It has become a tool and/or a format of psychotherapy that was not available at the beginning of our field. It has opened avenues and possibilities that can be quite significant in the enhanced treatment of our clients. However, there are also some potential pitfalls. These can be classified as confidentiality, technical, and relationship (Roy & Gillett, 2008).

One of the biggest potential pitfalls of email therapy is related to confidentiality and unwanted disclosures. At the beginning of therapy, perhaps in the informed consent, you might inform the client of strategies for keeping the emails protected. This can include only using an email that the client has sole access to, sending the email as an attachment that is password protected, only sending an email to the client and not to multiple participants (where they might see each other's names and/or email addresses), and not putting identifying information in the header of the email. If you are like us, you have accidentally sent an email to the wrong person or hit "reply all" when you only wanted to send the email to the original sender. While it is quite embarrassing to do so, when this happens in the therapeutic context, you risk ethical violations.

The Health Insurance Portability and Accountability Act (HIPAA), regulated by the U.S. federal government, is the national model for how protected health information is managed. This policy was established to protect individuals' private health information from being disclosed to other systems without permission from the person. HIPAA has established regulations on how to maintain confidentiality within a technologically based world. One guideline for maintaining HIPAA compliance within email therapy is to make sure you are sending email from a secure internet connection, rather than a public WIFI connection that you connect to at Starbucks or Dunkin' Donuts (we don't discriminate)! Another guideline is to utilize an encrypted email system. For example, your current Gmail email address would not be sufficient, because you would be responsible to pay a third party to maintain the encryption services. It is important to note that most free email platforms are not encrypted. Additionally, clients may authorize you to use a less secure form of email communication. If you choose this route, be sure to have additional documentation noting your clients' consent to this form of communication.

As discussed previously, emails are an asynchronous form of communication where the sender and receiver are reading and writing at different times (Suler, 2005). This can lead to a couple of technical pitfalls including communication disruptions and slow typing speed. When you send an email you do not know when the client will read it, or even if they received it. To offset this, you can set the preferences of your email so that you are notified when the email was delivered and when it was read. This way you can monitor the flow of the email exchange. A further technical issue is about how fast you type. Email therapy is usually easier—at least for time demands—for those therapists who are quick with their fingers. The more that you type, the better you will get at the skill of typing. If you are planning on engaging in email therapy, we recommend that you practice your typing skills, perhaps through an online typing skills program or on your own.

You should also develop a strategy for storing your emails. Not only should this email be password protected, but you should also be the only individual accessing this email. When using email therapy, you must establish a functional organization system to ensure you are not breaking confidentiality by sending the wrong message to the wrong client.

Email therapy may also lead to potential difficulties in the therapeutic relationship. In face-to-face therapy, we meet with our clients (usually) on a certain day and time for a prescribed length of time. The same may not be the case for email therapy. While you may arrange with the client when you would like them to email you and when you will email them, this does not prevent them from emailing whenever they wish. Some clients may send an excessive number of emails. If they do and you have planned when to email, a reminder would be in order. If you hadn't, then developing an agreement or timetable for communication will help to set the boundaries between the two of you.

The potentials of boundary issues when you contact a client via email "include inappropriate self-disclosure, inappropriate language (such as seductive content), breaches of confidentiality of the recipient patient or other patients, and billing issues (if e-mail contact is not billed, is it a social letter?)" (Gutheil & Simon, 2005, p. 954). Further, similar to a client overstaying the time of a session, emails may be an attempt by the client to extend the sessions. As previously mentioned, it is important to establish this structure of therapy in the initial emails.

Another potential problem of email therapy is that of overfamiliarity. People have become more informal in their exchanges when using technology. This issue of overfamiliarity is even more prominent when we engage in chats or text messages with our clients, as these forms of communication tend to be shorter, without greetings and salutations. A recommendation is for you to ensure that, at least on your end, you maintain a formality in your sent emails. This would include writing the client's name at the beginning of the email, using full sentences with proper punctuation, and having a closing salutation ending with your name. Figure 10.1 presents a sample of a therapist's email to their client that attempts to fulfill the suggestions and guidelines we've presented.

Emails are used by therapists regardless of theoretical orientation. While the intent and content may differ, there is likely quite a lot of overlap. For instance, Paxling et al. (2013) analyzed the email correspondence of cognitive-behavioral therapists working with clients dealing with generalized anxiety disorder. They were able to distinguish eight therapist behaviors: empathetic utterances, task prompting, psychoeducation, deadline flexibility, task reinforcement, alliance bolstering, self-efficacy shaping, and self-disclosure. There would be different behaviors for therapists from a different orientation. Regardless, your email therapy should be consistent with your theoretical model. And your therapy model needs to come through in how you write to your client. When you email your client, you should be as vigilant and thoughtful with what, when, and how you email as you do when you provide vocal communications during face-to-face sessions. What you write in an email will have an impact on the client, and you should attempt to utilize emails for the most therapeutic purposes you can.

Usually, when we email someone important information, we expect some type of response. So, how often must you check to see if a client has emailed you? The answer is dependent on what your agreement is with your client. Depending on how you will be using email with clients, it is important that you are upfront and clear about the use of emails and the frequency of reading and responding. For instance, you may let them know that you do not check your emails over the weekends or past 6 pm at night.

Establishing these ground rules early on provides a solid foundation for which to grow the therapeutic rapport. Being clear about expectations

From: CLIENT NAME <CLIENT'S EMAIL ADDRESS>
Date: DAY, DATE, AND TIME STAMP (I.E. Monday, June 26, 2023, at 3:39 PM)
To: THERAPIST'S NAME <EMAIL ADDRESS>
Subject: RE: MUTUALLY AGREED UPON NAMING CONVENTION

Hi there,

Happy Monday, I hope you had a great weekend. My apologies there was a delay in my response, this has been a very busy week. I realize this is only my second correspondence this week, our previous correspondence was on Wednesday. A lot has happened in the last few days, let me catch you up. This weekend was the trunk-or-treat event, and we carved pumpkins. It was such a busy weekend; I again did not have time for myself or to complete the "homework" I was supposed to do. After reflecting on this past weekend, I can see what you said about the fact that I always put the needs of others in front of my own.

I have to say, you had me thinking when you asked what my ideal self would look like or how would I know when I reached that point. I can honestly say, no one has ever asked me that question. I think that the best version of me would just be happy and content with her life and feel gratitude.

Thanks,

CLIENT NAME

From: THERAPIST'S NAME <EMAIL ADDRESS>
Date: DAY, DATE, AND TIME STAMP (I.E. Wednesday, June 28, 2023, at 10:42 AM)
To: CLIENT NAME <CLIENT'S EMAIL ADDRESS>
Subject: RE: MUTUALLY AGREED UPON NAMING CONVENTION

Good morning (or afternoon),

I hope you are having a good week and thank you for your response. How is your week going, still busy? Were you able to make some time for your morning meditations? You mentioned in your email on Monday that you were unable to do the homework. Would it be easier if we attempted less of a commitment? Would taking two mornings this week to complete your 10-minute guided meditation be more realistic? You know what, before we discuss further some behavioral changes, I have a weird question for you, but would appreciate it if you took a minute to think and then respond. Let's say you go to bed tonight and life is as is, however, when you wake up in the morning you are your ideal self; happy and content with life as well as feeling the warmth of gratitude, what would be different? What would your day look like? Walk me through it.

Once you have thought about what your ideal day and what your happy self would look like, take a moment and jot down a few things that you would have to change to achieve your best self.

Respectfully,

THERAPIST NAME AND CREDENTIALS
Primary Therapist
NAME OF PRIVATE PRACTICE/AGENCY
ADDRESS
Phone: 555-555-5555
Email: THERAPIST EMAIL ADDRESS

Figure 10.1 Sample of Email Correspondence between Therapist and Client Engaging in Online Therapy.

with your clients in this technical age goes beyond emails. Emails are just one form of technological communication you may have with your clients. Text-based chats are on the rise!

Chats

Chatting online with clients is another technological advancement in the mental health field. Where most text-based communications would fall under the asynchronous category, online **chats** offer a synchronous component of texting back and forth with a mental health provider in real time. In other words, this type of communication appears as a text-based dialogue between multiple people which takes place in the present moment. Chat therapy is most associated with online teletherapy platforms and utilizes the corresponding application, whether that be on a computer, through a tablet, or even a smartphone.

You are probably curious about how synchronous text-based chat therapy works. For starters, it is important to utilize a HIPAA-compliant chat application as not all chat platforms are completely secure. These applications can be found through a quick web search and usually will have an associated cost. When looking to establish yourself with a particular application, you should ask yourself, "What do I want to be able to accomplish with this app? Do I need multiple log-ins? Do I want a complete Electronic Healthcare Records application, or do I only want to utilize certain communication methods?" These questions will help you determine what features you want and don't want. For example, if your intent is to provide synchronous text-based chat services, you would need a Live Chat feature. You may also be interested in a text-messaging feature for you and your client to communicate outside of the live chat time. Certain applications will even provide an analytic report of your sessions.

Once the live chat application has been established, you would be able to supply your client with a link to a website and/or application that will provide access to the communication platform. Depending on the application used, the client may need to establish a password-protected profile. The link you provided to the client could also connect them to an online waiting room that only requests the client's name. In this case, the client can use a pseudonym if they prefer. When the mental health professional is ready to begin the live chat, the feature activates, and the session begins.

The motivating factors for this therapeutic intervention becoming more popularized echo the reasons discussed in the above sections regarding online therapy and emails. Online services are associated with lower costs, ease of access for people who may not be able to obtain face-to-face services, increased autonomy, control on behalf of the client, emotional distance from the therapist, and heightened anonymity. For example, some people find the act of meeting with a therapist so incredibly anxiety-provoking, they back out of the first session. Synchronous text-based chats can reduce the awkwardness and deescalate the tension of meeting with a stranger and talking about personal topics. Through text-based chat, a client who is guarded can engage with the therapist at their own pace without the awkward silence that can be experienced in face-to-face sessions.

A few considerations should be discussed about synchronous text-based chat services. Like email therapy, developing a therapeutic rapport with your client may be a bit challenging. One way we tend to communicate on text-based platforms is through emoticons and emojis (images that depict an emotion such as a happy face) and memes (humorous images, videos, or texts). Through these images, we are more accurately able to communicate the inflection of the message we are sending. When sending these images, it is important to keep in mind your role as the therapist and the appropriateness of the content. Avoiding overfamiliarity is important for maintaining professionalism and modeling therapeutic boundaries. Figure 10.2 displays a therapeutically appropriate synchronous text-based chat session.

An additional consideration to keep in mind when utilizing synchronous text-based chats is the reading and comprehension capabilities of your client. To navigate this, consider matching the client in their vocabulary, structure, and pace. Some clients may communicate in lengthy messages while others may send short thoughts or sentences. Facilitating a conversation around what messaging style the client finds most effective

Therapist: Good afternoon, John, are you there?

    Client: Hi, yes, I'm here.

Therapist: Great. Welcome to this evening's session. I've had a look at your questionnaires and noticed that your mood scores have improved slightly this week. How are you feeling at the moment?

    Client: I'm feeling OK, I think. My anxiety has subsided a bit, but I guess that is because I haven't put myself in any anxious situations.

Therapist: Wow. That is a big change for you. Congratulations on being able to do that. How were you able to make that choice?

    Client: At the weekend my parents were trying to get me to go to a party that I didn't feel comfortable going to and I told them I did not want to go. So I finally stood up for myself and didn't go to that party where I would have likely freaked out at.

Therapist: That's good to hear.

Figure 10.2 Sample of Chat Exchange between Therapist and Client.

can add to the clarity of the conversation, further enhancing the impact of the session.

Synchronous text-based chats are not for everyone. People who do not like to read or find it difficult to communicate through writing will find this form of therapy to be challenging. Although most of the chat applications are easy to use, the client should be able to easily navigate the chat features, or this may add to any frustrations they may already be experiencing. It is also important to mention that people navigating the challenges associated with anxiety, stress, relationships, and life changes may find this form of therapy helpful as it can be accessed anywhere and anytime it is needed. Someone experiencing elevated symptoms may need more intensive services.

On the same note, for someone going through a crisis, text-based chat may be their only way to communicate. Crisistextline.org is a free synchronous text-based chat service that connects the person in crisis with a trained crisis counselor. The crisis counselor works with the person experiencing the crisis in real time by asking questions, empathizing, and employing active listening skills. Through the conversation, the crisis counselor can determine the safety of the person, provide additional resources, and contact local officials if needed.

Overall, synchronous text-based chat therapy provides clients with an alternative way of receiving mental health services when the concept of meeting with someone face-to-face is not a fit. HIPAA practices are still maintained, and the privacy element can be thought of as enhanced due to the lack of verbal communication and the use of password-protected applications. It is also important to keep in mind the distinction between chatting in real time and utilizing text messaging as a form of communication. The difference in response time is vast, and being clear on what a live chat is versus a text message is imperative to the process.

Text Messages

As previously stated, **text messages** are an asynchronous form of communication because the sender and the receiver are not communicating at the same time. This form of communication in the mental health field can be used in a variety of ways, such as scheduling appointments and sending appointment reminders and providing additional support in between sessions, as well as an adjunct delivery system to the main form of therapeutic services. Text messaging is another form of therapeutic writing which requires a clear understanding of the technology and how to utilize it accordingly.

Before incorporating text messaging into your practice, it is important to understand your comfort level with the communication form and the

HIPAA limitations that go with it. Some helpful questions to consider are,

> What role do you see text messaging playing in your therapy practice? How might you want to utilize this form of technology? How will you navigate someone using text messages inappropriately? Do you have any concerns about safety issues? Will you be using a HIPAA Compliant Text Messaging app?

Through questions such as these, you will be able to determine if text messaging is a form of communication you want to include in your practice or not.

HIPAA was developed to protect the personal health information (PHI) of a client from being disseminated for public knowledge. As mental health providers, it is our duty to provide a secure platform for PHI to be sent and received through. Although HIPAA-compliant platforms exist, it is important to note that most free text messaging applications are not secure as they do not ensure confidentiality. Using text messaging services is permitted if you have validated consent from the client. This consent form should include a statement indicating the limitations of confidentiality specifically pertaining to the text messaging format, how text messaging may and may not be used throughout the course of therapy, a statement focused on an expected response time, and any financial aspects associated with the service.

Once the consent form has been signed, you are able to move on toward utilizing text messaging as a communication piece and enhancement toward therapeutic services. When using text messaging to schedule appointments and send appointment reminders, it is important to remain consistent in the timing of when the message is sent as well as the format of the message. One suggestion for doing so is modeling your cancellation policy. For example, if your cancellation policy indicates 24-hour notice is required, then sending a text message reminder should follow the same 24-hour policy. As for the format of any text message you may send, you want them to be clear, easy to read, and free of identifying information. When scheduling an appointment, it is always helpful to confirm the time and date at the end of the conversation. For example,

> Thank you for taking a few minutes to work on scheduling your next appointment. You are scheduled for October 31st at 2:00 pm. As you know, we will be meeting via doxy.me. Please keep in mind the 24-hour cancellation policy.

Text messages can also be used to enhance therapeutic engagement between sessions. One way of using text messages in this manner is when clients send quick thoughts and updates when not in session on topics they want to discuss in session. Clients should be made aware of what type of response they can expect from you and when. The understanding between you and the client may simply be that you won't respond to those types of messages but will make certain to bring them up in your next session. It is also important to set boundaries around when it is no longer appropriate to send text messages. Rizvi and Roman (2019) suggested that sometimes people, outside of therapy, utilize text messages to express their dissatisfactions and to convey their complaints. They usually do so without seeking help or asking questions. The use of texting in this manner is not useful for clients. When this happens, it would be imperative for you to communicate to clients what they can use the text exchange for so that your interactions can be more effective.

Using text messaging as an adjunct to the main delivery method of therapy services is similar to email therapy and synchronous text-based chat therapy in how it operates and why this therapeutic service is gaining popularity. Going back to The Online Disinhibition Effect (Suler, 2005), text messaging allows clients to remain invisible while establishing a therapeutic rapport. During this time the therapist may engage with the client through text messages until the client is comfortable enough to meet face-to-face. Due to the asynchronous fashion of text messaging, clients may feel more in control of their sessions and the flow of information being communicated. These factors amongst others contribute to the rise of text-based therapies.

The main difference between chat therapy and using text messages in therapy is that text messages are asynchronous. A few considerations to follow when using text messaging are deidentifying your conversations to strengthen the limited confidentiality provided in this communication platform. Establishing a cut-off time for text message communication is important for the therapeutic relationship and important

Therapist: Hello, how has your week been?
10/21/22 @ 2:00 pm

Client: Hi, so glad you texted. I wanted to tell you
I completed my guided meditations twice already this week!
10/25/22 @ 5:36 pm

Therapist: Good to hear, what has been different?
How have you been able to work the meditations
into your schedule?
10/25/22 @ 6:00 pm

Client: The last two days, I woke up telling
myself positive affirmations, like we discussed
and made it a priority for 10 minutes in the morning.
10/27/22 @ 5:45 pm

Figure 10.3 Sample of Text Message Exchange between Therapist and Client.

for your self-care. When using text messaging the therapy agreement documentation should be clear regarding the parameters of the treatment as well as the expectations of the client and the therapist. Interactions should be written with formality and consistency to maintain a professional stance. Figure 10.3 presents a sample of text message exchange between a therapist and a client.

Emoticons and Emoji

Text-based messaging brought a paradoxical twist to the field of mental health. The joining process with clients includes an emotional undertone which provides clients with a sense of whom they are working with and if they can trust the therapist. Computer messages do not convey the emotional tone of messages being sent; therefore, a lot of assumptions are made about the meaning of the text. This challenge of conveying emotions was solved through the invention of emoticons and, later, emojis.

As mobile phones and text messaging became one of the leading forms of communication, images depicting happy faces and sad faces were developed to assist in conveying the contextual meaning of the text-based message. Emoticons were developed first and come in the form of keystroke combinations whereas emojis are mini pictures. Through these images, the receiver of the message can pick up on the intent of the sender rather than having to infer the meaning.

Emoticons and emojis can be used to enhance all forms of text-based interventions. Therapists may find themselves also using memes and Graphics Interchange Formats (GIFs) to convey a reaction, thought, or emotion which are captioned videos or pictures of a specific genre and disseminated through social media. When using these types of technology to enhance text-based communications, it is important to remember who will be receiving these symbols and how they will connect to the meaning. One suggestion to enhance the clarity of utilizing emoticons, emojis, memes, and GIFs is passing out a chart in your intake paperwork that displays your most used symbols and what that symbol stands for. Figure 10.4 presents some common emoticons and their associated emojis.

Table 10.1 Sample Emoticons and Emoji Chart

Samples of Emoticons		Samples of Emojis	
Happy face	:-)	Happy face	😊
Sad face	:-(	Sad face	🙁
Mad	>:-(	Mad	😠
Wink	;-)	Wink	😉
Sealed lips	:-x	Sealed lips	🤐
Surprise	:-0	Surprise	😲

Technology Assignments

While we have primarily talked about the therapist's skills and knowledge of using and writing via technology, we also want to briefly present how you might get clients to write that doesn't involve you. One such possibility is having clients, specifically couples, go on electronic fantasy dates (Hertlein, 2016). Most therapists, and lay individuals as well, will suggest that couples who are having difficulties should go on a date as this will likely bring them back to the beginning of their relationship when they were courting one another. However, that budding romance probably occurred when things were a little simpler—perhaps no children, less stress, and more free time. The **electronic fantasy date** helps to increase intimacy within a couple without them having to have money or the ability to go on the date.

What is needed for an electronic fantasy date is the ability of both members of the couple to text one another. Luckily, in many places today, most people have smartphones that have texting capabilities. While in-person dates are temporally defined, starting and ending at specific times, the electronic fantasy date lasts much longer and has each member attempting to text positive thoughts and experiences.

Depending on the couple and their situation, you work with them to figure out who will initiate the date. You then explain that you want them to text each other at least eight times over the course of the day that the date was determined. They should write so that they are providing thick descriptions about what they are doing, feeling, and thinking on this fantasy date. The initiator of the date sends a text describing the beginning of the date. This might be picking the person up or meeting them in a specific location. For instance, they might write, "It is early evening, and I am dressed in a suit. I knock on the door, and you answer dressed in that beautiful orange and blue dress that makes your eyes shine."

The sender then texts about what they are doing on this date. Perhaps it is going on a walk together, to the beach, or to dinner. You might let them know when you introduce this activity that they can also text pictures of the places they are describing to help bring the date to greater life. Each subsequent text should describe the next phase of the date, where the location, activity, and personal thoughts and feelings will have changed. This occurs all the way until the last text which describes the ending of the date.

Based on the dynamics of the couple, you could assign two dates in the week or one date a week so that both partners are able to be the initiator/sender of the electronic fantasy date. The "date" and the feelings and experiences are then processed together in the next therapy session. While this is a useful technique for many clients, you might consider not using it if the couple had experienced some type of infidelity that was technology related (i.e., a virtual affair or an affair where there was a lot of texting between the two).

Websites

In today's day and age, most therapists who are in private practice, as well as those working in an agency, have information about themselves and their services posted on a website. This website is your potential client's first contact with you. Based on what you write, as well as how it visually looks, the person looking at your website may decide to further explore possible therapy with you or think that you are not the right fit for them. Thus, having a website that conveys who you are and what you do in a way that is informative and engaging is extremely important. Your landing page should be visually appealing with clear menu links.

When scanning a plethora of mental health facilities and private practice websites, you will notice similar information provided. When a potential client searches you out on the internet, they want to be able to quickly locate an overview of your therapeutic philosophy (see Figure 10.5), an explanation of the types of therapy you do and your potential specialties (see Figure 10.6), rates, accepted insurance plans (if any), hours of operation, an About Me section (see Figure 10.7), and a method of contact. The About Me section should include information on your therapeutic modality, what format you provide services through (in person, emails, chat, text messages, video conferencing), and areas of expertise. When discussing rates, you will often find a flat rate displayed with the caveat of a possible sliding fee scale based on need. If a practice accepts health insurance, the various plans would be listed. However, if the

Figure 10.4 Sample of Homepage for a Fictional Private Practice.

Figure 10.5 Sample of Webpage Explaining the Therapist's General Therapeutic Philosophy.

Figure 10.6 Sample of Webpage Describing the Therapist's Theoretical Orientation, Method and Location of Therapy, Rates, and Insurance Possibilities.

practice does not accept health insurance, you may find a statement clarifying the reason for that decision as well.

It is important to keep in mind how you refer to yourself regarding your license and state requirements. For example, in the state of Florida, Florida statute 491.0149, *Display of license; use of professional title on promotional materials*, discusses the way your license should be displayed and the words you can use to display your credentials on marketing materials, which includes a website. If this information is not displayed according to the state guidelines, you may appear to be noncompliant with your state's licensure protocol.

Remember, your website is an expanded business card. You want it to accurately display the therapist you are and the services you provide. The goal of your website is to market yourself to your populations of interest, another target to keep in mind when building the About Me section! You might also have in writing what past clients have written about you (ensuring that there is no identifying information present). Figure 10.8 presents a sample testimonial page on your website.

Figure 10.7 Sample of About Me Page on a Group Practice's Website.

Figure 10.8 Sample of Website Displaying Past Client Testimonials.

Technology Training

Most experienced therapists were trained to work with clients sitting right in front of them. While some therapists engaged in telehealth, it wasn't until the 2020 Coronavirus pandemic that most therapists dipped their toes into the technological waters. Many training programs scrambled to teach their students how to work in that medium. We won't talk here about videoconferencing but rather about the training for text-based technology interventions.

Murphy et al. (2008) developed a university training program for asynchronous email-based counseling. This program consisted of two levels. Level 1 teaches the cornerstones of cybercounseling, including ethics, technology, skills, and theory. Level 2 takes everything learned in Level 1 and emphasized their practical application.

While someone may be an excellent therapist when they are sitting across from a client, that does not necessarily translate into the online environment. There are different ways of being that occur via email than face-to-face, particularly that of joining. Many therapists learn how to connect with clients using proximity, vocalics, immediacy, etc. When working online, you will need to expand your skill set. The following provides some ways to increase your therapeutic presence when interacting with clients via email-only therapy.

Emotional bracketing helps provide the nonverbal aspects of communication. It is used primarily during joining when you are trying to display warmth. In conveying your thoughts and feelings, you can put these in brackets in your writing. Here is an example:

> It has been three weeks since we last conversed and I have been concerned for you [said with a serious tone]. The last time we talked, you were quite worried about your children's reaction when you told them about the divorce. I was wondering how that went, especially how it went for you since you've been scared not to disappoint them [I'm giving you a few minutes for you to consider this].

When clients come to your office, they take in the surroundings with all their senses. They see how it is decorated, hear the sounds, smell the air, feel the firmness or softness of the couch, and perhaps don't taste much. Clients don't get these stimuli at home when they are online and only read your emails. **Descriptive immediacy** brings the client into your office by painting a picture of you and the scene. This should help promote the connection between the two of you. The following is an example of descriptive immediacy:

> As a write this, I am sitting in my office where the sun is shining and the green of the trees just outside the window are bright and vibrant. It is a nice warm day here in Fort Lauderdale.

Descriptive immediacy helps to personalize the exchanges you have with clients. It shifts you from being an anonymous typist to a real person. The more the client feels a connection to you, the more they are likely to engage in the therapeutic process.

Ethical Considerations

The use of technology is ever-increasing in psychotherapy. With this increase comes an increase in considerations about the ethical implications of their use. Most professional organizations have some type of guidance when dealing with technology-assisted professional services. For instance, the American Association of Marriage and Family Therapy ethical code 6.1 is on Technology Assisted Services and states:

> Prior to commencing therapy or supervision services through electronic means (including but not limited to phone and Internet), marriage and family therapists ensure that they are compliant with all relevant laws for the delivery of such services. Additionally, marriage and family therapists must: (a) determine that technologically-assisted services or supervision are appropriate for clients or supervisees, considering professional, intellectual, emotional, and physical needs; (b) inform clients or supervisees of the potential risks and benefits associated with technologically-assisted services; (c) ensure the security of their communication medium; and (d) only commence electronic therapy or supervision after appropriate education, training, or supervised experience using the relevant technology.

Perhaps the most significant ethical concern is with privacy. Titov (2010) recommended that therapists talk with their clients about the security of emails and how they might take precautions so that other people do not read the emails if the client does not want them to. For instance, it is probably better to have the client use their own personal email rather than a work email. If the client is using a shared email account or one through their school or work, there is the potential that other people who have technological oversight of that email system may be able to go in and look at the emails.

The use of technology may not be appropriate in all situations. Murphy et al. (2008) cautioned that therapists should encourage face-to-face meetings when clients are having serious mental health issues, crisis situations, distortions of reality, and suicidal situations. Roy and Gillett (2008) concurred that email therapy is usually not recommended for those who are abusing drugs and alcohol, have psychotic symptoms, are in life-threatening situations, and are at risk of harm to themselves or others.

One of the biggest issues when conducting therapy online is the location of the therapist and client. Before teletherapy, it was usually quite clear (at least in the United States) that a therapist could only practice within the state that they are licensed. The advent of videoconferencing availability has opened the possibility of working with clients wherever in the world they may be. This opportunity is even easier when texts, chats, or emails are used rather than video. You and/or the client can be at home, on vacation, or working outside of your residential state or country. It will be important for you to check the national and international licensing laws (if there are any) for what the laws and rules are for working either from that locale or with a client who is currently in that locale.

When a client comes to your office, we tend to have a good sense of the identity of the client. While many therapists do not ask clients to show proof of identity (e.g., a driver's license or a passport), we know each week we are talking to the person we talked with the previous week. However, the more that we solely use text-based communication, the less we can confirm that what we are saying to a person is being received by the person we are attempting to talk to. When we send a text to a client's phone, other people in the vicinity might be able to look at the screen and read it. An email may sit in a client's inbox and be available for others to read. Further, in the last ten years or so, the phenomenon of catfishing has come to the forefront. This is when a person takes images from another person, such as photos you might have on a social media site, and uses those pictures to create a new identity for themselves. Without looking at photo identification and using video you cannot confirm the identity of your client.

Another potential issue in providing psychotherapy services via technology is that of remuneration—will you and how you will get paid? More insurance companies are covering online therapy. However, they may only do so when video is used. Each client will have to check their coverage, which may be based on the insurance company and location. Further, while a 45- to 60-minute session might be reimbursable, the time that you took to compose and send an email or text message may not. You should be very clear with your client from the very beginning of therapy about how you will use technology and the associated costs for your time. You might charge a flat fee which entails a session and various technology correspondence. Alternatively, you might charge for certain durations, such as in 10- or 15-minute increments. An open and clear discussion of how you operate will be very important in developing a trustworthy and transparent therapeutic alliance. Because of the potential for misunderstandings to happen with chats, texts, and/or emails, you might consider printing out all your written correspondence with clients and putting these in the official record.

Summary

This chapter touched on only a few therapeutic technological resources, such as emails, chats, text messages, and computer-assisted interventions. As technology progresses, the modes in which we conduct therapy sessions will continue to change and modify with the population. As therapists, we adapt to our clients and utilize innovative modes of therapy. A prime example of this is when we transitioned to teletherapy during the COVID-19 pandemic. These forms of asynchronous and synchronous session formats have been easier for clients to communicate openly, more accessible, and affordable.

References

Fairburn, C. G., & Patel, V. (2017). The impact of digital technology on psychological treatments and their dissemination. *Behaviour Research and Therapy, 88*, 19–25.

Gutheil, T. G., & Simon, R. I. (2005). E-mails, extra-therapeutic contact, and early boundary problems: The internet as a 'slippery slope'. *Psychiatric Annals, 35*(12), 952–960.

Hertlein, K. M. (2016). "Your cyberplace or mine?": Electronic fantasy dates. In G. R. Weeks, S. T. Fife, & C. M. Peterson (Eds.), *Techniques for the couple therapist* (pp. 182–185). Routledge.

Murphy, L., MacFadden, R., & Mitchell, D. (2008). Cybercounseling online: The development of a university-based training program for e-mail counseling. *Journal of Technology in Human Services, 26*(2/4), 447–469.

Murphy, L. J., & Mitchell, D. L. (1998). When writing helps to heal: E-mail as therapy. *British Journal of Guidance & Counseling, 26*(1), 21–32.

Paxling, B., Lundgren, S., Norman, A., Almlöv, J., Carlbring, P., Cuijpers, P., & Andersson, G. (2013). Therapist behaviours in internet-delivered cognitive behaviour therapy: Analyses of e-mail correspondence in the treatment of generalized anxiety disorder. *Behavioural and Cognitive Psychotherapy, 41*, 280–289.

Reiter, M. D. (2010). Solution-focused marathon sessions. *Journal of Systemic Therapies, 29*, 33–49.

Rizvi, S. L., & Roman, K. M. (2019). Generalization modalities: Taking the treatment out of the consulting room—Using telephone, text, and email. In M. A. Swales (Ed.), *The Oxford handbook of dialectical behaviour therapy* (pp. 201–215). Oxford University Press.

Roy, H., & Gillett, T. (2008). Email: A new technique for forming a therapeutic alliance with high-risk young people failing to engage with mental health services? A case study. *Clinical Child Psychology and Psychiatry, 13*(1), 95–103.

Suler, J. (2005). The online disinhibition effect. *International Journal of Applied Psychoanalytic Studies, 2*(2), 184–188.

Titov, N. (2010). Email in low intensity CBT interventions. In J. Bennett-Levy et al. (Eds.), *Oxford guide to low intensity CBT interventions* (pp. 287–293). Oxford University Press.

Chapter 11

Writing for the Legal and Medical Contexts

Lori Pantaleao, Shaelise Tor, and Michael D. Reiter

For most of this book, we have presented you with ideas about how you write to clients or get clients to write for themselves or others. We now expand the field a little bit and talk about how you are likely to write about clients in two specific contexts, the legal and the medical contexts. First, we present the legal context and the various factors you are likely to experience when writing for judges and/or attorneys. We then focus on the medical context and considerations when writing to medical professionals. We understand that most of you may not frequently write in these contexts. However, you are likely to periodically find yourself being asked to write a communication, note, or report about a client who is heavily involved in legal and/or medical issues. We hope that the ideas presented in this chapter will be an introduction for you to legal and medical writing so that you can ethically and professionally communicate in these contexts.

Psychotherapy Writing in the Legal Context

How Is Legal Writing Different from Traditional Clinical Writing?

As a mental health professional, you will do a lot of writing! While writing to your client or for the standard documentation that goes into the client's official file (e.g., progress notes), there are some general guidelines to follow which will contribute to readability and ease of comprehension. Ensuring the conciseness and completeness of the documentation is important to communicating the overall intended message. Maintaining chronological order within clinical documentation is also essential as it assists with displaying the progression through the treatment process (positive or negative). These significant elements for clinical writing are mirrored in all forms of writing completed by healthcare providers.

You may find that there are times when you are working with a client, and you receive a request from someone in the legal system for

DOI: 10.4324/9781003294702-11

information about them. Such letters can be used for multiple purposes, and the reason for the request will determine the style in which the summary is written and the depth of the information provided. Mental health professionals are often tasked with writing clinical case summaries, letters to be used in the courts, letters for social security determination, gender affirmation surgery referral letters, and, sometimes, Employee Assisted Programs (EAP). Writing for these various populations requires an understanding of the purpose of the requested documentation, knowledge of your audience, remaining within the scope of your practice, and the utmost professionalism. This section of this chapter discusses what should be included in your documentation, the difference between the various types of legal documentation, and offers general guidelines focused on how to prepare the requested documentation.

When writing for legal purposes some of these elements are amplified more than others. Lawyers and judges intentionally read clinical documents because they need specific information to assist with making educated decisions in the context of their professional duties. Legal writing differs from traditional clinical writing because you are customizing the format of the report to fit the context of the information being requested. When undertaking the task of legal writing, it is important to keep in mind that the courts' emphasis is focused on the effectiveness of the letter and what information it provides.

Many individuals believe the purpose of legal writing is to persuade. However, therapeutic writing for legal documentation is vastly different as it is used to simply provide information to the requesting party. Miscommunication typically occurs between parties within the legal system and mental health professionals because we do not typically "speak the same language." It is this cross-disciplinary communication gap that needs to be bridged. This gap can be bridged through careful consideration with the use of language and appropriate guidelines.

While most therapists will only periodically encounter the legal system and need to produce a document to be sent to someone in the legal context, other psychotherapists have more frequent contact. Some therapists, particularly clinical psychologists, may function within the forensic world and may need to write a report that will be used in the legal systems. Some of the areas this would occur include when clients are divorcing, victims and offenders of maltreatment, criminals postincarceration, those deemed incompetent, and others (Ackerman, 2006). **Forensic psychologists** utilize their knowledge to assist in the judicial system and in criminal manners. They work closely with judges, attorneys, and other law professionals. They make assessments of individuals, interview people involved in court cases, engage in forensic report writing, and testify in court when needed. While forensic psychologists primarily work in the legal field, this section of this chapter is intended for all psychotherapists as you will likely find yourself needing to provide written documentation to someone in the legal context at some point in your career.

Subpoenas and Court Orders

As discussed throughout this book, you are required to hold clients' personal information confidential. You are not allowed to talk to other people, verbally or in writing, about your client. However, there are a few situations where you do have to break confidentiality, such as when there is talk about child abuse, harm to self, or harm to others. You will also break confidentiality when there is a court order. However, this will not be done behind the client's back. Any letters and reports that you send to individuals involved in the legal system should be talked about with your client so that your role in their life is clear and overt.

Let us take a minute to make a distinction between subpoenas and court orders. A **subpoena** can be initiated by an attorney or the Court. While you will need to respond to either, for attorney-initiated subpoenas, you do not have to agree to the request that is in that document. The request is likely for you to provide the initiator of the subpoena with your client's records. While you do have to respond to a subpoena, such as showing up at court on a certain day/time, you do not have to necessarily disclose confidential information. A **court order** is a legal mandate that has been documented and signed by a judge. The document dictates what measures need to be taken by the clients involved and what services they may need to obtain. If you receive a court order from your client, review the document and determine if your services will meet the needs of the client. If so, make sure to obtain release forms for the various points of contact you may be required to report to.

If you are delivered a subpoena, slow down, take a breath, and think about what your ethical obligations are. Based on the situation, you should likely check with your client, letting them know that you received the subpoena and what is being requested of you by whom. Some clients may have worked with their lawyer and have signed a release form with them. If so, it will be important for you to gain access to that release form and have a copy of it in your files. If your client does not want you to release information based on the subpoena, you can contact the client's attorney to have them fill out the appropriate paperwork to quash the subpoena.

When your client and you agree to submit documentation from the subpoena, you will likely not send all your clinical records regarding the client but rather a summary of the treatment. You will only want to send information that is pertinent to the subpoena or the court order. The rule of thumb is to provide as minimal information as possible while still fulfilling the request. Whatever information is sent to the court, you should not alter or destroy the documents that comprise your client's clinical record.

How to Write Clinically, So Others Will Understand

As mental health practitioners, to be able to bridge that gap between the language of our profession and the legal world, we must first understand the purpose of clinical summaries and letters, as this form of written documentation promotes communication between clients, providers, and other parties involved (Salmon et al., 2016). The main difference between these different types of reports relates to the depth of information shared. In order to provide clarity, let's review a common scenario for writing a clinical document as a psychotherapist. We will then use this case scenario to amplify the differences between a clinical summary and a letter.

Case Scenario

A family system, consisting of a biological mother, biological father, and son, initiated services at your thriving private practice, four months ago. As this is a reunification case, you have been requested to provide clinical documentation to the Guardian Ad Litem. The son has no interest in being unified with his mother, due to a history of negative interactions with each other. However, his mother is aggressively attempting to build a relationship between them by utilizing the legal system. Thus, this has created a growing resentment and contributed to the disconnect between the two. The father in this scenario is supportive of his son and encourages him to voice his own opinion of the situation.

Clinical Summaries

The Guardian Ad Litem requests a clinical summary from you regarding your sessions with the family system. How do you start? What information do you put in a clinical summary? We will explore the use of a clinical summary with the case scenario provided above.

First, let us review what a clinical summary is. A **clinical summary** is a written description of the status of a clinical case. This description is used in lieu of providing the client's entire medical record, in an effort to maintain client-therapist confidentiality. There are various reasons you may be requested to complete a clinical case summary, but the structure remains the same. Let's explore some guidelines for completing clinical summaries. Guidelines to follow when completing a clinical summary are to incorporate the following key elements: client history, assessment, observations, current status, and treatment plan progression.

Clinical summaries should include:

- Client's demographics:
  - Patient name
  - Provider's office contact information

- Initiation date and completion date
  - If services are in progress indicate that accordingly
- Location of services rendered
- Updated medication list
- Clinician's report:
- Reasons for seeking services
- How the client meets the criteria for the diagnosis by:
  - Describing the client's symptoms
  - Duration of symptoms
  - Functional impairment
    - Alternative diagnoses that were considered and ruled out (if any)
- Treatment plan goals, what you are working toward

Clinical Summary

Client Name: Son
Date Of Birth: **/**/***
Client Address: 123 Main Street, USA
Client Telephone Number: ***-***-****
Beginning Date of Therapy: **/**/2023
Ending Date of Therapy: TBD
Type of Sessions: Family Sessions

Diagnosis:
F41.1 Generalized Anxiety Disorder

Clinician's Report:
SON'S NAME began treatment on **/**/****, due to REASONS FOR SEEKING SERVICES. SON'S NAME was diagnosed with F41.1 Generalized Anxiety Disorder. Behaviors that indicate this include LIST SYMPTOMS SPECIFIC TO YOUR CLIENT, DURATION OF SYMPTOMS, AND FUNCTIONAL IMPAIRMENT.

SON'S NAME continues to work towards RELATED TREATMENT PLAN GOALS, as evidenced by (GIVE AN EXAMPLE). He is working towards achieving his updated treatment plan goals.

SUMMARY OF TOPICS COVERED. The anxiety levels the client experiences negatively impact his daily functioning.

Current Medications:
REPORT ANY UPDATED MEDICATIONS YOUR CLIENT SELF-REPORTS.

_____
Provider Name

_____   _____
Provider Signature   **Date**

Figure 11.1 Clinical Summary Sample.

- Summary of topics covered
  - If appropriate you can indicate the time and location of the next appointment
- Please note that this document should be on letterhead which includes your agency/private practice logo and contact information (address, phone number, email, fax number, etc.)

Figure 11.1 provides a sample of clinical summary for you to gain a sense of how it might be formatted and what it might contain. We have kept this sample general so that you may more easily fill in the areas with the specifics of your clients who may be in need of a clinical summary.

Examples of when you may be asked to complete a clinical summary are drug court, family court, and disability determination, just to name a few. Regardless of the context in which you are writing the clinical summary, it should present a clear and concise status update of your client. Utilizing this format allows you to provide the specific information being requested, without providing extraneous information. If more detailed information is being requested from the legal system, one suggestion we have is clinical letters.

Clinical Letters

Clinical letters are a more comprehensive form of legal documentation that mental health practitioners are requested to complete. These letters require more detail to gain an understanding of the system of which the client is a part and what impacts they are experiencing because of this. For example, utilizing the reunification case scenario described above, a comprehensive description and professional recommendation may be required by the Guardian Ad Litem to present in court. Let's explore some guidelines for completing clinical letters below.

Clinical letters should include:

- Client's demographics:
  - Patient name
  - Provider's office contact information
  - Initiation date and completion date
    - If services are in progress indicate that accordingly
  - Location of services rendered
  - Updated medication list
- Clinician's report:
  - Reasons for seeking services
  - Client diagnosis
    - How the client meets the criteria for the diagnosis by:
      - Describing the client's symptoms and onset
      - Duration of symptoms

Clinical Letter
Citrus County Courts

April 20, 2022

Jane Doe
Guardian ad Litem
123 Main Street
Hollywood, FL 33023

Re: The Johnson Family
Case #: 12345

Dear Ms. Doe,

I, PRACTITIONER NAME, am writing this letter to update you as the Guardian Ad Litem for CLIENT CASE NAME. THE CLIENT and her mother, MOTHER'S NAME, were clients at FACILITY NAME from DATE to DATE. THE FACILITY NAME is a community-based mental health clinic. The clinic offers relational therapy services to the community on a sliding fee scale rate. The sessions are facilitated through various means and structures.

This case was brought to THE NAME OF THE FACILITY through a court order from Judge NAME of the STATE OF THE CASE Court system.

MOTHER NAME, AGE, initiated services at the FACILITY on DATE. Her reason for seeking services was to initiate the court-ordered reunification process with her AGE-year-old son, SONS NAME. MOTHER'S NAME individually attended NUMBER of sessions in anticipation of her son's beginning the family reunification sessions. These sessions were held on the following dates: XXXXXX. The court order specifically stated (INCLUDE SPECIFIC COURT ORDER REQUIRMENTS SESSION STRUCTURE HERE). During the course of our work, I met with MOTHER'S NAME for NUMBER sessions during which time she provided a historical overview of the challenges she faced with OTHER BIOLOGICAL PARENT and her eldest son, SON'S NAME. She also discussed her expectations of reunification therapy, which included an improved relationship with her son to spending more time with each other. She also referred to working with an individual therapist (INCLUDE OTHER THERAPEUTIC ATTEMPTS REGARDING REUNIFICATION).

FATHER'S NAME, AGE, also initiated services at the FACILITY on DATE. His reason for seeking services was to begin the court-ordered reunification process between his AGE-year-old son, SON'S NAME, and his biological mother, MOTHER'S NAME. FATHER'S NAME individually attended one session on DATE. During this session, FATHER'S NAME discussed his concern for his son's mental health and his son's unwillingness to work with more therapists. FATHER'S NAME verbalized his anxiety surrounding MOTHER'S NAME claims of parental abuse. According to FATHER'S NAME, he cannot force SON'S NAME to attend therapy sessions and explained how he encourages his son to contact his mother at scheduled times. ADD CASE SPECIFIC DETAIL HERE.

SON'S NAME, AGE, began attending services at the FACILITY on DATE. SON'S NAME met with THERAPIST to get acquainted with one another and discuss the reunification process. This was followed up by a second session on DATE. Prior to services beginning, SON's NAME agreed to attend three sessions with the THERAPIST. After the three sessions focused on building rapport, SON'S NAME verbalized not being willing to meet with his mother and he was working with a therapist individually and did not want to continue meeting with the reunification therapists. As a result, THERAPIST sought clarification from the court before proceeding with reunification services.

Family Sessions were initiated on DATE, and follow up sessions were held on DATE, DATE, and DATE. During the course of our work together, the following themes emerged throughout our sessions:

- SON'S NAME is being forced to communicate with his mother even though he is adamantly opposed based on previous adverse childhood experiences
- SON'S NAME stated that his mother initiated the problems for the family.
- SON'S NAME stated that his father strongly encouraged him to remain in contact with his mother.
- MOTHER'S NAME did not verbalize an understanding of how her actions contributed to the current situation. Nor did she take responsibility for the results of her decisions.
- MOTHER'S NAME continues to blame "the father" for SON'S NAME not communicating and visiting her.
- SON'S NAME was very transparent that he is choosing to not interact with his mother and makes these decisions independent of his father's requests.

In addition, on DATE, THERAPIST, spoke to (DISCUSS OTHERS INVOLVED IN THE SYSTEM THAT MAY HAVE CONTRIBUTED TO THE CASE). IF APPOPRIATE INCLUDE A SUMMARY OF THE CONVERSATION YOU HELD WITH EACH PARTY INVOVED.

My professional opinion is SON'S NAME is an extremely articulate, bright, insightful, and determined, AGE-year-old. At this present time, SON'S NAME is unwilling to reunify with his mother for reasons he articulately stated throughout our sessions which he based on past experiences within their family system. He never wavered from this standpoint. He responded to his mother's conversations in therapy from an extremely mature and steadfast posture.

It is my professional opinion that continuing services at this time would not benefit this case and further add to SON'S NAME adverse childhood experiences.
Although AGE years old, SON'S NAME appears to have the intellect and motivation to clearly express his concerns for his mental well-being.

Thank you for your attention to this matter.

Respectfully,

Bruce Banner

Bruce Banner, Ph.D., LMFT
Positive Ripple Effects

Figure 11.2 Clinical Letter Summary Sample.

- - Functional impairment
  - Alternative diagnoses that were considered and ruled out (if any)
- A comprehensive overview of the client
  - Strengths
  - Relationships
  - Life situations
  - Cultural influences
  - All participating systems (e.g., school, family, legal, mental health, medical doctor, support)
  - Health concerns and their potential interaction with the diagnosis
- Treatment plan goals, what you are working toward
- Summary of topics covered
  - If appropriate you can indicate the time and location of the next appointment
- Clinician's recommendation:
  - Areas/expressed ideas for further development (enhance and support lifestyle change)
  - Client considerations based on self-report
  - Your professional recommendation on the direction of the case
- Please note that this document should be on letterhead which includes your agency/private practice logo and contact information (address, phone number, email, fax number, etc.)

Figure 11.2 provides a sample of clinical letter.

Examples of when you may be asked to complete a clinical letter are comprehensive assessments, substance abuse evaluations, reunification, or custody family system cases, just to name a few. Similar to clinical summaries, clinical letters should be easy to read by all systems involved and clearly indicate the relevant information. In contrast to one another, a clinical letter provides a more comprehensive overview of the case.

Considerations and Tips

So, how do you know when to write a clinical summary versus a clinical letter? Who makes this decision? Well, that would be YOU in collaboration with other systems involved. No pressure, we got this! Given the case scenario above, a clinical summary would be appropriate for a court status hearing focused on the identified client's progress. On the other hand, a clinical letter would be used for a reunification review with the Guardian Ad Litem. It is pivotal to communicate with all systems involved when determining which form of clinical writing you will use.

Some ethical considerations when writing clinical documentation for legal settings encompass fees, maintaining Health Insurance Portability and Accountability Act (HIPAA) compliance for client safety, and a communicated timeline to fulfill the request. If this is not already indicated on your treatment consent form, best practices indicate you should discuss the associate fees with your client prior to providing the documentation. Do not start writing the summary or letter until you have the client's agreement to the associated fees in writing.

According to HIPAA 1996, you must obtain a release of information form signed and completed by the client prior to contacting other systems involved in the case. This release must include a specific point of contact and include their direct contact information. Without securing permission from the client to share their information, you cannot verify they are your client, let alone complete any documentation.

Another important aspect to consider when fulfilling requests for clinical documentation is the timeline for when the document is needed. Best practices indicate you should have a timeline structure embedded in your treatment consent form, to avoid any confusion as to how quickly a request can be filled. For example, your form may say something to the effect of, *please allow two to four weeks for any clinical document request to be completed.*

Some tips to consider when writing clinical documentation are to be clear and concise. What this means to you is that the written information comes across to the reader as easy to comprehend and straightforward. The reader does not have to second guess the meaning of the words being chosen to describe the scenario.

Another tip is to consider your reader. You are likely writing to one of three audiences: mental health professionals, non-mental health professionals, and nonprofessionals (Ackerman, 2006). Depending on which audience you are writing to, you will provide different information. When writing for mental health professionals you will need to ensure you include any diagnostic labels, psychological test names, and the associated scores, as well as other mental health terminology. If you are writing for non-mental health professionals, you should include the diagnostic assessment and recommendations. However, you will probably not explain the actual scores and subtest names since there is a greater likelihood that they will be misunderstood. Instead, you might use generic labels (e.g., "test of cognitive impairment"). Reports written for nonprofessionals should be written with as little medical and psychological terminology to try to minimize the possibility that the report is misunderstood or misinterpreted. If you do provide diagnostic considerations, you should clearly explain what these mean. There will also be times when you will be writing to all three audiences. At these moments, Ackerman (2006) recommends that you write with a balanced approach, writing for the non-mental health professional. When doing so, you will be utilizing specific and accurate terminology to clearly convey a message. In addition, be sure to structure the document according to the needs of the requestor within the agreed-upon timeframe.

We have provided you with an introduction to writing in the legal context. In your career, when you are asked to write for this arena—and you *will* likely be asked to at some point in your career (and much more often if you are working in forensic psychology)—these explanations and suggestions should orient you in the right direction. However, we just want to give a word of caution. Please consult other psychotherapy professionals and perhaps even lawyers when writing whatever document is requested of you. As with any skill, it takes time and repetition before you understand what is required and develop the necessary skills.

Psychotherapy Writing in the Medical Context

In the first half of this chapter, we presented why psychotherapists may need to write for the legal context and provided recommendations for the various types of documents that you may be asked or required to write. Now we shift to talk about writing within the medical context. As a psychotherapist, there will be times when you are working with medical professionals or your client is dealing with serious medical issues. In this capacity, you may need to write to communicate with your client, their family member, or someone in the medical field.

While this section of this chapter is primarily focused on the aspects of writing a psychotherapist will conduct when working within a medical context (i.e., writing to doctors, patients, or other affiliated healthcare professionals), we will briefly explain that therapists working with clients dealing with medical issues can utilize client-written letters to assist them in dealing with their illness. This is especially important since many people dealing with chronic illness experience a loss of independence and the ability to use their voice to express themselves (Signs, 2015). We encourage you to review the material presented in Chapter 8 on Client Writing Therapy for ideas of how you might utilize and modify the ideas presented in that chapter when working with clients dealing with medical illnesses.

Most psychotherapists work with a range of clientele, presenting many concerns that can be understood through a diagnostic lens, where the clinician can assess the client's problems through the use of the diagnostic criteria in the DSM-5-TR or the ICD-10. Many of our clients, besides psychological and emotional difficulties, are also experiencing physical difficulties. Thus, they are involved with many healthcare professionals. As such, holistic treatment will require conversation among these various professionals.

> The practitioner who engages in dialogue only with others in the same discipline or who share a similar theoretical view is not as well grounded as those who make an effort to relate to the broad

spectrum of individuals involved with the whole person and his/her psychological well-being from birth to death

(Anchor, 1991, p. 3)

It is incumbent upon you to be able to engage your clients and the significant professionals your client's psychological and physical health is predicated on.

In this section, we present an overview of medical psychotherapy and medical family therapy, two subspecializations in the psychotherapy field. While these sections describe these two specialties, we want to reiterate that you do not have to identify as either one to find yourself needing to write notes, letters, or reports to clients or medical personnel for the betterment of your clients.

Medical Psychotherapy

Anchor (1991) explained, "Medical psychotherapy is an interdisciplinary enterprise which serves as a vehicle for the assessment and treatment of inpatients and outpatients with psychiatric, behavioral, and/or medical difficulties with a psychological basis" (p. 18). This interdisciplinary process may include aspects of clinical psychology, counseling, medicine, psychiatry, nursing, pharmacology, nutrition, education, behavioral medicine, social work, rehabilitation, and ethics. For those engaged in **medical psychotherapy**, there is usually a treatment team that functions together to provide the widest catchment for patient care. Communication amongst the variety of professionals is key to effective treatment.

Medical psychotherapy developed based on patient needs, with the increased appreciation of a mental health professional's usefulness in the healthcare setting. There are three main areas in which psychotherapists are involved in the healthcare field (Anchor, 1991). The first is surrounding prevention, where the therapist assists in working with patients to decrease behaviors that are related to risk factors for disease. Second, psychotherapists provide direct patient service. Here, they provide counseling and therapy to assist in psychological and emotional mental health and well-being. Third, psychotherapists work in the healthcare field by assisting patients through rehabilitation, where they help people restore functions that were hampered by physical disability or trauma.

Mace and Healy (2011) described some of the clinical and educational issues medical psychotherapists primarily address:

The dangers and risks of inexpert interventions; using understanding of brain, body and autonomic nervous system functioning in accounting for the clinical consequences of multiple traumas; the place of family in personal psychotherapy; the economic implications of intensive and team-based treatment; the influence of training on boundary violations; the need for methodical investigation alongside the use of evidence-based practice; the development of expertise in psychological and psychosomatic dangers of personality disorder; and idiosyncrative responses to therapy in the presence of commonly prescribed psychotropic medications.

(p. 303)

Many medical psychotherapists have a psychiatric background. However, clinicians who are not psychiatrists are also involved in addressing the above practice issues of helping our clients who are having some type of medical issue.

Medical Family Therapy

Let's switch now and talk about what Medical Family Therapy (MedFT) is and how it is different from "regular" psychotherapy and family therapy. You might ask yourself the following questions: am I doing medical family therapy if one of my clients has an illness? How will my clinical documentation be different as a medical family therapist? According to the originators of MedFT, "all human problems are biopsychosocial systems problems" and Medical Family Therapy brings this unique perspective to the therapeutic work with families (or individuals) (Doherty et al., 1994). That is, MedFT is a whole subfield of the broader field of Marriage and Family Therapy that attends to not only the relationships among family members but also the fact that each individual is a biopsychosocial spiritual system of themselves and operates in some sort of integrated way. While traditional family therapy has focused on relationship and systemic underpinnings of mental health issues, medical family therapy also considers the overlap of the biomedical and psychosocial (Doherty et al., 1994). Again, traditional family therapy has tried to understand individuals within systems, keeping pathology at arm's length, while medical family therapy sees the same individuals within systems, recognizing that there are biomedical aspects of the individual and family's experiences.

A medical family therapist considers both medical and mental health conditions and the delivery of the care is through collaborative teams (Doherty et al., 2014). This subfield requires a basic understanding of some chronic illnesses and medical jargon. Usually, medical family therapists are located in a healthcare facility. The main family therapy system concepts (circular interactions, boundaries, etc.) are combined with medical knowledge to bridge the mind-body gap (Doherty et al., 1994). In addition, medical family therapists must have an awareness of self that goes beyond the traditional self-of-the-therapist model to include an awareness of relationships and emotions related to healthcare experiences and settings (McDaniel et al., 2014). These therapists need an awareness of the potential triggers that therapy brings and the additional layer of personal triggers related to health issues and the healthcare system. Ways to identify these triggers may be similar to other training tools. The use of a **Medical Genogram**, for example, could facilitate a trainee's awareness and identification of potential biases or triggers. A medical genogram is similar to other genograms (see Chapter 9) while more explicitly including graphical representations of medical conditions such as any medical illnesses, causes of death, hereditary traits, and other factors that might put individuals at risk for health issues. These symbols might include heart disease, diabetes, cancer, Alzheimer's, asthma, autism, depression, high blood pressure, etc. Currently, the American Association for Marriage and Family Therapy has a list of competencies outlined for MedFTs that provides a brief overview of some of the required skills and knowledge needed to identify as and implement MedFT (AAMFT, 2018).

Another aspect that makes medical family therapy unique is the collaborative and multidisciplinary aspect. In medical family therapy, you hold many roles. In fact, one Medical Family Therapy text outlined nine potential roles of a MedFT (Falke & D'Arrigo-Patrick, 2015). In contrast to a community mental health clinic where you may be collaborating with other mental health professionals (LMFTs, LCSWs, and LMHCs) or maybe even psychiatrists, in medical family therapy you are also working with providers who are not experts in mental health but in another subject area. One individual client may have a primary care physician as well as specialty providers such as a neurologist, a gastroenterologist, and a psychiatrist who all work in different settings. They could potentially work in different medical systems as well, but you are their assigned medical family therapist. You will provide that collaborative and zoomed out, holistic perspective. You may also facilitate communication across the medical professionals, given your unique skillset. You just may find yourself the one in charge of the whole communication chain.

Consider this example: your clients, Tiffany and Tom, are in couple's therapy with you, discussing their struggles with fertility and their recurrent miscarriages. You may collaborate with Tiffany's OB/GYN who originally diagnosed her infertility and has been treating the recurrent miscarriages, Tiffany's reproductive endocrinologist who is assisting her in assessing hormones and providing fertility treatments, her rheumatologist who diagnosed her Celiac disease symptoms (an autoimmune disorder that can be associated with fertility issues), and her gastroenterologist who is providing management of her Celiac disease symptoms. All these specialists operate independently, yet as a systems-trained clinician, you can see the intersections and overlap. Each individual provider (including you) is treating an aspect of Tiffany's fertility struggles. You may have to communicate (either verbally or through written communication) with each provider to stay updated on the current treatment recommendations, and in return, you may be providing updates to the rest of the team. In addition, you may find that when communicating with the gastroenterologist, he is a bit harsh in the way that he speaks about Tiffany. She may have mentioned in her session with you that she feels judged by him and that maybe if she had made dietary changes sooner, she would not have had so many miscarriages. You may engage in communication with the gastroenterologist who fosters his empathy for Tiffany and her situation and challenges his perspective. Often, physicians do not get the same people skills training that therapists do. You may be able to help repair Tiffany's relationship with the provider through that conversation in a better effort to support her overall mental health and well-being and this could be reflected in her medical record.

You will both have to write encounter notes (outlined in a section below) based on these conversations. When we work systemically, we can write systemically and use less pathologizing language as well. In some places, where only one encounter note is needed and you were the initiator of the encounter, you would be able to write an encounter note where you discuss the presenting problem with a more systemic lens and write things like "Therapist and GI provider met to discuss pt's current poc (plan of care). Provider mentioned that the current medication was dc (discontinued) and therapist facilitated exploration of other contributing issues to pt's current dx."

Why Documentation Is Important

You may ask, why is documentation so important for Medical Psychotherapy/MedFT? This is a great question. Part of being a good clinician, in general, is keeping good records. That is why it is in almost all organizations' Codes of Ethics. For instance, the American Psychological Association's (APA) code of ethics has a whole section on record keeping and fees. Code 6.01 is about the documentation of professional and scientific work and states:

> Psychologists create, and to the extent the records are under their control, maintain, disseminate, store, retain, and dispose of records and data relating to their professional and scientific work in order to (1) facilitate provision of services later by them or by other professionals, (2) allow for replication of research design and analyses, (3) meet institutional requirements, (4) ensure accuracy of billing and payments, and (5) ensure compliance with law.

Think about why we keep therapy notes. It's for a variety of reasons: we want to be able to keep track of what is going on in the case, track progress toward collaboratively set goals, identify interventions and their outcomes, and make sure we are fulfilling our role as therapists as aligned with our chosen theory. In addition, we keep notes to have a record to refer to when we are thinking about where to go next as we guide our clients through the therapeutic journey.

With Medical Psychotherapy/MedFT, documentation becomes even more important because it is a way to document the coordination of care. Typically, in the 2020s, clinics are using some version of an electronic health record (eRecord, Epic, Nextgen, etc.). Though rare, you may operate in a clinic that is still functioning with paper health files, so written documentation becomes even more important to track information. In addition to less paper waste, an electronic health record creates ease for coordination of care and collaboration across disciplines. Sometimes, the mental health and physical health records are separated by the "glass wall" and require providers to acknowledge when they are "breaking" the wall to access the records. In some locations and systems, these records are available to both sides, and sometimes the patient/client as well. This is more typical in a fully integrated healthcare setting (McDaniel et al., 2014). The way that this electronic health record is managed will vary across health systems and across clinics.

One last consideration of Medical Psychotherapy/MedFT that will influence this book's focus on documentation is whether the setting is outpatient, co-located, or integrated (McDaniel et al., 2014). Collaboration may happen in any setting, that is, working with other care providers to provide care for the same patient. In a co-located setting, you have two (or more) kinds of medical care located in the same place. You may have, for example, a mental health and a family medicine clinic located in the same building. A fully integrated healthcare setting is one where all the providers are integrated into one place and hold equal roles in the collaborative team; care is not differentiated between the specializations but treated as a system (McDaniel et al., 2014). In integrated care, providers will share documentation and communicate frequently for the greater good of the patient (Doherty et al., 1994). It is important to identify what kind of system you are operating in, to know who has access to the notes and what kind of language to use. Integrated will mean that all providers have full access to your notes; co-located will mean that they have access to some but not all; and collaborative could mean that they have access, but depending on the type of clinic, they may not.

The Treatment Recommendation Letter

A significant consideration when working with patients who are experiencing medical and psychological issues is noncompliance. That is, the patients are not following through with the treatment and intervention plan. If this happens with one of your clients, you might consider drafting a **treatment recommendation letter** (Lewis et al., 1991). Treatment recommendation letters are used when a healthcare patient is non-compliant. Noncompliance behaviors range from the mild (lateness for appointments) to the dangerous (refusing hospital evaluation for lethality).

In essence, a treatment recommendation letter is a contract between therapist and client around the issue of the client's mental health as a means to increase and structure their compliance to treatment. This form of contract attempts to explain to the client (first in writing and then through discussion) applied psychological concepts as well as ethical and legal considerations. The treatment recommendation letter takes medical and professional language and presents it in a language the client can understand. This is quite important since clients may not follow through if psychological and medical jargon is used because they do not understand what is being asked of them. The treatment recommendation letter attempts to address noncompliance factors by improving patient understanding, soliciting their involvement, and highlighting similar belief sets between patient and therapist (i.e., "The fact that you have headaches for which your physician can find no physiological cause does not mean the pain is not real. Stress can be a factor. Let's examine that possibility") (Lewis et al., 1991, p. 192).

When writing the treatment recommendation letter, there are a few factors to consider that will make the letter more useful to gain the client's compliance. You need to consider the vocabulary/reading level of patients. If there are multiple people (i.e., couple or family), it is best to write for the person with the lower vocabulary/reading level. You might then also consider if the patient is ready to listen to you as you explain your appraisal of pathology outlined in the letter. Lewis et al. (1991) provided the following guidelines to consider when writing the letter:

* Wording the letter to increase motivation
* What to put in the letter to lessen the chance of someone else reading it
* Speculations concerning unconscious or nondisclosed events (i.e., childhood sexual abuse) are both ethically and therapeutically ill-advised because they are unsubstantiated and frightening to new patients
* No more than two to three pages
* Be as specific as possible
* Address the presenting concerns of the consumer
* Use the patient's title

They suggest that the letter be eight paragraphs. Depending on the context in which you are working and the type of client you have (i.e., individual, couple, or family), you might need to make modifications to this format. Here, briefly, is what is usually contained in each paragraph.

November 17, 2023

Salvador White
6789 Tilo Boulevard
Los Angeles, CA 90001

Dear Mr. White,

This letter is in relation to our therapy meetings these past four weeks. It is based upon those meetings, your medical records, and consultation with past service providers.

I want to thank you for being open and participatory in your sessions. On two of those sessions (October 19th and November 2nd), you arrived more than 15 minutes late. You had also not shown up for your session on October 26 and did not inform our office of not coming.

You came to our center after two different stays in the psychiatric hospital. You mentioned that you were hoping to work on what you called "living a stable life." Your goals were to be medication compliant (which you stated you had not been up to this point), decrease feelings of anxiety, improve your relationship with family members, and not want to self-harm.

I want to also talk about some of your personality strengths. It is important to note that you were the one to initiate coming to our center. This is a demonstration of your desire to change. In session, you have used humor, which in some ways is a useful coping strategy.

I just want to remind you of some of our clinic's administrative policies. We ask that if you are not going to attend a session you contact us at least 24 hours in advance, otherwise, you will be charged the full fee. Also, we will not meet with you if you arrive after 20 minutes late. Please make sure that you attend and are on time for your sessions. On our end, our goal is to ensure that you do not have to wait once your scheduled time arrives. Also, in session, we discussed a safety plan. Please make sure that you keep this available to you in case you ever need it.

We realize that your mental health is very important to you and that you are trying to get your life into a stable place. We are very appreciative that you've chosen to come to our clinic during this journey in your life. From working with many clients, we know that the journey becomes easier with more consistent visits as we are better able to address all your treatment goals. We look forward to continuing this journey with you.

Respectfully,

Virginia Johnson

Virginia Johnson, Psy.D.
Hope and Healing Center

I have read the above letter, understand it, and agree to abide by its guidelines.

_____   _____
Salvador White   Date

Figure 11.3 Sample of Treatment Recommendation Letter.

1 The dates of services and explanation of what the therapist's impressions are based on (such as psychological testing and previous medical records)
2 A reinforcement of cooperation and an explanation of how the client's behaviors helped provide an understanding of the client.
3 A focus on the presenting problems and associated symptomology.
4 A focus on the presenting problems and associated symptomology.
5 A focus on the presenting problems and associated symptomology.
6 Descriptions of personality strengths. Lewis et al. (1991) recommend that you have as many strengths as you have treatment goals so that they are balanced.
7 Overview of administrative issues (such as fees, policies, limits of confidentiality, and emergency processes).
8 Appreciation of the client's initial cooperation and encouragement for them to make decisions regarding their treatment.

Figure 11.3 presents an abbreviated sample of treatment recommendation letter.

Some Considerations for Medical Psychotherapy Notes

As you know from Chapter 2, all psychotherapists must write progress notes when working with patients. This is the case when working with medically related patients. Knowing the kind of system we are in shapes the way that we write these notes. We want the notes to reflect what happened in the session with enough detail to support the billing code for insurance but not so much detail that everyone is accessing the patient's private information. Another question to ask is, how would my client feel if they read this note? Again, in this age of technology, it is not unheard of for patients to be able to legally access their electronic health records through a portal and have access to read the notes. Are you using language that is respectful of the patient? Are you providing enough detail to support your medical billing code? These are some questions to guide yourself as you are writing.

Now let's return to the idea that medical psychotherapy is about collaborative relationships. Multidisciplinary means multiple providers, by definition. There is a common saying "there are too many cooks in the kitchen" but in the case of medical psychotherapy, you have a sense of who is chef, sous chef, etc. All providers are contributing but in varying capacities. You are all working together for the good of one meal, or, in this case, one family. Therefore, all providers will need access to the recipe, the medical record. If they are not able to physically access it, due to electronic health record barriers, not being fully integrated, or that rare paper record case, then you as the therapist will need to provide information via phone, fax, or handwritten communication.

In terms of language, you want to be clear and concise. As therapists, we will have much more detail in our heads, and we understand that there are complex processes that occur. For the purposes of the documentation, however, we want to be clear, concise, and organized. This is important when collaborating with other professionals as well. When discussing a mutual patient (with a signed release of information form) we want to make sure we are providing the most minimal clinically relevant information. We want to be a part of the treatment team, but the other medical professionals don't need to know the details of our patient's trauma history, for example. If that trauma history is clinically relevant to the patient's care, then we would want to discuss it with the most minimally appropriate, clinically relevant details.

Let's return to our client, Tiffany. During the course of working with the couple, you find out that Tiffany has a history of sexual assault. She shares the story with you, with the support of her husband. She has questions about how her experience of sexual assault may have physically impacted her, potentially contributing to her infertility struggles beyond the impact of the Celiacs alone. She doesn't know how to talk to her provider about this and you spend some time in session figuring out how she will address it in her upcoming visit. When you write the note for this session, you would not describe the sexual assault in detail, even if Tiffany shares those details with you. You would however write something like, "Patient disclosed history of sexual assault. This therapist provided empathetic listening and validation as patient shared her story. Session focused on supporting patient to follow-up with provider about health-related questions." In addition, if Tiffany allows permission (verbally and through a written release), you may reach out to the OB/GYN to let them know that you have a recent treatment-related concern and that Tiffany will be following up with him. You would then write an encounter note.

One last consideration for collaboration: physicians often have patients scheduled back-to-back and their training has oriented them in a way to listen for relevant details and come to a quick conclusion to provide a diagnosis. This may shift the way that we write and the way that we speak to physicians because we need to provide information that is necessary for clinical care, but make sure that we get those details across before they check out or must run to the next patient. We will also have to have some level of medical record literacy and comprehension ourselves. Shorthand is all things that may show up in medical records. Figure 11.4 presents a few that may be helpful to know.

Encounter Notes

An encounter note is created every time you have an encounter! An encounter could be a walk in the hallway discussing a relevant change

Sx......................symptoms
Dx......................diagnosis
Hx......................history
Prn......................as needed
PCP.................primary care physician
c/o.................complaining of
dc....................discontinued
poc..................plan of care

Figure 11.4 Some Useful Medical Shorthand.

in your patient's symptoms with the provider who prescribed the medications (making sure not to use identifiers in order to protect patient privacy) or it could be a phone call with the provider. Encounter notes are important because ideally in places where records are not integrated, each provider will still have written documentation of that conversation that now lives in the patient's chart. Even in places where it is integrated, having two encounter notes for the same encounter written from two discipline-specific perspectives will be beneficial for long-term coordination and collaboration of care. An encounter note should include the two providers who talked (you and the other providers), the bare minimum about what was discussed (i.e., providers discussed an update on patient medication), and the follow-up plan (i.e., will stay in touch prn). Here is an example of the body of the text for the encounter you (the psychotherapist) had with Tiffany's OB/GYN:

> Therapist spoke with pt's OB/GYN per discussion in session. Therapist informed provider about relevant updates to pt's medical hx. Therapist communicated potential correlation between pt's medical hx and current sx of infertility. We will follow-up prn or after pt's next visit.

Letter Writing for Gender-Affirming Treatments

Recently, psychotherapists have been one of a few healthcare professionals eligible to write letters supporting a transgender client's desire for gender-affirming medical treatments. Usually, this endorsement letter comes from a psychiatrist, psychologist, or other licensed psychotherapists. As therapists, we are usually not in the gatekeeper role for one of our clients to receive medically necessary treatment (Budge, 2015). Thus, we have rarely been making these types of assessments or writing these types of letters. However, our society is changing, and more clients are likely to seek our services for these types of assessments and letters.

Most therapists lack the training and experience needed to work with transsexual clients (Coolhart et al., 2008; Coolhart et al., 2013). These authors have developed an assessment tool to assess transgender clients' readiness for gender transition. They have constructed one tool for adult clients and one tool for youth clients. We will not go into the assessment aspect here but we recommend that you do if you find yourself working with a transgender client who desires gender transition. The World Professional Association for Transgender Health (WPATH) has developed Standards of Care (currently on version 8) that promotes clinical guidance on working with transgender clients based on the best available science and professional consensus. The remainder of this section will talk about ideas about writing the actual letter for gender-affirming treatments.

In order to write a letter for hormone therapy, clients need to meet several criteria, including (1) the capacity to make an informed decision to consent to treatment, (2) being 18 years old (although provisions may be made for someone 16 or 17 with parents' permission), (3) documentation of persistent gender dysphoria, and (4) control over medical and/or mental comorbid conditions (Lev, 2004; Unger, 2016).

Budge (2015) provides several suggestions for writing letters around supporting a client's desire for medical transition. These include:

- Having conversations with them about their insurance company and medical plans (i.e., whether they will engage a specialist or generalist).
- Being familiar with the most recent WPATH Standards of Care.
- Contacting the client's chosen doctor or medical clinic to find out what their requirements are for hormone or surgery letters.
- Being overt with the client about the assessment and evaluation process and what information would be included in the letter.
- Being overt with the client about the gender dysphoria and/or gender identity disorder diagnoses and that these will be included in the letter.

Coolhart et al. (2008) recommend using terms such as assigned gender and preferred gender. They defined these terms, "Assigned gender refers to that which was assigned to the person when they were born. Preferred gender refers to the gender the person experiences internally and wishes to transition to externally" (p. 308).

Lev (2004) suggested that the format for the letter for recommendation include the following areas:

1 **Client identification:** The client's legal name, nickname, address, phone number, and other contact information. Further, this would include demographics such as ethnicity, race, religion, and other pertinent information. Lastly, the client should be described by their preferred pronoun.
2 **Reason for referral:** This section describes why the client is seeking medical treatment as well as what assessments have been conducted.

3   **Familial history:** Pertinent information about the client's family of origin should be provided, describing the client's childhood history. As much as possible, this information should be obtained through contact with the client's family members.

4   **Current living situation:** This area provides information about the client's present functioning, including whether they are in a romantic relationship, marital status, whether they have children and are in a parental role, and whom they live with. This section should describe the length, quality, and functioning of the client's interpersonal relationships.

5   **Work and education:** This section describes the client's school and post-secondary education. It would include any learning difficulties or developmental challenges. Further, the client's work history and current employment should be explored. The therapist will discuss the likelihood of the client maintaining their work status throughout the transition and their plans for continued work.

6   **Gender issues:** Here, the therapist documents the client's history with their relationship to their gender. It includes a discussion of how the client experienced gender issues as well as their trajectory regarding gender expression.

7   **Social support:** This section presents the client's social supports, including family, friends, connection to the transgender community, hobbies, and social activities.

8   **Psychosocial stressors:** The therapist documents any medical and/or mental health issues. Various areas to write down (which would have been explored in the assessment) include the client's relationship to drugs and alcohol, history of physical and mental abuse/domestic violence, suicidality, legal history, and previous therapy.

9   **Summary:** This last section describes the therapist's observations of the client and provides a recommendation for the client, which may include further psychotherapy, gender-assisted treatments, or other recommendations.

Remember that this letter is based on an extremely thorough assessment. Before you begin the assessment, we encourage you to consult with therapists who have conducted gender-assisted treatment assessments as well as base your work on established standards of care. You should also consult with more experienced therapists once you have written a draft of your recommendation for treatment letter to ensure that you provide the information appropriately.

Summary

Psychotherapists will occasionally write to communicate with people outside of the therapeutic context. As a therapist, it will be important for you to know your legal obligations when writing to people other than your client, specifically when there is a court order for information. You may also need to write to people in the medical context so that you can coordinate care for your client when they are experiencing medical issues. In both the legal and medical context, it is important to inform your client about what you are writing and whom you are writing to as it may impact the therapeutic relationship.

References

Ackerman, M. J. (2006). Forensic report writing. *Journal of Clinical Psychology, 62*(1), 59–72.

American Association for Marriage and Family Therapy. (2018). *Competencies for family therapists working in healthcare care settings.* Retrieved from www. aamft.org/healthcare.

Anchor, K. (1991). Introduction to medical psychotherapy. In K. N. Anchor (Ed.), *The handbook of medical psychotherapy* (pp. 3–24). Hogrefe & Huber Publishers.

Budge, S. L. (2015). Psychotherapists as gatekeepers: An evidence-based case study highlighting the role and process of letter writing for transgender clients. *Psychotherapy, 52*(3), 287–297.

Coolhart, D., Baker, A., Farmer, S., Malaney, M., & Shipman, D. (2013). Therapy with transsexual youth and their families: A clinical tool for assessing youth's readiness for gender transition. *Journal of Marital and Family Therapy, 39*(2), 223–242.

Coolhart, D., Provancher, N., Hager, A., & Wang, M. -N. (2008). Recommending transsexual clients for gender transition: A therapeutic tool for assessing readiness. *Journal of GLBT Family Studies, 4*(3), 301–324.

Doherty, W. J., McDaniel, S. H., & Helpworth, J. (1994). Medical family therapy: An emerging arena for family therapy. *Journal of Family Therapy, 16*(1), 31–46.

Doherty, W. J., McDaniel, S. H., & Hepworth, J. (2014). Contributions of medical family therapy to the changing health care system. *Family Process, 53*(3), 529–543.

Falke, S. I., & D'Arrigo-Patrick, E. (2015). Medical Family therapists in action: Embracing multiple roles. *Journal of Marital and Family Therapy, 41*(4), 428–442.

Lev, A. I. (2004). *Transgender emergence: Therapeutic guidelines for working with gender-variant people and their families.* The Hawthorn Clinical Practice Press.

Lewis, J., Stokes, D., & Bolton, S. (1991). The treatment recommendation letter: A standard of care techniques. In K. N. Anchor (Ed.), *The handbook of medical psychotherapy* (pp. 191–206). Hogrefe & Huber Publishers.

Mace, C., & Healy, K. (2011). Medical psychotherapy: A specialty for now. *The Psychiatrist, 35*, 301–304.

McDaniel, S. H., Doherty, W. J., & Hepworth, J. (2014). *Medical family therapy and integrated care* (2nd ed.). American Psychological Association.

Salmon, C., O'Conor, R., Singh, S., Ramaswamy, R., Kannry, J., Wolf, M. S., & Federman, A. D. (2016). Characteristics of outpatient clinical summaries in the United States. *International Journal of Medical Information, 94*, 75–80.

Signs, T. L. (2015). The art of letter writing in medical family therapy. *Journal of Family Psychotherapy, 26*(3), 243–246.

Unger, C. A. (2016). Hormone therapy for transgender patients. *Translational Andrology and Urology, 5*(6), 877–884.

Chapter 12

Article and Grant Writing in Psychotherapy

Pei-Fen Li, Kelsey Railsback, and Michael D. Reiter

Throughout this book, we have primarily talked about writing for documentation or therapeutic purposes. In this chapter, we shift our goals and talk about writing for larger audiences. Therapy is a process that needs to be continually enhanced and refined and this happens when we, as professionals, pass on knowledge to one another. This happens by engaging in research and disseminating findings and clinical experiences to other therapists.

In this chapter, we put together thoughts and suggestions for you to be able to successfully write grants, articles, and even books. Using our collective experience which spans the writing of 12 books, over 10 book chapters, over 30 journal articles, and various accepted grants as well as being the editor, editorial assistant, special sections editor, and reviewers for over 10 different journals and 3 books, we hope to share some of what we've learned with you so that you can more effectively write and publish since we believe that knowledge not shared is knowledge that's wasted.

Writing for Journals

As a master's or doctoral student, are you trying to get published? Have you engaged in clinical work that you think might be useful for other people to know about? Have you conducted research that you'd like to publish? Have you thought about submitting your work and ideas to a journal? Are you wondering what journals tell authors? This section will cover how to write an article on clinical issues, and how to get it accepted by an academic journal.

Therapy students often struggle with publication. One reason students become overwhelmed with the idea of writing for publication is simply that they are unfamiliar with the process. We would like to offer you our perspectives on what the journals are looking for and how to increase the likelihood of your article being published.

Chapter 8 introduced you to the idea of therapeutic journals. This type of journal is for anyone's use, where people keep track of their thoughts,

DOI: 10.4324/9781003294702-12

usually for their own purposes. Most likely, they don't want anyone else to read what they've written. We are now going to present a different type of journal, an academic journal. **Academic journals** are magazines that publish articles whose intended audience is a specific research or clinical community. They are usually published three to five times per year and each journal has maybe five to twenty different articles per issue.

Most people in the lay community will never open let alone read an article that is in an academic journal. However, these journals are the primary medium in which knowledge and information are discussed in many professions. Academic journals help clinicians, scientists, and practitioners keep up to date on the most recent conceptualizations, techniques, and research in a specific field. There are journals for medicine, law, mathematics, arts, humanities, social sciences, and, of course, psychotherapy. In each field (and there are journals for a much wider variety of fields than this), there are multiple different journals. Psychotherapy has hundreds of journals, including *American Journal of Psychotherapy*, *Journal of Counseling Psychology*, *Journal of Cognitive Psychotherapy*, *Journal of Marital and Family Therapy*, *Journal of Systemic Therapies*, *Journal of Arts and Psychotherapy*, *Journal of Consulting and Clinical Psychotherapy*, *Journal of Clinical Social Work*, *Psychoanalytic Psychotherapy*, *European Psychiatry*, and the *International Journal of Systemic Therapy*. This is just a very small sampling of the journals that are out there. Each journal has a different focus. Some are based on the various models of psychotherapy (i.e., cognitive-behavioral, psychoanalytic, gestalt), some on the client type (i.e., group, family, individual, or couple), and some are based on the treatment setting (i.e., private practice, residential settings, hospitals). There will be at least one, but most likely a lot more (since there is overlap in the aims and scope of each journal) different journals that your article would be suited for. Your job will be to figure out which journal is most appropriate for the content of your piece.

Most journals, at least the ones that you would want to publish with, are **peer-reviewed**. What this means is that once you send your manuscript to the editor of that journal, they will send it out to peers—people in the same field who know about the topic that you wrote about. Using a reviewing guide that each journal has, they will review your document to ensure that it is written well, accurate, and contributes something to the field. Usually, there are three peer reviewers who do so through a **blind review process**, meaning that your name is removed from the document so they do not know who wrote it, which allows the reviewers to be more objective in their review. Individually, they will send their comments back to the editor along with their suggestion of what to do with the article. The journal editor will then consider the feedback from all the reviewers and make a final determination about the article. This decision is usually (1) not to publish, (2) publish with significant revisions, (3) publish with minor revisions, and (4) publish with no revisions. This last decision is extremely rare. Most peer reviewers usually have many comments and suggestions of how to make your article better.

Once you get the decision from the journal editor, you can then choose whether to go along with the suggestions, challenge the suggestions, or send your article to a different journal. Keep in mind, you should not send your article for review to different journals at the same time. Only send your article to one journal and wait for their decision. And as Tom Petty once said, "the waiting is the hardest part." You should not expect a quick turnaround from when you submit the article to when you receive the decision. Most journals take at least two months since the peer reviewers are usually faculty members at universities who have classes to teach, student papers to grade, their own research to conduct, and their own publications to write. Some journals may take more than half a year to get back to you. Whichever journal you submit to, please be patient. In the following section, we provide some potential steps for you to take when thinking about submitting an article for publication.

Step 1: Decide Which Is the Best Journal for Your Article

Choose reputable journals. One thing that you might think about when submitting to a journal is the journal's **impact factor**. This factor is a numerical number that focuses on the average number of times that articles from that journal were cited in the last couple of years. The higher the impact factor, the more respected the journal. Impact factors will change based on the field. In most fields, scores above a one are good. Keep in mind that not all journals have an impact number and just because a journal has a low impact number it doesn't mean that the articles published in it aren't good.

Be wary if a journal is asking you for money to publish your article. The article should be published based on its merit, not on your finances. However, there are times when journals will only publish if you pay a publishing fee. This usually happens when it is an **Open Access journal**, which allows anyone to download the article for free (whereas traditional journals are based on a subscription service that university libraries tend to pay so the students and faculty at the university have access to those journals). Most people will not publish in Open Access journals since this can be quite expensive. Those who do tend to have grant money for their research that covers the fees for publication.

Step 2: Research the Submission Instructions

Journals will provide you with a checklist of what they require. Look for "call for submissions," "instructions to authors," "the submission process," and similar language to find exactly what you need to do. In addition to the article, most journals will request an abstract with keywords. They will also want to know pertinent information about you and any additional authors you worked with to write the article. Articles are most often requested in Microsoft Word or PDF formats.

Step 3: Understand Their Content Expectations

Familiarize yourself with the journal by reading the journal's "About" page which should list the Aims and Scope of the journal. Further, you should review their recently published articles. Journals will also highlight some articles that represent their brand (e.g., clinical work with marginalized populations), so explore their most downloaded articles and other articles they are featuring. Your article will not be accepted if it strays too far from the brand.

Step 4: Identify Their Formatting Standards

Unless explicitly stated otherwise, write your article in the most current APA format. At the time we are writing this, the standard is APA 7. Keep your headings in accordance with APA levels of heading (i.e., Level 1, Level 2, and so on), but we recommend removing any Microsoft Word heading styles you may have applied to your draft. These styles may make it easier to navigate a longer paper and automatically connect it with a table of contents; however, they can create more of a formatting headache for the production editor. This same concept applies to any other linked items: avoid them. Keep your work in plain text whenever possible. The only exception may be digital object identifier (DOI) hyperlinks (not URL) in the reference page; this makes it easier for a reviewer or editor to check that your links match the source material.

Step 5: Know Your Worth

What are you contributing to the journal? Adopt the attitude that your work is helping contribute to their journal rather than an attitude that they are doing you a favor by publishing your article. The journal should publish a paper *from* you, not *for* you. Journals need content. You provide that content, and with how the system is set up, you are not getting paid (at least by the journal) for the hard work that you put into the article. Thus, know that journal editors want you to submit. And that they want you to submit quality work. The next section highlights some ideas about ensuring that your manuscript is well written which may smooth the acceptance process.

Editing Your Article for Publication

Giftwrapping

If you are like us, then you have forgotten someone's birthday once or twice only to remember in a panic that you need to procure a gift ASAP. What do you do? You first find an item you think they will like. You then wrap the item in such a way that lets the recipient know it is a present for them rather than something that was just lying around. Regardless, giftwrapping is key. You can either get a gift bag with tissue paper or use giftwrapping paper to wrap your tidy box. If you are going the extra mile, you add a bow.

If you are submitting your work for publication, you either have crafted this piece for the journal or it was something you had already written that was lying around. Regardless, you need to pay attention to how you present the material to the journal. It needs to be polished if they are going to receive it as a gift.

Now, giftwrapping can be a tedious step, which is why many companies allow you to request a giftwrapping service either in person or at an online checkout. If you don't use a professional editor, you need to take your work as seriously as a professional would. You increase your chances of having your work accepted if it is packaged nicely. You *significantly* increase your chances of having your work accepted if it is packaged impeccably. In our capacity as journal editors or reviewers, we have downgraded the quality of many submissions because the author(s) did not take the time to ensure that the basic formatting and writing quality of their article was as good as they could make it. In today's age, it is extremely easy to use spell check, grammar check, and other online programs that will help you with the formatting and quality writing of your article. If writing is an issue for you, then yes, somehow procure yourself an editor to help you *before* you submit your article. Whatever you do, our advice to you is this: add a bow.

Know Their Standard

This brings us to standards and expectations. If you want your work to look professional, you must know what the journal thinks professionalism looks like. Journals will almost always want your work formatted in the most up-to-date APA standard (i.e., APA 7). If you submit a paper that has no regard for a unified standard, your work can appear chaotic. People are constantly judging and making determinations with limited data. It's not their fault—we're all just people. But without adhering to the standard, you will likely come across as someone who (a) doesn't care, (b) is incompetent, or (c) is both.

Now, we've been writing, reading, and editing papers and articles since 2000. In all that time, we've never seen a paper where nothing needed to be changed. Authors with the fanciest credentials have had the silliest errors, and even papers that would get an A in the classroom will have a plethora of mistakes or formatting issues. The idea is to get as close to perfect while keeping in mind that there is no absolute perfection that you can achieve. Nova (2013) explained that writing is the collision between what one wants and what one gets. He related this to a quote he had read from Robert Graves, "There is no such thing as good writing, only good rewriting" (p. 24).

A journal will have professional reviewers and editors who go through your work before it is officially published, but don't use that as an excuse to put forth less effort. As an extreme example, if a reviewer sees an article with 40+ errors, they will lose faith in the credibility of the author even if the content is good.

Know Your Audience

Besides having an appreciation for which journal tends to publish in the content area of your paper, you'll also want to think about who your intended audience is. You will write differently if you are writing for the general public, undergraduate students, graduate students, or professionals in the field. Kekäle et al. (2009) recommended that journal authors explain their ideas and findings in plain language. The purpose of journal articles is to disseminate information. If the reader does not understand what you are writing, you will have a publication under your belt, but the field is not enhanced.

Use Your Resources

Before you submit your article, check it for flow, organization, grammar, and mechanical writing errors. If you are at a university, it likely has a writing center; use that! If you are out in the field, there are many online resources. For instance, Grammarly is accessible to anyone with access to the internet and is often available to students for free or discounted rates via their institution. Don't forget Google is a resource too, and you can use Google as an editing tool to look up any formatting, mechanical, or grammatical issues. Your final resource should be your writing support group (e.g., friends, mentors, and colleagues). Ask someone to look over your article before you submit it. The more times they can review it, the better. In fact, the more people you have who are willing to look over your paper, the better. You want as much feedback as possible. Bauer and Hammer (1996) found that greater levels of feedback from peers were associated with higher article quality. Writing can be vulnerable, and sometimes we feel very exposed when someone reads our work but try to overcome any hesitancy you have in this regard by focusing on the desired result: quality work.

We will just briefly talk about **plagiarism**, which is using someone else's words or ideas without appropriate recognition of that person(s) through citing. You should keep quotations to a minimum, especially lengthy quotes that would need to be block quoted. Most of your introduction section should include a significant number of paraphrases. Provide the citation in the sentence when you first present that person's ideas. Make it clear that these are the other person's ideas rather than yours. What you will do in the article is integrate other people's ideas to help provide a foundation for your own ideas and your own take on the matter. There are several websites available for you to upload your article to check that there is no plagiarism. You should use these. However, you should also know that you do not need to use these by not using anyone else's words in your paper unless they are in quotation marks!

Appreciate the Importance of Practice and Repetition

Some people take a very long time to write a paper because they try to make the article perfect as it moves from their brain to the page. You should go into the writing process knowing that whatever gets on the page is the very first draft. There will likely be many drafts of your paper before you submit it to the journal. We call these *iterations* and all good papers have gone through many iterations before they see the light of day. As Caterjian (2013) explained, "Publication writing often improves with repeated practice whereby there has been unbiased or objective support from, often colleagues regarding structure, composition, comprehension and flow" (p. 56).

If English Is Not Your First Language (And You Are Submitting an English-Language Paper, Of Course)

Don't fret! If you follow the packaging guidelines and have good content, the editor(s) will comb through and correct any obvious errors. But what you want to make sure comes across is that you tried. Think back to the giftwrapping example. If we present a birthday gift to someone, and it is haphazardly wrapped with crumpled, holiday wrapping paper, it appears that we did not put forth any effort for their gift. They may or may not be offended, but the gift will not be received in the same way. If you can tell I made small mistakes wrapping the gift—the wrapping paper just barely doesn't fully cover the entire box—it is easily forgivable. If you want to be sure your paper is well written, our advice in this circumstance is to have a native English speaker review your work and let you know if anything seems slightly off.

What Journals Tell Authors

After you submit your paper, there are potentially two steps: the first is that your article is reviewed, and the second is that it is edited. The journal reviewer will read your article and see if it is a good fit for their journal. However, if your editing isn't up to snuff, it doesn't matter how good your content is, a reviewer may send it back to you.

Some journals will go into extensive detail about why your paper was rejected, but if it looks to them like you didn't try, the reviewer will be less likely to give you detailed feedback. The amount of feedback you receive will be based on the journal's prestige, the number of reviewers currently working, and how much effort it appears you applied.

After your work is approved, some journals will have an editor who will comb through the article. One or more editors may do copyediting followed by production editing to make sure it is up to the journal's standards. Remember that some reviewers become editors and vice versa; some do both jobs. This is even more reason for you to make sure your gift is impeccably wrapped! If you are hoping they won't catch something—you are going to be disappointed. It's their job to look for mistakes. It's your job to submit excellent work.

Writing the Article in the First Place

By the time you sit in front of your computer to start writing, you already have expectations of what your experience will be like. Many graduate and doctoral students have trained themselves over their college careers to develop an unhealthy attitude toward writing. Students often practice unhelpful habits—such as pulling all-nighters—that lead them to anticipate hardship and exhaustion. Some students have only taught themselves to produce work under the pressure of an intense deadline. These are habits you need to unlearn. You can replace them by following the question recipe of "what" and "how."

Question 1: What Type of Writing Are You Doing?

Keep in mind that writing to get an article published in a journal is a different process than writing to submit a school assignment before the due date. Many people try to bulldoze through their writing, but you need a different approach when you are **writing on spec**. This is a phrase in the writing community that stands for "writing on speculation." You are writing on spec when you have received neither a contract nor a promise of publication. Thus, if you are writing an article with hopes of getting it published in a journal, you are writing on spec because the journal has not committed to publishing your work before you have written it. When you haven't been hired to write, there's no hard deadline and nobody waiting on you to submit the article, so you must keep yourself accountable. You must create your own boundaries, and it's often hard to enforce those on yourself.

Question 2: How Will You Approach Your Writing?

There are many techniques writers have employed to help them actually get words on the page, but one of the most common is called the **Pomodoro Technique**. The Pomodoro Technique is an example of approaching writing by time intervals rather than by word count. Broken down, the technique is really about motivation. If you tell yourself, "I have to write 5,000 words right now," that will be overwhelming. But if you say, "I have to write for 25 minutes right now," you create a context that allows you to succeed. You'll feel more refreshed at the end of the day, and you may end up with an article.

Don't focus on the outcomes that are measurable (i.e., word or page count). Just focus on time. It's about the 25 minutes, not about the words per day. You should think of the experience like getting back into the gym to lift weights: start small and slowly build up your strength. Go slowly. You can't end the day exhausted and overwhelmed because that will build up and make you associate writing with being exhausted and overwhelmed. You can't write if you don't have the motivation.

You should also know when to stop. Our recommendation is to take inspiration from Earnest Hemingway. He always liked to end his writing day when he knew what came next, not when he ran out of ideas. When he started writing the next day, he would start right where he left off. Any moments of struggle belong in the middle of your process. You should stop when you feel energized by ideas.

Question 3: How Much Can I Write about My Clients?

Psychotherapy journal articles usually focus on promoting theory and practice. While there are articles that are quantitative studies where you are sharing participant responses en masse and will not have to worry about any individual identifying information, many psychotherapy articles highlight techniques used during a session, using one or two cases to exemplify the intervention. This is perfectly fine and highly encouraged as reading about new techniques in journal articles helps the field move forward. So, what are some of the considerations you will need to keep in mind when you are writing about your cases?

When you write about a case you must make sure that there is no identifying information that would allow a reader to figure out who the client is. For instance, if you say that the client is the founder and president of the most influential social media platform, the list of possible people who this might be is quite limited. There would be too great of a chance that people might figure out who the client you are talking about is. Thus, it is your responsibility to change the identifying information (e.g., age, gender, sexual orientation, occupation) so that the client you are talking about remains anonymous. Just make sure that somewhere in the document (perhaps in parentheses or as a footnote) you let the reader know that you've changed the information.

When you write about your clients, you do not have the freedom that a fiction writer does. In fiction, there is the freedom to write whatever one wants. In writing case studies, you need to consider the welfare of others. Just like when you are writing case notes, you should always have in your head the notion, "Am I comfortable having my client read this?" While you want to be as accurate as possible about what happened in the case, there are times when a few liberties can be taken (to change important information that may threaten anonymity). However, there are a few journals that publish case studies but want them to be fictional. In this manner, you can present the whys and hows of the technique you are promoting while preventing any possible disclosure or harm to come to an actual client.

Journal Article Format

When constructing a research article, you'll want to follow the standard format that almost all professionals in most scientific fields utilize. This organizational scheme—sometimes referred to as the **IMRaD** structure—is used by those in the social sciences, natural sciences, engineering, and computer sciences. By formatting your article in this way, it becomes easier for you to disseminate the information you want and for the reader to know what to expect when they are reading it. If you are currently in school, you will be taking a research methods course where you will cover this format. Or if you are out in the field and are reading articles to update your knowledge and skills, these articles are most likely structured in the following manner.

For any of you who want to get a doctoral degree, you will be writing a dissertation. The format we are covering is the same format you will use for that (just that your dissertation will be about five to ten times as long as the article). In fact, many people publish a shorter version of their dissertation as a separate article. If you decide to do this, just keep in mind that you must rewrite it to avoid self-plagiarism.

The good news is that this standard format is not new to you. You have encountered it many times previously, starting from the science fair that you participated in during elementary or middle school. But moving forward when you want to convey information to a mass of readers, you will want your headings sections to guide you in the structure of the article. We will present the standard IMRaD format here; however, depending on the type of article you write, you might not use it. Theory pieces and case studies may have their own format, but what we present is what you will most likely see when you read or write a journal article (and will most likely be used in your grant proposal).

The standard IMRaD format for journal articles is:

- Introduction/Literature Review
- Methodology
- Results
- Discussion

Your **introduction** section can include your personal concern for the problem/topic and how you came to be interested in doing the research study. You will include relevant cultural context and general information about the topic here. Your **literature review** section will include only the highly relevant studies or groups of studies for your point (e.g., the first study on the topic, a major study that agrees with your point, a major study that disagrees with your point, and a reputable recent study on that matter). What you are trying to do in this section is provide the reader with enough information to see why you will be doing what you are doing and set up enough information to be able to understand how the results of your study fit (or don't) within what is known out there. Your **methodology** will explain why you chose the specific method you are using and the specific steps you took. This section should be so detailed that the reader will be able to conduct the same exact study (just with different participants). Your **results** section presents your findings for your reader, and your **discussion** section recaps what you've discussed in context (how your results relate back to the literature review), the implications of your study, and areas for future research and development. While it is not in the acronym, your journal article will begin with an **abstract** (a brief overview of the paper—usually around 150 words) and end with a **reference** list. Let's try applying this to a fictional study, using a simple between-subjects design regarding the impact of schizophrenic individuals' contact with dogs on their emotional well-being.

First, you should draw the reader into the article, perhaps explaining how many people (either in the country you are located or in the world) own animals. You might also talk briefly about the issue of people's emotional well-being. Whatever you write, within the first paragraph or two, you should explain to the reader the purpose of the paper. It is very important to have a purpose statement so the reader is understanding why they will be reading what comes next and can better contextualize it to the primary topic. For instance, the last sentence of your introduction might be, "Given that.32% of the population struggles with schizophrenia, the purpose of this study is to explore the impact that daily contact with a therapy dog has on schizophrenic individuals' emotional well-being."

Next, your article should explore what is currently known about the impact of people's connections to animals. You might discuss dog culture in the US and how having a dog is a common experience. Second, you would talk about how many studies already exist exploring the positive impact that pet-assisted therapy has on people. You would point out any differences and similarities to your research and explain why your research fills a gap (i.e., offers something new—in the case of our hypothetical study, it is the use of animal-assisted therapy with schizophrenic individuals). Your introduction/literature review section will end with your research question/research hypothesis. When you think about the literature review, imagine a V where you start with the more general and will end with the more specific. You should show how what you did fills the hole in the literature.

In the methods section you would talk about the criteria of inclusion for your study (who was a potential participant and who wasn't)—for instance, you might have included people who were 18 and over and who were diagnosed with schizophrenia while excluding people who self-reported having a phobia of dogs. You would then explain how you recruited your participants and the procedure you followed throughout the study (i.e., random assignment to either the animal-assisted intervention or a control condition).

In the results section, you present the data. This usually comes narratively, numerically, and visually. This is the section that has the most figures as you will display your results through figures and tables while also describing what the results were. In the discussion section, you will then put these results into context. How much did they coincide with the literature that you presented at the beginning of the paper? How did they differ? How do you make sense of your results? Did they support your hypothesis? Counter it? What did you learn? Last, you would talk about implications and future areas for researchers, animal-assisted therapy, or any other population you felt could benefit from your research.

The last thing you write for the article will be the first thing that people read, the abstract. This is the shortest section of your article but perhaps the most important because it will determine whether people read your article or not. You want the reader to be intrigued about what is in the article. Given this, take time to carefully construct your abstract. Your **abstract** will mirror your article in terms of what information you present and in what order you present it. Make sure the structure of the abstract follows the structure of the paper. You will also want to cater your tone to your chosen journal and keep the abstract simple. Here is a sample abstract (we have made up the citation):

Animal-assisted therapy (AAT) has become increasingly popular in a variety of inpatient and outpatient settings (Simmons et al., 2022). While previous studies have focused on using dogs, cats, and horses to increase individuals' moods, the current study investigates utilizing dogs in therapy with patients diagnosed with schizophrenia. A between-subjects pre-post experimental design evaluated the effect of the daily contact between people and dogs on therapy patients. Measures included a variety of determinants of emotional well-being. Analysis indicates a significant increase in well-being (p<.05) for those participants who interacted with a dog daily for two weeks. This AAT program resulted in increased emotional well-being for those diagnosed with schizophrenia leading to suggestions for increased contact between people and animals across a range of treatment contexts.

Now let's analyze the abstract line by line.

1 Animal-assisted therapy (AAT) has become increasingly popular in a variety of inpatient and outpatient settings (Simmons et al., 2022).
   - You'll want to avoid using too many citations in your abstract but having one citation may lend to your credibility. In this case, the citation gets it across to the reader that this research affects a large portion of the population.
2 While previous studies have focused on using dogs, cats, and horses to increase individuals' moods, the current study investigates utilizing dogs in therapy with patients diagnosed with schizophrenia.
   - This sentence is an acknowledgment that this is not a novel idea for a study, yet this approach to studying this topic is novel. Include what is unique about your study that makes it worthwhile and contributes to the literature.
3 A between-subjects pre-post experimental design evaluated the effect of the daily contact between people and dogs on therapy patients. Measures included a variety of determinants of emotional well-being.
   - Here you briefly explain your chosen methodology and the processes you took to conduct your study.
4 Analysis indicates a significant increase in well-being (p<.05) for those participants who interacted with a dog daily for two weeks.
   - This sentence highlights the information that most readers will want right away. What were the results of your study? What did you find?

5 This AAT program resulted in increased emotional well-being for those diagnosed with schizophrenia leading to suggestions for increased contact between people and animals across a range of treatment contexts.

- Here you are reinforcing the interest and utility of your study across populations.

Perhaps the last thing that you will do before sending your article to a journal is to create a title. Your title should clearly explain what your paper is about. Depending on the journal and the content of your article, you might become very creative with your title. When people are looking through the contents page of the journal or through online search engines, your title is the first thing they will encounter. You want to make sure that your title draws the reader in and gets them intrigued about reading more. For our example study, we might have the following titles:

- *The Impact of Daily Contact with Dogs on Schizophrenic Individuals' Emotional Well-Being.*
- *Dog Therapy: Barking Up the Right Tree*
- *Feeling Better through Canine Contact: Treating Schizophrenia through Animal-Assisted Therapy*

Writing for Grants

So far in this chapter, we have provided general guidelines for psychotherapists to write for publication. We may have gotten ahead of ourselves a little bit because before you have the information that you want to convey in the article, you needed to engage in clinical, research, or philosophical pursuits to obtain that information. For a think piece, you may not need any funding. However, if you are to engage in research, especially with a large population, and depending on if you need any equipment (e.g., biofeedback, access to certain tests or measures, an fMRI), you will likely need money to do so. And, if you are like us, you would prefer to use someone else's money instead of your own, as some research studies can be extremely expensive. This section of this chapter will discuss why a psychotherapist might want to pursue a grant, where and how to start writing a grant proposal, its essential components, and the types of grant funding resources.

Why a Psychotherapist Pursues a Grant??

Psychotherapists devote their time and effort to clinical work, training, and education. Throughout years of clinical experiences, they develop wisdom and knowledge about how to do their work better. To broaden the impacts of their work, psychotherapists might become supervisors who provide training and education for beginning or junior clinicians. Some of them are clinical directors who run a clinic in the community. No matter their roles, they might encounter a situation: where do they find resources to support training and education for clinicians? Where can they bring more financial resources to support their visions and dreams that bring more benefits and positive impacts to people in the community? As clinical directors, how can they use resources to enhance the infrastructure of the clinic and the quality of care provided to clients in the community? These questions lead psychotherapists and clinical directors to the following practical question: where can they find these financial resources? Who are those grantors willing to support their dreams and visions? Psychotherapists' great clinical experiences, ideas, and visions might align with some grant funders' missions and can provide effective interventions to address community issues. Their proposed interventions might assist grant funders in solving the community issues they are concerned about. A grant can support clinicians' training activities and education and enhance the clinic's reputation. It also brings the gaps between clinical research and practices when research is done based on real-world experiences.

Where and How to Start Writing a Grant Proposal?

An excellent place to start writing a grant proposal is to look for a grant opportunity, a grant funder. There are government and private-sponsored funders (Bauer, 2015). Each type of funder has its mission and goals and provides different types of grants. Each funder will also provide submission guidelines on its website. A grant seeker should check out the types of grants they want to pursue to see if the funders' missions match the proposed project and ideas. Usually, a grant funder is seeking someone who can provide innovative and effective intervention to solve an issue they are concerned about in the community. For example, due to the tremendous and negative impacts of COVID-19 on people in the community, the National Institute of Health has released many grant funding opportunities for research on studying innovative interventions to improve the health and well-being of vulnerable clinical populations. Another example is the Organization for Autism Research. This organization is funded by a community that cares about people on the spectrum, their family members, and service providers. They support research on increasing the quality of life of those on the spectrum. In addition, it is even helpful to review an awarded project to gather more information (e.g., its title, research designs, targeted clinical populations, the identified problem, and the funders' preferred choice) and get some inspiration about creating your own. Grant seekers are also encouraged to contact previous grant awardees to consult their successful grant-seeking experiences. Program officers also welcome grant seekers' contact and inquiry for more information (e.g., advice on submission requirements and grant-seeking suggestions).

Public and Private Funding Opportunities

Bauer (2022) highlights the different natures between public and private funders. She mentions that public funding sources refer to those funds from the federal government (e.g., the National Institute of Health, the National Science Foundation, and the Substance Abuse and Mental Health Services Administration) and state and local governments. Public fundings often have the most money to support grant seekers, so it attracts many competitors. They provide many resources for assistance and can support both the direct and indirect costs. It often requires grant seekers to follow specific submission rules and regulations. Grant seekers often receive grant reviewers' feedback if they receive a rejection.

Private funding opportunities refer to funds from non-profit foundations, professional associations, special interest groups, or faith communities (Bauer, 2022). They have less money to fund grant seekers than public funding sources and often do not support indirect costs. However, private funding is often mission-driven and can easily match clinical institutions or programs with similar missions. It can increase opportunities for those clinicians who pursue smaller grants and those beginning grant seekers.

Before writing a grant proposal, grant seekers should research and gather information about grant funders on their websites, the types of grants they want to pursue, grant application materials, and any requirements or regulations to decide which funding source is most appropriate. However, no matter the types of grants they seek, grant seekers want to prepare a solid and convincing proposal to increase their funded opportunities.

Basic Components of a Grant Proposal

Locke et al. (2014) highlight that there are three functions that a grant proposal serves. The first is communicating grant seekers' ideas and plans to grant funders. The grant funders and reviewers use this information for review and evaluation to decide if the grant proposal is applicable in real-world settings. Second, a grant proposal serves as a plan for action. It contains thorough and careful planning and implementation of the study. It shows the grant seekers' visions of carrying out the proposed project. Third, it is a contract between the grantee and grant funders. Once granted and approved, the grantee will follow its agreed plan to implement the proposed project. The followings are some essential components of a grant proposal. However, a reader might want to revise them based on the submission guidelines specific to different types of grants.

Introduction

This section is an opening statement to introduce the proposed ideas/projects to the grant funders and reviewers. It is a synopsis of essential components in a grant proposal. A good introduction uses factual information to highlight the importance of the identified problem to catch grant reviewers' attention. It also gives grant reviewers an outline of what to expect in their following reading.

Problem Statement

This section provides more contextual information about the identified problems that need further attention, solutions, and intervention. The problem statement highlights the nature and severity of the problem and its significant impacts on people in the community. It is better to provide statistics and information to support and state the presented problem. Doing so assists the grant reviewers in seeing the severity and impacts of the identified problem in the community. A good problem statement persuades grant reviewers to acknowledge the difficulties and challenges that must be resolved, provoking their "anxiety" to solve the problem. There are several questions you should consider while writing up this section. What is the presented problem in the community? What factual/statistical information shows its prevalence? What are some of the negative impacts of the problems, and how do they impact whom (such as individuals, couples, families, communities, specific vulnerable populations, or underprivileged and minority groups)? Why is this a significant issue for whom, and how urgent is it to solve it? Is this identified problem something the grant funders would be concerned about and interested in seeking a solution for?

Literature Review

This section provides detailed background information about the presented problem, proposed solutions, and intervention. A literature review summarizes what has been done in the field and identifies the gaps in the literature. In grant writing, grant seekers use literature to support their proposed arguments: why is it essential to conduct this proposed intervention project for those who need it the most? They use current literature and empirical studies to identify the significant impacts of the identified problem on individuals, couples and families, and specific populations and explain why it is necessary to address the issues. In addition, the grant seekers summarize the literature on current treatment trends for the identified problems and highlight their limitations. Because of these limitations of current treatments, the grant seekers propose alternative interventions and treatments to address this gap. Using empirical studies to support the effectiveness of the proposed intervention on other clinical populations or problems is even better and gives a positive outlook of the proposed solution.

The grant seekers might want to search the literature about the following questions: what are some existing programs/interventions that have been developed to address this problem? Are there any limitations to those existing programs/interventions? What is the uniqueness of the proposed intervention/program? Are there any empirical studies to support the effectiveness of the proposed intervention? Is there any evidence-practice or research to show and support its effectiveness for other clinical populations? How can the proposed intervention or program further address/compensate for the identified weakness/limitations of the existing program/interventions?

Goals vs. Objectives

Both goals and objectives should be pertinent to the problem statement. The proposed project's goals provide a bigger vision of what your proposed intervention aims to accomplish (O'Neal-McElrath et al., 2019). The objectives provide detailed outlines of what changes the impacted clinical populations would gain after participating in the proposed intervention. One way to structure objectives is to use **SMART (Specific, Measurable, Achievable, Relevant, and Time-bound)** guidelines. Specific objectives refer to any specific changes the targeted populations will gain after completing the project. Measurable objectives provide direct evidence of project success and outline step-by-step tasks to reach the goals. Achievable objectives refer to the grant seekers proposing a real solution to the identified problem. The relevant nature of objectives refers to the notion that each objective contributes to obtaining the overarching goals. Finally, the time-bound objectives define the degree of change for the proposed intervention within a specific time frame. The "smarter" the objectives are, the more convincing your proposed project is.

Methods

The methods section explains what grant seekers will do to accomplish their goals and objectives. Grant seekers need to answer the following questions: what specific activities and proposed interventions will they execute to accomplish the project goal? Where will those activities be conducted? Who are the personnel (e.g., professionals or staff) to carry out those activities? Who are the participants to receive the proposed intervention? What types of data will be collected to assess if the project goal is achieved and demonstrate the proposed intervention's effectiveness?

Proposed Interventions and Specific Activities

This section provides detailed information about the grant seekers' proposed intervention to achieve the goals and objectives and justifies their choice of the proposed intervention. It outlines the phases, the nature of interventions, the number of sessions, and when and where they will be conducted during a particular time. For example, a grant seeker proposes a solution-focused online group to support parents raising a child on the spectrum during the pandemic. The grant seeker would explain the benefits of solution-focused oriented interventions, outline the number of group sessions, specify the duration of each group session, and summarize what discussed topics or specific solution-focused interventions would be used during the intervention period. The grant seekers would also highlight any required administrative activities that support the intervention, such as recruiting staff or volunteers.

Personnel

The grant seekers must specify all key project staff and professionals, such as principal investigators, collaborators, consultants, subcontractors, and statisticians. It is essential to describe those personnel's educational background, skills they have, the roles and responsibilities they play in the project, the tasks they will do, etc. Often times, all personnel's resumes are attached in the appendices. This is important so the grant reviewers have contextual information about who will carry out the project and if they can do so.

Participants

Most clinically oriented grant projects will involve interactions with targeted clinical populations, whom we call the participants. The grant seekers explain their sampling methods (e.g., how they will recruit potential participants) and list the inclusion (who is eligible to participate in the project) and exclusion (who is not eligible) criteria of participants. Grant seekers need to ensure that participants' qualifications are connected to the problem statements and their impacted populations mentioned at the beginning of the proposal.

Locations

The grant seekers need to describe where they will conduct the proposed interventions. A safe space is essential to ensure all staff and participants' safety and confidentiality. When the proposed interventions are provided online for a reasonable reason (e.g., the impacts of COVID-19), the grant seekers need to specify its online modules and any HIPAA compliance. Some physical locations require grant seekers to buy insurance to protect all staff and participants' safety, which needs to be considered in the budget planning.

Data Collection and Analysis

The grant funders often want to know if the money they pay is cost-effective. The grant seekers need to detail the methods of data collection and analysis to evaluate the outcomes of the proposed intervention. The type of evaluation methods (e.g., quantitative or qualitative) that the grant seekers use depends on the research questions they propose concerning their problem statement and goals and objectives. For example, let's say a grant seeker wants to know how the solution-focused online group reduces parental stress during the pandemic time. Using quantitative assessments to measure parent participants' stress levels before and after the online group intervention is appropriate. Appropriate quantitative analyses will then evaluate whether the participants' stress decreased to a statistically significant level. However, if the grant seeker wants to know the participant's experiences in the group and gather their feedback to improve the quality of online group service further, a qualitative interview with the participants to understand their participation experiences and seek their feedback to improve the group service is necessary.

Budget

O'Neal-McElrath et al. (2019) state that "a budget is the proposal narrative reflected in numbers" (p. 75). Their statement captures a budget's function and the proposal's continuity. The grant funders often provide some guidelines for budget formation and regulation on their public website (e.g., the maximum funded budget, what items can be funded or not). The grant funder might also provide a budget template for grant seekers. The grant seekers should also check out those awardees' granted amount of money and have some knowledge about how much money they can plan in the budget.

In addition, each clinical organization and institution has its principal regulation of the budget use or reimbursement. The grant seekers need to consider those organization rules while budgeting so the granted money can be well-used. The grant seekers also need to consult their clinical organization regarding budget planning. For example, if the grant seekers need to hire administrative staff to assist with the project, how much annual salary will be budgeted to hire staff at the organization? Are there any fringe benefits they need to include in the budget, such as overtime compensation or insurance? When is the fiscal year to start for hiring the staff?

The budget includes direct and indirect costs. **Direct costs** refer to all expenses that can be easily identified for a specific project or activity (O'Neal-McElrath et al., 2019). Direct costs include but are not limited to salaries and fringe benefits of all key personnel (e.g., consultants, statisticians, interventionists, research assistants), materials and supplies, travel expenses, project-specific space rental, participants' costs, recruitment or advertisement cost, consultation fees, miscellaneous costs, etc. **Indirect costs** refer to incurred costs for the joint objectives of the organization. They can mean those costs for supporting general operations of your clinic, such as administrative staff costs (e.g., human resource services, accounting service), legal consultation costs, rental space costs, facility maintenance costs, the costs of any utilities, and technology support.

Finally, the grant seekers should provide a reasonable and detailed written narrative to explain their budget planning and use. The budget number is not self-explanatory. It requires the grant seekers to justify why they think it is necessary to request this much money and explain the purposes of each budget item. The grant funders want to know if the money they fund can be reasonably located where it should be and benefit those needed clinical populations. The budget planning and justification should echo other sections in the proposal. For example, if a grant seeker hires a statistician to evaluate the outcome of the proposed intervention, this should be listed in the budget. Good budget planning provides a quick summary of a grant proposal in numbers.

Dissemination

Supposedly, grant seekers successfully receive the grant, implement the proposed project, and reach their established goals and objectives. It is good to disseminate what they and the funding source have achieved and share the research findings with those who will use this information in their practice. The grant funders usually support and like the grant seekers to disseminate research findings in the field and have the public recognize their name and contribution. In this section, the grant seekers provide their plans about how they will tell others about the project in a public setting. Some common dissemination strategies include but are not limited to presenting papers or posters at national or international conferences, conducting a workshop, developing courses or seminars, writing a book or training manuals, publishing articles in a journal or newsletters, attending press releases or webcasts, etc.

Summary

Psychotherapists provide clinical services to individuals, couples, families, groups, and various organizations and agencies. Sometimes they engage in research to determine best practices for various clinical populations. Those clinicians who are engaging in research may need funding to be able to complete the project they want in the way they want to. When this happens, they will need to write a grant and submit it to a grant funder. Each grant funder will have specifics of what is needed in the proposal, but we provided here some of the classic and usual guidelines. Once the project is finished, or you have engaged in other types of clinical work, we encourage you to write up your findings in an article and submit it to a journal or some other place where you can disseminate your ideas as our field is predicated on growing through therapists passing on what they have learned.

References

Bauer, D. G. (2015). *The "How To" grants manual: Successful grantseeking techniques for obtaining public and private grants.* London: Rowman & Littlefield.

Bauer, M. (2022). *Finding grant opportunities.* https://sharkmedia.nova.edu/media/L%26L+-+Finding+Grant+Funding+%2802-02-22%29/1_6nrbc84w.

Bauer, T. N., & Hammer, L. B. (1996). Help received during the journal article writing process: The outcomes of quality and quantity. *Journal of Social Behavior and Personality, 11*(2), 213–224.

Caterjian, A. (2013). Editorial special: Writing a journal article. *Australian Journal of Clinical Hypnotherapy and Hypnosis, 35*(2), 55–63.

Kekäle, T., de Weerd-Nederhof, P., Cervai, S., & Borelli, M. (2009). The "dos and don'ts" of writing a journal article. *Journal of Workplace Learning, 21*(1), 71–80.

Locke, L. F., Spirduso, W. W., & Silverman, S. J. (2014). *Proposals that work: A guide for planning dissertations and grant proposals.* Sage Publications.

Nova, C. (2013). By heart. *The Atlantic*, June 11.

O'Neal-McElrath, T., Kanter, L., & English, L. (2019). *Winning grants step by step: The complete workbook for planning, developing, and writing successful proposals.* John Wiley & Sons.

Index